The Research Report Series of the Institute for Social Research is composed of significant reports published at the completion of a research project. These reports are generally prepared by the principal research investigators and are directed to selected users of this information. Research Reports are intended as technical documents which provide rapid dissemination of new knowledge resulting from ISR research.

Sex Role Attitudes among High School Seniors

Views about Work and Family Roles

A. Regula Herzog
Jerald G. Bachman

Survey Research Center
Institute for Social Research
The University of Michigan

1982

ISR Code No. 9014

This publication was prepared with funding from the National Institute of Education under Contract No. NIE-G78-0036.

The opinions expressed in this publication do not necessarily reflect the positions or policies of NIE.

Library of Congress Cataloging in Publication Data

Herzog, A. Regula (Anna Regula), 1941-
    Sex role attitudes among high school seniors.

    Bibliography: p.
      1. High school students--United States--Attitudes--Longitudinal studies. 2. Sex role--United States--Longitudinal studies. 3. Sociology--Research. I. Bachman, Jerald G. II. Title.
LC208.4.H47   373.18'1   82-3144
ISBN 0-87944-275-1 (pbk.)   AACR2

Published in 1982 by:

The Institute for Social Research
The University of Michigan, Ann Arbor, Michigan

6 5 4 3 2 1

Manufactured in the United States of America

Sex Role Attitudes among High School Seniors:
Views about Work and Family Life

Parts of this report have been previously published. Parts of chapter 5 were published in a paper by Herzog, A.R., "High school seniors' occupational plans and values: Trends in sex differences 1976 through 1980," in Sociology of Education, 1982, 55, 1-13. Appendix A was published in a paper by Herzog, A.R., and Bachman, J.G., "Effect of questionnaire length on response quality," in Public Opinion Quaterly, 1981, 45, 549-559.

ACKNOWLEDGEMENTS

This is the final report of a two-year project, sponsored by the National Institute of Education, on high school seniors' sex role attitudes and the relationship of those attitudes to various plans for adult roles. The project was based on data from an ongoing series of national surveys entitled "Monitoring the Future," directed by Lloyd Johnston and Jerald Bachman. The grant from the National Institute of Education provided funding for conducting analyses of those data, and for writing this report and a number of journal articles. We are grateful to Dr. Mary Lou Randour, the original project officer for this project, and Dr. Jean Miller, the present project officer, for their support. We are much indebted to Pamela R. Kittel and Deborah H. Poinier, who have provided capable research support to this project, including data management, computer analysis, table and graphics preparation, documentation, editing and supervision of manuscript preparation. The data collection was competently organized by Mary Bewley and Bill Diedrich. Invaluable clerical assistance in producing this report and related articles was provided by Mary Beth Danneffel-Mashruwala and Karen M. Donahue. Many other staff members of the Monitoring the Future project gave generously of their expertise and time, including our two colleagues Drs. Lloyd D. Johnston and Patrick M. O'Malley. Finally, this project would not have been possible without the help of the many seniors who throughout the years participated in the Monitoring the Future study and in our special data collection. We extend our thanks to all of them.

GUIDE TO DATA TABLES

Entries in the chart below are table numbers. For example, distributions and trends in attitudes about equal opportunities for women appear in Table 3-1.1. In order to find the page location for any table consult the List of Tables that begins on page xi.

	Based on Monitoring the Future samples of high school seniors, 1976 through 1980			Based on special long form samples of about 1,000 seniors in 1978		
	Response distributions for M, F, 1980; Mean values for M, F, 1976-1980; Time trends and sex differences	Correlations with sociodemographic (i.e., background) factors	Interrelationships involving items and/or indices	Correlations with sex role attitudes	Correlations with division of labor preferences	Correlations with educational and occupational views
CHAPTER 3. **SEX ROLE ATTITUDES**						
Equal Opportunities for Women	3-1.1	3-2.1	3-3			
Patriarchical Family Structure	3-1.2	3-2.2	3-3			
Encouraging a Daughter's Independence	3-1.3	3-2.3	3-3			
Effects of Working Mother on Children	3-1.4	3-2.4	3-3			
Effects of Working Wife on Marriage	3-1.5	3-2.5	3-3			
Importance of the Parenting Role	3-1.6	3-2.6	3-3			
Conventional Marriage and Extramarital Sex	3-1.7	3-2.7	3-3			
Overall Index of "Traditional Sex Role Attitudes"			3-3			
CHAPTER 4. **PREFERRED DIVISION OF LABOR IN FAMILY**						
Division of Paid Work, Couple without Children	4-1.1	4-2.1	4-3	4-4.1		
Division of Paid Work, Couple with Preschool Children	4-1.2	4-2.2	4-3	4-4.2		
Division of Child Care, Husband Works	4-1.3	4-2.3	4-3	4-4.3		
Division of Child Care, Both Spouses Work	4-1.4	4-2.4	4-3	4-4.4		
Division of Housework, Both Spouses Work	4-1.5	4-2.5	4-3	4-4.5		
CHAPTER 5. **EDUCATIONAL AND OCCUPATIONAL PLANS**						
Educational Plans	5-1.1	5-2.1		5-3.1&2	5-3.1&2	
Role of Paid Work	5-1.2	5-2.2		5-3.3&4	5-3.3&4	
Occupational Values	5-1.3	5-2.3	5-4.1			
Perceptions About Success Potential	5-1.4	5-2.4	5-4.2	5-3.5	5-3.5	
Preferred Work Settings	5-1.5	5-2.5				
Occupational Aspirations	5-1.6			5-4.3	5-4.3	5-4.3
Prestige of Aspired Occupation	5-1.7	5-2.6		5-3.6	5-3.6	
CHAPTER 6. **MARITAL AND FAMILY PLANS/EXPECTATIONS**						
Likelihood of Getting Married	6-1.1	6-2	6-3	6-4.1	6-4.1	6-4.1
Likelihood of Staying Married	6-1.2	6-2	6-3	6-4.2	6-4.2	6-4.2
Preferred Timing of Marriage	6-1.3	6-2	6-3	6-4.3	6-4.3	6-4.3
Preference for Having Children	6-1.4	6-2	6-3	6-4.4	6-4.4	6-4.4
Preferred Number of Children	6-1.5	6-2	6-3	6-4.5	6-4.5	6-4.5
Preferred Timing of First Child	6-1.6	6-2	6-3			

TABLE OF CONTENTS

LIST OF TABLES

LIST OF FIGURES

Page

EXECUTIVE SUMMARY

This report deals with high school seniors' sex role attitudes, and with seniors' plans and preferences for education, work, and family roles. We examine each of these areas in some detail, we explore ways in which they are interrelated, and we consider the extent to which there have been changes across the five senior classes from 1976 through 1980.

Our primary source of data is the Monitoring the Future project, which conducts large and nationally representative surveys of seniors on an annual basis. The Monitoring the Future sample each year totals more than 16,000 seniors; however, much of the survey material is divided among five different questionnaire forms. Thus, for most of the findings presented here, the underlying numbers of cases are about 1,500 males and 1,500 females for each of the graduating classes of 1976 through 1980. These relatively large numbers of cases, and the opportunity to replicate patterns and/or observe trends over five cohorts, give us a good deal of confidence in the findings. An important additional data source is a survey of about 1,000 seniors in 1978, which employed a much longer questionnaire permitting an exploration of interrelationships among many of the survey measures which appeared on different forms in the Monitoring the Future surveys. (An extensive discussion of both data sources is presented in Chapter 2.)

Sex Role Attitudes and the Concept of Traditionality

We conceive of sex role attitudes as opinions and beliefs about the ways that family and work roles do, and should, differ by gender. We have found it useful to view such attitudes as ranging along a continuum from traditional to non-traditional, where "non-traditional" attitudes are those which do not urge differences in roles or opportunities based on gender.

The conceptual framework which guided this research assigns a key position to sex role attitudes as representing the cumulative impact of a wide range

1

of socialization factors, and as in turn impacting on plans and preferences for education, occupation, marriage, and family. (See Chapter 1.)

We found it both necessary and desirable to develop a number of separate measures of sex role attitudes. Most of them could be characterized as ranging from traditional to non-traditional, and several of them were fairly strongly correlated. Nevertheless, the research findings confirmed our expectations that sex role traditionality/non-traditionality does not readily reduce to a single scale. (Chapter 3 presents the analyses of the sex role attitude measures.)

Equal Opportunities for Women. Overwhelming majorities of both male and female seniors believe in equal pay for equal work, and in equal educational opportunities for both sexes. Large majorities also agree, or agree mostly, in the concepts of equal opportunities for jobs, and for leadership roles as executives or politicians. There are important sex differences, to be sure, with larger proportions of females than males favoring complete equality of opportunities. Nevertheless, we are struck as much by the similarities between sexes as by the differences. Although responses to these items on equal opportunities for the sexes are correlated strongly with other sex role attitudes, we considered it important for conceptual reasons to treat these views as a separate dimension in our analyses.

An Index of Sex Role Traditionality. A number of questionnaire items dealt with what might be termed "sex role stereotypes"--notions about husbands making all the important decisions, wives caring for home and children rather than working outside, and the like. For these items, as in the case of the equal opportunities ones, there are more males than females at the "traditional" end of the continuum. There is, however, a much wider range of opinion in this area than in the equal opportunity domain. Thus, for example, a majority of males, and more than one third of the females, agree or agree mostly that "it is usually better for everyone involved if the man is the achiever outside the home and the woman takes care of the home and family." But only about 30 percent of the males, and half that many females, agree or agree mostly with the notion that "the husband should make all the important decisions in the family." A total of 16 items dealing with such sex role stereotypes were found to intercorrelate substantially, and they also showed generally similar patterns of correlations with other measures (e.g., strong religious commitments, political conservativism). Accordingly, these items were com-

2

bined to form an index of sex role traditionality which figured prominently in our later analyses.

Views on Parenting, Conventional Marriage, and Extramarital Sex. We examined seniors' views along a number of other dimensions which might be described as covering a range from traditional to non-traditional; however, the meaning of the term changes somewhat for these dimensions, and so do the patterns of relationship.

For example, the importance of parenthood--for both fathers and mothers--is endorsed by large majorities of both male and female seniors. The sex differences are quite small, with slightly larger proportions of females giving strong endorsement to the parenthood role (which might be considered the more "traditional" position, at least where women's roles are concerned).

Views about marriage and extramarital sex are mostly "traditional" among male seniors, and somewhat more so among females. Relatively few agree with the statement that "having a close intimate relationship with only one partner is too restrictive for the average person;" and most are not willing to question marriage "as a way of life." The sex differences are largest in responses to the item, "It is usually a good idea for a couple to live together before getting married in order to find out whether they really get along." Male seniors are split just about evenly in terms of agreement versus disagreement; whereas one third of the females agree, and more than half disagree. The sex difference noted above certainly fits the stereotype of females resisting male suggestions for sexual relationships outside of marriage; thus what may in one sense be viewed as greater "traditionality" on the part of the females may in another sense be viewed as resistance to sexual exploitation.

As we said earlier, one could attempt to apply the notion of traditionality to the views on conventional marriage and extramarital sex; but as we have just illustrated, the term is somewhat distorted by such an effort. Our preference, therefore, has been not to conceptualize these views as sex role attitudes, even though they involve some closely related matters.

Recent Trends in Sex Role Traditionality. Seniors' views about equal opportunities for women changed rather little during the late seventies-- support remained consistently high. Many of the other items also showed little in the way of trends. But some of the items most central to our definition of sex role attitudes--opinions about division of paid work and housework, and about the effects of mother's work on her children--have undergone some change in the non-traditional direction during the last five years. These changes have occurred at about an equal pace for both sexes, leaving the substantial sex differences on these items largely unchanged.

One other trend may be worth noting here. While female views have shown little change, male seniors have shown a modest increase in support of conventional marriage. As a result, the gap between males and females is only about half as large for the class of 1980 as it was for the class of 1976. Thus, during the latter half of the seventies we do not detect any evidence of erosion of young people's commitment to marriage; and there may actually be some movement back toward it on the part of young men.

Correlates of Sex Role Traditionality. As we report in later sections of this summary, sex role traditionality is related to various plans and preferences for work, marriage, and parenthood. We note here the patterns of correlation with a number of other dimensions.

The largest and most consistent differences in traditionality appear between males and females; as noted at several points above, female seniors are in most respects less traditional than males.

Sex role traditionality also occurs to a lesser than average degree among those seniors bound for college, those with high grades, and those whose parents were college educated.

Greater than average traditionality appears among seniors who report a strong commitment to religion, those with conservative political views, and (to a slight extent) those from more rural backgrounds. A number of racial differences appeared, some of which are too complicated to summarize here; in most respects blacks are less traditional than whites.

Preferences for Dividing Family Responsibilities
(or, Who Should Be Employed and Who Should
Care for Home and Children?)

The questionnaire items discussed in the previous section deal largely with seniors' impressions about sex roles for people in general. Now we consider a series of items dealing with seniors' personal preferences for sharing the responsibilities of mar-

riage and parenthood. Each question in the series asks
the respondent to imagine being married, and to consider the acceptability of several different arrangements for sharing paid employment child care, and house
care. (Chapter 4 presents the analyses of these
items.)

Working Wives OK, but Small Children Change
Things. When thinking about being married with no
children, most seniors (both male and female) consider
it desirable or acceptable for the wife to work half-
time or full-time outside the home. But if they
imagine having one or more pre-school children, their
preferences for outside work by the wife shift substantially: the most frequently preferred alternative is
that the wife not work at all outside the home, with a
second choice being that she work only half-time.
About two thirds of the males, and nearly as many of
the females, reject as "not at all acceptable" the idea
of both husband and wife working full-time when pre-
school children are part of the family.

Little Enthusiasm for Sex Role Reversal. One
logical alternative to a wife reducing outside employment in order to care for children would be for the
husband to do so, or for both to reduce to half-time
employment. Such departures from the traditional pattern of a full-time employed husband receive little endorsement from high school seniors. In particular, any
arrangement involving a husband working less than the
wife is overwhelmingly rejected by both males and
females. Furthermore, sex role reversal is no more
welcome where child care and housework are concerned;
well over half of both male and female seniors reject
as unacceptable any situation in which the husband does
more than an equal share, and fewer than three percent
rate any such situation as desirable.

Sex Differences in Primary Responsibilities.
There is considerable evidence in the responses of
seniors suggesting a preference for egalitarianism.
First choices are often for equal sharing of child and
house care, even when the husband has a full-time job
and the wife does not work outside the home. But the
second choices, or next most acceptable alternatives,
most often move in the traditional direction. In other
words, while there seems to be a tendency toward sharing of duties between marital partners, the final
responsibility still seems to rest with the one partner
who traditionally held that particular duty. Thus, a
husband's help in child care is very welcome even to a
point of equal involvement with the wife; but the final
responsibility still appears to rest with the wife.
She is the one expected to reduce or give up outside

5

employment; and she would probably be blamed most if
anyone judged child care to be inadequate. By the same
token, the involvement of the wife in paid work is
widely accepted; but it is still the husband who is expected to maintain full-time employment irrespective of
his family situation. He is the one likely to be held
accountable, and to feel the greatest psychological
burden, if economic support for the family is not adequate.

Greater Flexibility for Wives than for Husbands.
We have noted that a fairly considerable range of
latitude exists in preferences concerning outside
employment for wives. To be sure, there is considerable limitation for wives when they have children
in the pre-school years. But when no children are involved, the range of options is wide. More specifically, only a small proportion of male seniors (16 percent) reject as unacceptable a marriage in which the
wife holds no outside employment, and a similarly small
proportion (19 percent) rule out a full-time employed
wife. The employment options for males are much more
narrowly constrained, however. Females overwhelmingly
reject any arrangement in which the husband is not
employed, and large proportions (60 percent or more)
reject an arrangement in which the husband works half-
time while the wife works full-time. It should be
added that very few males indicate a preference for
such an arrangement either. Whether some male
preferences might change, given a climate of greater
acceptability, must remain a matter for speculation;
although other attitudes have shifted to some extent,
seniors' preferences regarding the husband's work role
have not changed during the late seventies.

Sex Differences in Preference Patterns. As noted
above, there is a high order of agreement between male
and female seniors about the husband's employment--both
prefer that he be employed full-time. As for the
wife's employment, particularly in the case involving
no children, many males would accept a variety of working arrangements by the wife; however, the females tend
to prefer arrangements in which the wife works full-
time or at least part-time. This difference, with the
females averaging somewhat more egalitarian than the
males, shows up to some extent along the other dimensions for allocating family responsibilities. Nevertheless, the more dominant conclusion we draw from
these particular data is that males and females show
what may be a surprising extent of agreement in their
views about sharing responsibilities, especially when
it comes to the widely shared preferences for family
arrangements in which the mother of young children is
not employed full-time outside the home, and for the

6

involvement of both parents in caring for their children.

   Trends and Correlates. The preferences for division of family responsibilities have not changed substantially during the late seventies. Those trends which have occurred, which involve employment of wives or sharing of housework and child care, are in an egalitarian direction.

   Preferences for egalitarian arrangements are somewhat more likely among those high in academic ability, planning to complete college, and politically liberal. These findings are distinctly stronger for female seniors than for males, perhaps in part because the females' own working preferences or career plans affect their preferences for division of responsibilities to a greater extent than is true for males.

   One set of background factors shows strong relationships with views about working mothers. Respondents who are black, as well as respondents whose own mothers spent much time working outside the home, are much more likely than other seniors to consider it desirable--or at least acceptable--for a wife with preschool children to be employed. Thus it appears that those most exposed to the example of working mothers have not reacted negatively to that experience; instead, they show a greater than average willingness for their own children to have the same experience.

   As expected, the index of sex role traditionality described earlier (and detailed in Chapter 3) showed fairly substantial correlations with the personal preferences for division of family responsibilities. Those seniors whose general sex role attitudes were highly traditional were least likely to express preferences for egalitarian arrangements in their own future marriages.

Educational and Occupational Plans

   The educational plans of male and female high school seniors are not very different, on the average. A majority expect to finish a four-year college program; and attendance at graduate or professional school after college is rated as probable by a gradually increasing minority (36 percent of males and 31 percent of females in the class of 1980).

   Turning to occupational plans and attitudes, it appears than young women take work as seriously as young men do. It is mostly in items which introduce

7

family roles that differences appear between the sexes; young women show a greater likelihood of attributing very high importance to family and children, and a greater willingness to modify work roles for the sake of their family roles. Young women are also more likely than young men to regard the occupational values of altruism and other-orientation as important.

The largest differences between the sexes appear in specific occupations that seniors expect to occupy at age 30, and to a lesser extent in preferences for different work settings. The sex differences in categories of occupational aspiration parallel the existing occupational segregation in the labor force. While substantial proportions of both males and females select the general category "professional without doctoral degree," we suspect that some of the specific occupations in this category such as registered nurse, librarian, and social worker attract mostly females, while others such as engineer, architect, and technician attract mostly males. The traditionally male occupation of craftsman or skilled worker is chosen by 22 percent of male seniors but only one percent of females. The picture is reversed for the occupation of clerical or office worker (20 percent of females, two percent of males). Females are far more likely than males to rate working in a social service organization as desirable, and they are also more likely to give positive ratings to working in a school or university. By far the most popular working arrangement among both sexes would be self-employment, but this is especially true for males. The least popular work setting for both sexes is military service. Considering that this is a traditionally male work setting, and that substantially more males than females <u>expect</u> to serve in the military, the sex differences in ratings of the <u>desirability</u> of military work are surprisingly small.

One of the ways of quantifying the difference between male and female occupational expectations is the index of segregation. For the class of 1976, about 50 percent of the males (or females) would have had to change plans in order for the two distributions to become identical. The level of sex segregation in occupational plans, as measured by this index, has declined appreciably during the last five years, so that for the class of 1980 only about 36 percent of the males (or females) would need to change plans to make the two distributions identical. (Given the fact that our list of occupational preferences is quite general, however, it is likely that the sex segregation is noticeably larger than the above percentages would suggest. Nevertheless, we consider the trend data to be indicative of some genuine change in this area.)

One other trend of considerable importance is the steadily decreasing proportion of young women who expect to be full-time homemakers at age 30. Among those expecting to complete college, the proportion has remained consistently low (five percent in 1976, and four percent in 1980); but among the non-college bound, the drop has been substantial (from 22 percent in 1976 to 13 percent in 1980, and down to 9 percent for the class of 1981). Since virtually no males expect to be full-time homemakers at age 30, the declining numbers of females expecting to do so represents another kind of convergence--another way in which occupational aspirations are less sex segregated.

Correlates of Educational and Occupational Plans. Educational plans are affected by a number of well-known factors such as abilities and parental education. We noted earlier that those planning to complete college are also lower in sex role traditionality; however, the traditionality measure (and other sex role attitude measures) provide no additional prediction of college plans once we take account of abilities and parental characteristics. Thus, contrary to our expectations, sex role attitudes seem to have rather little direct bearing on the educational aspirations of young women.

Our exploration of the correlates of occupational plans replicated the usual findings with respect to the prestige of aspired occupations; prestige is strongly associated with academic ability and college plans, and to a lesser degree with parental education. There is also a clear tendency for those with more traditional sex role attitudes to report lower occupational aspirations; however, we find again that this association seems due almost entirely to the negative correlation between traditionality and academic ability, etc.

Among young women the measure of sex role traditionality does show a substantial correlation with plans for being a full-time homemaker at age 30; and this relationship is not at all diminished when controls are introduced for ability and college plans. A parallel finding is that females scoring high on the traditionality scale score relatively low on a measure of "job centrality" (indicating whether work, and doing a good job, will be a very central part of one's life). In other words, females' decisions about whether to be employed at all, and their expectations about how central a role work will play, are related to sex role traditionality independent of ability and college plans.

9

In sum, although we had expected that sex role attitudes would play an important part in the educational and occupational aspirations of young women, we find rather little evidence in support of that hypothesis. Sex role attitudes may play a part in the decision about whether to be employed at all (at age 30) and whether work will be a very central part of life. But we could not find clear evidence that sex role attitudes make an independent contribution to the status of women's occupational aspirations.

Marital and Family Plans

When it comes to plans or expectations about marriage and family, most seniors could fairly be characterized as squarely in the mainstream of conventional values. In overwhelming proportions they expect to be married, to stay married to the same person (though many are not certain about this), and to have children (two or three). Most of those who do not clearly expect to be married are not opposed to the idea; rather, they state that they "have no idea" about whether they will marry--a sentiment somewhat more frequent among male seniors than among females.

Correlates of Marital and Family Plans. Young blacks--especially young black women--are more skeptical than whites about the possibility of getting married and about the stability of marriage. Respondents with strong religious commitments, and those with conservative political views, are particularly likely to expect stable marriages. Religious commitment is also positively correlated with the likelihood of having children and the number of children preferred.

Among the several measures of sex role attitudes, the most consistent predictor of marriage and family plans is, not surprisingly, the measure of the importance of parenting. This is positively correlated with both male and female seniors' expectations that they will get married, stay married to the same person, and have children. While the measure of sex role traditionality shows a very modest positive relationship with plans for having children, it shows no clear association with likelihood of marriage. On the other hand, there is a strong tendency for females who are low in traditionality to plan relatively late marriages. This matches an even stronger tendency for women planning to complete college also to plan relatively late marriages, but the link between traditionality and early marriage plans remains even when college plans are controlled.

One of the problems in searching for correlates of marriage and family plans is that such plans do not show much variation at the very general level--the overwhelming majority of seniors expect to marry and have children. But the expected timing of marriage does vary, and turns out to be related to a number of other plans and attitudes. College plans, aspirations for high prestige occupations, and the belief that work will be very central in one's life are all predictors of plans for a relatively long delay prior to marriage. Each of these relationships appears for male seniors, but each is stronger among females. Another predictor of expected marriage timing among females, but not among males, is sex role traditionality. Those females with more traditional views about sex roles in general are likely to plan on relatively early marriages, a relationship which remains fairly strong even with other factors such as college plans controlled. It thus appears that among young men, and perhaps even more so among young women, there is an effort to sequence role commitments according to priorities: if education and work are to be important, and thus require extensive time and effort, then marriage is expected to be postponed.

Summing Up: Key Findings and Conclusions

The preceding pages reviewed our findings on a chapter-by-chapter basis. Now we highlight a few themes which appear with some consistency throughout this volume.

There are Important Differences--and Similarities--in the View of Males and Females. We have noted a fairly consistent tendency for higher proportions of females than males to show non-traditional or egalitarian responses. But we have also noted some exceptions, and we have noted that in many respects the similarities in the responses of males and females are more impressive than the differences. Both sexes tend mostly to favor equal opportunities for men and women; but the proportions are somewhat larger among the female respondents. Both sexes clearly prefer a marriage in which the mother of young children holds no outside employment, or in any case not more than a half-time job; but support for this traditional view is just a shade stronger among the male respondents.

The data we report thus provide plenty of ammunition for those who wish to stress differences, as well as for those who wish to focus on similarities. Is the glass half empty or half full? Since we fully expected

11

to see substantial differences, our own reaction has been to be a bit more impressed by the similarities. Especially when it comes to preferences for sharing of family responsibilities, we find a sufficient range of overlap, and a sufficient degree of tolerance for a range of alternative patterns, that we are fairly sanguine about the prospects for harmony as these seniors marry and actually set about the business of sharing the burdens of marriage and parenthood.

Some Trends Away from Traditionality. Most of the measures reported here have not shifted very substantially during the late nineteen-seventies, and many have not moved at all. But those changes which have occurred are almost all in the less traditional direction. In some cases the trends for males and females are parallel, so that what differences there are remain fairly constant. In other cases, there has been some convergence. Importantly, there are no significant instances of any gap between the sexes growing wider during the late seventies.

Restrictions of Flexibility Remain--for both Males and Females. One widely used survey item asks respondents whether they agree or disagree that "It is usually better for everyone involved if the man is the achiever outside the home and the woman takes care of the home and family." This item clearly states the traditional restrictions on both males and females--the males should work full-time outside the home and the females should take care of the home. There are substantial sex differences in responses to this item, with males tending more toward the traditional side. But for both sexes there is a very wide spread of opinion, which stands in sharp contrast to many other items, such as those dealing with equal educational or occupational opportunities. Indeed, female seniors in 1976 were split just about evenly between those who agreed and those who disagreed with the above statement; and by 1980 there was still a substantial minority of female seniors agreeing with the statement.

Our findings suggest that young people are in large measure committed to the principle of equal opportunity, but not to any principle of identical family roles. If women want higher education, they should be given the same opportunities as men. If they do the same work as men, they should get the same pay. And if a woman wants to be an executive or politician, she should not be considered any less seriously because she happens to be female. But for most people most of the time, these seniors seem to be saying, there are distinct advantages in the traditional family role arrangements. And when it comes to their own future mar-

12

riages, the overwhelming majority prefer to maintain some traditional role distinctions. They want an arrangement in which the husband consistently works full-time outside the home; any other alternative is ruled out. When small children are part of the family, they want a wife who is not spending large portions of her time working in outside employment. The degree of agreement between male and female responses on these two role restrictions is far more impressive than the small differences that exist. Thus there remain important restrictions on the flexibility of both males and females, and to a very large degree these restrictions seem to be internalized and thus self-imposed by the time a young person reaches the end of high school.

How Useful is the Concept of "Traditionality"? Given our heavy reliance on this concept, and our extensive use of a measure of traditionality, it seems appropriate that we try to assess its value in the light of what we have learned in these analyses. We should at the outset acknowledge a point which is better made in Chapter 3 than in this brief summary: traditionality is a rather complex dimension, and it may be helpful to place some limitations on it--at least when attempting to develop measures. Our own index of sex role traditionality is an effort to summarize opinions and beliefs about the ways that family and work roles do, and should, differ by sex.

We have noted some limitations in the utility of this concept of sex role traditionality. In particular, it does not seem to provide any additional prediction of educational and occupational aspirations, once we take account of what appears to be more fundamental factors (such as parental education, grades, etc.). But in other respects it has lived up to our expectations. It correlates with quite a number of background factors, attitudes, values, and plans, mostly in directions that were consistent with our conceptualizations. Thus we have found it to be a useful concept, from both theoretical and analytic standpoints.

Guide to Using this Volume

This executive summary has provided an overview of our findings. The much more detailed presentation in the chapters which follow has been designed to accommodate those readers who wish to be selective as well as those who prefer to cover all the material.

Chapter Organization. The first chapter presents a conceptual overview with an emphasis on sex role at-

titudes. (Other chapters also include conceptual background and literature review specific to the topics
covered.) The second chapter provides a fairly complete description of the methods of data collection,
sample characteristics, and a comparison between the
two sources of survey data used in this report. Chapter 3 begins our substantive reporting with measures of
sex role attitudes. Then, in Chapter 4, we examine
high school seniors' preferences for division of labor
between husband and wife when they imagine their own
possible marriage. Chapter 5 deals with seniors' actual plans and expectations for further education and
future employment, as well as a wide range of attitudes
about work. Chapter 6 focuses on seniors' plans and
expectations for marriage and parenthood.

Analysis Format and Guide to Data Tables. A
standard analysis format is followed in Chapters 3
through 6. For each of the measurement areas within a
chapter, we provide several standard tables of data.
The first such table in each case includes (a) the complete wording of the questionnaire items, (b) the
response distributions for males and females in the
senior class of 1980, (c) mean values for males and
females for the senior classes of 1976 through 1980,
and (d) correlation coefficients indicating the
strength of sex differences and the strength of trends
from 1976 through 1980. The second standard table
presents the correlations between each questionnaire
item (or index) and a set of background
(sociodemographic) factors, as well as the variance accounted for by the entire set of background factors,
using combined data from the senior classes of 1976
through 1980.

The two standard data tables described above make
use of data from the large and nationally representative Monitoring the Future project. Many of the
remaining tables are based on the special survey of
about 1000 seniors in 1978, designed to permit a wider
range of correlational analyses. The third type of
standard table examines interrelationships involving
the items and/or indexes which appear within a particular chapter. The fourth type of standard table,
employed in Chapters 4 through 6, presents bivariate
and multivariate relational analyses in which background factors, sex role attitudes, and other relevant
measures, are examined as predictors (or correlates) of
the various plans and attitudes concerning marriage,
parenthood, education, and occupation.

The standard tables described above cover a wide
range of survey material, some of which is discussed
extensively in the text, and some of which is treated

14

much more briefly. Our selection of which topics to
treat in greater detail has been influenced by the
findings themselves, and also by our own biases. It is
partly with a view toward those readers with other
biases and emphases that we have been fairly exhaustive
in our presentation. As an aid to those who wish to
access the tables directly, we have prepared a summary
chart which appears on page vi of this report. A
glance at that chart may provide a useful review of the
several types of tables outlined above, as well as an
overview of the topic areas covered in Chapters 3
through 6. We hope it proves to be a helpful tool for
those using this report as a reference volume. (In-
cidentally, all tables are grouped together at the end
of each chapter to permit easier access.)

CHAPTER 1

CONCEPTUAL OVERVIEW: THE IMPOR-
TANCE OF SEX ROLE ATTITUDES

In today's society the work and family roles of women remain quite different from those of men. While most men are in the labor force continuously throughout their adult life, many women work on an intermittent and part-time basis. Men's careers typically develop upward, while women's work lives show less of an orderly advancement (Rosenfeld, 1978). On the other hand, women obviously devote a major part of their time and effort to raising their offspring and taking care of domestic duties, and therefore have less energy to devote to a career. It has been argued that this division of labor is based on the different biological functions of the sexes: women bear children; men have great physical strength to bring to strenuous work. Today these biological arguments are only mildly convincing, if at all. The decline in the number of children a woman bears, in combination with the increase in life expectancy, results in a rather small part of her life being devoted to child rearing. With regard to men's greater physical strength, most occupations now require little if any physical labor. Of course, this division of labor has gained other significance. It has been argued that keeping women from the production of economic goods in a materialistically focused society has the effect of keeping them from access to power, independence, and the like, and thus results in a social stratification by sex.

These two elements—division of labor and social stratification by sex—are the two key elements of what is usually referred to by the concept of "sex roles" (Scanzoni and Fox, 1980). The "traditional" or "sexist" pole of the sex role attitude continuum refers to sex-segregated division of labor and unequal opportunities; the "modern," "egalitarian," or "nontraditional" pole refers to egalitarian division of labor and equal opportunities.

Presently, sex roles appear to be undergoing substantial changes. One indication is the rapidly changing public opinion towards these matters (Mason,

17

Czajka, and Arber, 1976; Parelius, 1975; Thornton and Freedman, 1979). Another indication is the increasing participation of women in the labor force who thereby increasingly share the breadwinner role with men (U.S. Bureau of the Census, 1976; U.S. Department of Labor, 1975a).

At the same time, other aspects of sex roles have changed curiously little. For example, although women participate in larger numbers in the labor force, they maintain conspicuously large differentials in pay (Featherman and Hauser, 1976; Treiman and Terrell, 1975b) and authority (Wolf and Fligstein, 1979) compared to men, and they continue to work largely in a few heavily female-dominated occupations such as service, clerical, and a few professional jobs (Blau and Hendricks, 1979; Davis, 1980; Fuchs, 1971; Oppenheimer, 1968). Also, the participation of women in the breadwinner role has not prompted substantially increased participation of men in child care and housework; husbands of working wives spend just about the same amount of time in those activities as do husbands of nonworking wives (Meissner, Humphreys, Meis, and Scheu, 1975; Robinson, 1977).

In essence, many substantial differences between the roles of the sexes persist, despite the lack of biological justification. The mechanisms by which these differences are maintained must include social values and attitudes that are transmitted through family, school, and peer group settings, and that guide young men and women when they form their occupational and family plans. (These same values probably also affect employers when they define positions and hire employees for those positions, thereby resulting in structural barriers to equality.) Briefly, while we do not deny that some of the current differences in work and family roles are explainable in terms of structural factors, we believe that personal plans and preferences during the transition to adulthood play a critical role in the development of these differences, by mediating the socialization influences of parental home, of school and of peer group on subsequent attainments.

A similar conceptualization of plans has been successfully applied in the status attainment literature. Plans have been assigned a predominant role within the theoretical framework of the status attainment model. Research in that tradition has quite consistently demonstrated that educational and occupational plans are affected by characteristics of the family--particularly parental SES and educational level--and by personal characteristics--particularly abilities (Alexander and Eckland, 1974; Bayer, 1969a,b;

Marini and Greenberger, 1978a,b; Sewell and Shah, 1968), and that those plans in turn exert a moderate effect on early attainments (Featherman and Carter, 1976; Otto and Haller, 1979; Sewell and Hauser, 1975; Sewell, Hauser, and Wolf, 1980).

The status attainment model, however, was developed solely on young men, and has provided less insight into the attainment process of young women. As suggested by some, the attitudes and plans that are particularly relevant to the female role in this society should be included to make the model more relevant for young women (Alexander and Eckland, 1979; Sewell, 1971; Treiman and Terrell, 1975b). Such attitudes and plans might include marital and family plans and attitudes about the proper roles of the sexes.

While the attitudes women hold about the proper roles of the sexes and the expectations they develop for marriage and family life are of obvious importance in understanding women's planning of their education and their occupation, it is our contention that some impact might even be expected for young men's educational, occupational, and family plans. For example, some level of financial independence associated with holding a job and having completed schooling is important in planning marriage and starting a family. Moreover, Pleck (1976) has argued that even among men family and work roles are likely to interfere with each other. Therefore, young men might also anticipate a certain amount of role conflict and plan their future roles accordingly. In sum, we would argue that sex role attitudes, marital and family plans should be included into status attainment models certainly for young women, but preferably also for young men.

The studies that have incorporated marital and family plans, unlike the traditional literature on status attainment, tend to utilize small, specialized, and often exclusively female samples. Although not entirely consistent, this research demonstrates a certain level of interrelatedness between the various plans. For example, some studies suggest that plans for timing of marriage are related to educational aspirations, for young women more so than for young men (Bayer, 1969a, b; Gaskell, 1977-78; Shea, Roderick, Zeller, and Kohen, 1971). Other studies indicate that fertility plans of young women are related to their planned labor force participation (Gustavus and Nam, 1970; Waite and Stolzenberg, 1976; Westoff and Potvin, 1967; Whelpton, Campbell, and Patterson, 1966), their career commitment (Falbo, Graham, and Gryskiewicz, 1978; Farley, 1970;

McLaughlin, 1974), and the sex-typicality of their occupational plans (Aneshensel and Rosen, 1980).

Several alternative interpretations remain, of
course, after demonstrating such interrelationships.
First, the direction of causation remains undetermined,
given that cross-sectional data have been used by most
of the relevant studies. Secondly, the relationship
could be altogether spurious, i.e., be caused entirely
by a common, causally prior predictor. This possibility can be investigated with cross-sectional data
(and in some studies has been), using multivariate
analysis techniques, provided that a measure of the
postulated common predictor is available in the data.

Much of the evidence suggesting a relationship
between general sex role attitudes and plans for adult
roles is also based on small and often unrepresentative
samples and mostly bivariate analysis procedures. According to those studies, sex role attitudes are related to some of the marital and fertility plans as
well as to educational and occupational plans (Aneshensel and Rosen, 1980; Eagly and Anderson, 1974; Gaskell,
1977-78; McLaughlin, 1974). This is consistent with
the view that plans are part of a more general
ideological orientation and the interrelationships between them reflect an effect of underlying ideology
rather than a recognition of the incongruence between
the specific roles. But such a notion needs to be
tested explicitly in a multivariate analysis framework.
If the relationships between the various plans are
reduced or eliminated when sex role attitudes are controlled, this suggests that their interrelationships
were in fact created by their simultaneous
relationships to sex role attitudes. More concretely,
women with non-traditional sex role attitudes tend to
respond along non-traditional lines to a number of different plans and preferences; and vice versa for women
who hold traditional attitudes. We need to take the
argument one step further. Since we conceptualize sex
role attitudes as well as various plans to be outcomes
of socialization, it is possible that they are all affected by a powerful socialization variable. For example, religiosity is likely to have an effect on sex
role attitudes, as well as on marital and family plans
and women's labor force participation plans. This possibility also needs to be tested in a multivariate
analysis framework.

In sum, the research reported here has been
guided by the following conceptualization of the formation of plans. Adolescents' educational, occupational,
marital, and family plans, including plans about the
timing of those events, incorporate some of the cumula-

tive impact of (a) previous socialization experiences in family, school, and peer group, as well as (b) personal attitudes and characteristics. Moreover, such plans are likely to impact on subsequent marriage and childbearing patterns, since at this critical stage in their lives young people make decisions which set the stage for much of their future lives (Otto, 1979; Spenner and Featherman, 1978). While their impact on later attainments documents the significance of plans in the process of role attainment, this report focuses only on the structure of those plans and on their formation.

Our research examines a variety of relevant socialization dimensions: mother's education, father's education, whether the respondent lived with the father while growing up, whether he or she lived with the mother while growing up, whether the mother worked when the respondent was growing up, and the degree of urban density of the setting in which the respondent grew up. The research also examines personal characteristics: race, academic abilities, political orientation, religious commitment, frequency of dating a person of the opposite sex. Sex role attitudes are viewed as a major factor in the formation of plans. They are conceptualized as outcomes of socialization experiences and personal characteristics, but at the same time we hypothesize that they will contribute to the explanation of plans for adult roles (i.e., educational, occupational, marital, and family plans). On the other hand, we postulate no single causal sequence between the various plans. We believe that these plans develop in close conjunction with each other, involving multiple reciprocal causation. It is our firm conclusion based on the analytical literature that such complex causal patterns cannot be sorted out with the cross-sectional data which are available to us, and that such a task would be very difficult even with panel data.

Figure 1 lays out the conceptual framework that guided our investigations. As the figure indicates, we postulate sex role attitudes as a major intervening factor between socialization/personal factors on one hand and various plans on the other hand. Otherwise, we do not specify any causal sequences between the plans and preferences shown on the right side of Figure 1. Although we are convinced that there is a complex pattern of interrelationships among the various plans, involving most likely reciprocal causation, we are equally convinced that our data--and most other available data--are not suited to sort out such complex patterns of interrelationships as we expect to exist between these plans. Thus, we limit our analyses to a three-step causal sequence as indicated in Figure 1.

Given the prominent role that sex role attitudes assume in this framework, they assume a focal position in the report being introduced and discussed right after the introductory chapters. For reporting and organizational purpose only, we also impose an order on the set of plans that we discuss in this report. We start with plans for the division of labor in the family, then proceed to discuss educational and occupational plans, and conclude with the discussion of marital and family plans.

Figure 1

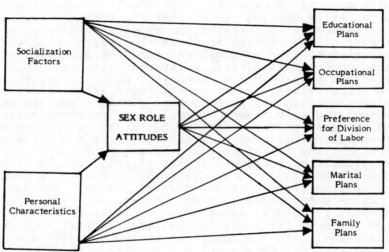

CHAPTER 2

METHODS

THE MONITORING THE FUTURE PROJECT

Most of the data for the present study are
provided by a nationwide study of high school seniors,
called "Monitoring the Future, A Continuing Study of
the Lifestyles and Values of Youth." The study is
being carried out by the Institute for Social Research,
operating under a series of grants from the National
Institute on Drug Abuse. Although the survey coverage
includes extensive measurement devoted to drug use and
directly related topics, a great many other topics are
included. Of particular importance to the project
reported here are a variety of plans, expectations, and
attitudes about marriage, parenting, education, work,
and the management of family responsibilities.

Research Design[1]

The basic research design involves annual data
collections from high school seniors during the spring
of each year, beginning with the class of 1975. Each
data collection takes place in approximately 125 public
and private high schools selected to provide an accurate cross section of high school seniors throughout
the United States.

The present report focuses on the surveys of
seniors in the five graduating classes of 1976 through
1980. (Although many of the questionnaire items
reported here were included in the 1975 survey, differences in format and response rates reduce
comparability--thus the decision to begin with the
class of 1976.)

---

[1] A more extensive description of the research
design may be found in Bachman and Johnston (1978).

Reasons for Focusing on High School Seniors.
There are several reasons for choosing the senior year
of high school as an optimal point for monitoring the
plans and attitudes of youth. One is that the completion of high school represents the end of an important
developmental stage in this society, since it demar-
cates both the end of universal public education and,
for many, the end of living in the parental home.
Therefore, it is a logical point at which to take stock
of the cumulated influences of these two environments
on American youth.

Further, the completion of high school represents
the jumping-off point from which young people diverge
into widely differing social environments including
college, business firms, military service, and homemaking. But these environmental transitions are not the
only important changes which coincide with the end of
high school. Most young men and women now reach the
formal age of adulthood shortly before or after graduation; more significantly, they begin to assume adult
roles, including financial self-support, marriage, and
parenthood. In other words, young people's careers
start taking a variety of forms after the completion of
high school; and plans play an important role in
directing these career lines.

Finally, there are some important practical advantages to building a system of data collections
around samples of high school seniors. The last year
of high school constitutes the final point at which a
reasonably good national sample of an age-specific
cohort can be drawn and studied economically. The need
for systematically repeated, large-scale samples from
which to make reliable estimates of change requires
that considerable stress be laid on efficiency and
feasibility; the present design meets those require-
ments.

One limitation in the present design is that it
does not include in the target population those young
men and women who drop out of high school before
graduation (or before the last few months of the senior
year to be more precise). This excludes a relatively
small proportion of each age cohort--between 15 and 20
percent (Golladay, 1976, 1977). For the purposes of
estimating characteristics of the entire age group, the
omission of high school dropouts does introduce certain
biases; however, their small proportion sets outer
limits on the bias. For the purposes of estimating
changes from one cohort to another, the omission of
dropouts represents a problem only if different cohorts
have considerably different proportions who drop out.
However, we have no reason to expect dramatic changes

24

in those rates for the foreseeable future, and recently
published government statistics indicate a great deal
of stability in dropout rates since 1967 (Golladay,
1976, p. 62; 1977, p. 81).

Sampling Procedures

The procedure for securing a nationwide sample of
high school seniors is a multi-stage one. Stage 1 is
the selection of particular geographic areas, Stage 2
is the selection of one or more high schools in each
area, and Stage 3 is the selection of seniors within
each high school.

Stage 1: Geographic Areas. The geographic areas
used in this study are the primary sampling units
(PSUs) developed by the Sampling Section of the Survey
Research Center for use in the Center's nationwide
interview studies. These consist of 74 primary areas
throughout the coterminous United States. In addition
to the 12 largest metropolitan areas, containing about
30 percent of the nation's population, 62 other primary
areas are included: 10 in the Northeast, 18 in the
North Central area, 24 in the South, and 10 in the
West. Because these same PSUs are used for personal
interview studies by the Survey Research Center, local
field representatives can be assigned to administer the
data collections in practically all schools.

Stage 2: Schools. In the major metropolitan
areas more than one high school is often included in
the sampling design; in most other sampling areas a
single high school is sampled. In all cases, the
selections of high schools are made such that the
probability of drawing a school is proportionate to the
size of its senior class. The larger the senior class
(according to recent records), the higher the selection
probability assigned to the high school. When a
sampled school is unwilling to participate, a replacement school as similar to it as possible is selected
from the same geographic area. Schools remain in the
sample for two consecutive years, after which time a
new school is sampled. Each year half of the sample
schools are replaced.

Stage 3: Students. Within each selected school,
up to about 400 seniors may be included in the data
collection. In schools with fewer than 400 seniors,
the usual procedure is to include all of them in the
data collection. In larger schools, a subset of
seniors is selected either by randomly sampling
classrooms or by some other random method that is convenient for the school and judged to be unbiased.

Sample weights are assigned to each respondent so as to take account of variations in the sizes of samples from one school to another, as well as the (smaller) variations in selection probabilities occurring at the earlier stages of sampling.

The three-stage sampling procedure described above yielded the following numbers of participating schools and students:

	Class of 1976	Class of 1977	Class of 1978	Class of 1979	Class of 1980
Number of public schools	108	108	111	111	107
Number of private schools	15	16	20	20	20
Total number of schools	123	124	131	131	127
Total number of students	16,678	18,436	18,924	16,662	16,524
Student response rate	77%	79%	83%	82%	82%

Questionnaire Administration

The actual questionnaire administration in each school is carried out by the local Survey Research Center representatives and their assistants, following standardized procedures detailed in a project instruction manual. The questionnaires are administered in classrooms during normal class periods whenever possible; however, circumstances in some schools require the use of larger group administrations.

Content Areas and Questionnaire Design

Drug use and related attitudes are the topics which receive the most extensive coverage in the Monitoring the Future surveys; however, the questionnaires also deal with a wide range of other subject areas including attitudes about government, social institutions, race relations, changing roles for women, educational aspirations, occupational aims, marital and family plans, as well as a variety of background and demographic factors. Given this breadth of content, the study is not presented to respondents as a "drug use study," nor do they tend to view it as such.

Because many questions are needed to cover all of these topic areas, much of the questionnaire content is divided into five different questionnaire forms (which are distributed to participants in an ordered sequence that insures five virtually identical subsamples). About one-third of each questionnaire form consists of key or "core" variables which are common to all forms. All demographic variables, and nearly all of the drug use variables are included in this "core" set of measures. This use of the full sample for drug and demographic measures provides a more accurate estimation on these dimensions and also makes it possible to link these dimensions statistically to all of the other measures which are included in a single form only.

Representativeness of the Sample

The samples for this study are intended to be representative of high school seniors throughout the 48 coterminous states. We have already discussed the fact that this definition of the sample excludes one important portion of the age cohort: those who have dropped out of high school before nearing the end of the senior year. But given the aim of representing high school seniors, it will now be useful to consider the extent to which the obtained samples of schools and students are likely to be representative of all seniors.

We can distinguish at least two ways in which survey data of this sort might fall short of being fully accurate: (1) some sampled schools refuse to participate, which could introduce some bias; and (2) the failure to obtain questionnaire data from 100 percent of the students sampled in participating schools could also introduce bias.

School Participation. Depending on the year, from 66% to 80% of the schools initially invited to participate agree to do so; for each school refusal, a similar school (in terms of size, geographic area, urbanicity, etc.) is recruited as a replacement. The selection of replacement schools almost entirely removes problems of bias in region, urbanicity, and the like that might result from certain schools refusing to participate. Other potential biases are more subtle, however. If any single factor were dominant in most refusals, that also might suggest a source of serious bias. In fact, the reasons for a school refusing to participate are varied and are often a function of happenstance events; only a small proportion specifically object to the drug content of the survey. Thus we feel fairly confident that school refusals have not seriously biased the surveys.

Student Participation. Completed questionnaires are obtained from about 80% of all sampled students in participating schools. The single most important reason that students are missed is that they are absent from class at the time of data collection, and in most cases it is not workable to schedule a special followup data collection for such absent students.

In addition to absenteeism, student nonparticipation occurs because of schedule conflicts with school trips and other activities which tend to be more frequent than usual during the final months of the senior year. Of course, some students refuse to complete or to turn in the questionnaire. However, the SRC representatives in the field estimate this proportion at below 3 percent, and perhaps as low as 1 percent.

THE SPECIAL (LONG FORM) DATA COLLECTION

Rationale for the Special Data Collection

Although the Monitoring the Future data provide a rich resource for descriptive and trend analyses, they are less well suited for extensive correlational and multivariate analyses, because of some of the design features of the Monitoring the Future study. Specifically, questions in the annual survey are located in five different questionnaire forms. This means that except for demographic and some drug use questions, which are included in each of the five forms, questions can only be related to questions that appear in the same questionnaire form.

In order to deal with this problem, an additional data collection was conducted in the spring of 1978. This involved a "Long Form" questionnaire which included nearly all of the questions contained in the five Monitoring the Future questionnaire forms, thereby permitting a much wider range of correlational analyses.

28

Selection of Schools for Participation in the Long Form Data Collection

Working from the listing of schools which had participated in previous Monitoring the Future data collections, we selected a set of nine schools which, taken together, approximated the distribution of the 1976 Monitoring the Future sample with regard to region, urban density, and school size. Within this stratification, schools were selected not randomly, but so as to exclude schools which (a) would be asked to participate in a future Monitoring the Future sample, (b) were currently part of a special sample designed to test the effects of marijuana law changes, or (c) had proven to be particularly troublesome in previous questionnaire administrations. Of the nine schools initially invited, three refused to participate and were replaced with others conforming to the same general specifications. In five of the small and medium sized schools, questionnaires were distributed to the entire senior class; in one small and three large schools, students were randomly selected by classroom or home room. The overall response rate was 75 percent.

Table 2-1 shows that the distributions on region, urban density, and school size are very similar along the stratification variables for the Long Form respondents and the 1976 Monitoring the Future sample, which was used as the basis for stratification, and more importantly, the 1978 sample, which will frequently be used in conjunction with the Long Form respondents.

The Long Form Questionnaire

The Long Form questionnaire combined the materials from the five Monitoring the Future forms, deleting only duplicates of items that were repeated in several or all of the forms. In addition, a few variables related to sex role and work attitudes that were not retained after the 1975 or 1976 surveys were included in the Long Form questionnaire.

Procedures of the Long Form Data Collection

The selected schools and students were approached in much the same way as in the Monitoring the Future study. Three important differences should be noted: schools were paid a $100 honorarium; students were paid $5 for their participation; and, of course, the questionnaires were much longer than those in the Monitoring the Future surveys.

Following the procedures of the Monitoring the Future study, the specific arrangements for questionnaire administration were made by the local Survey Research Center representatives. These include visiting the schools before the scheduled administrations and handing out materials to teachers and students (the materials were identical to those used in the Monitoring the Future study, but the pamphlet to teachers included an extra page describing the specifics of this data collection).

The administrations were conducted by the local Survey Research Center representatives and their assistants. Unlike most of the Monitoring the Future administrations, Long Form administrations were conducted at the same time for all the eligible seniors from each school. Such "mass" administrations were necessary since they imposed the least inconvenience on the part of the schools when scheduling three-hour administration periods for large numbers of seniors. The actual administration time was approximately 2 1/2 hours.

COMPARISON OF THE LONG FORM DATA WITH THE MONITORING THE FUTURE DATA

The comparison of the two data sets follows two major lines of inquiry. First, the two data sets were compared on responses to a standard set of demographic, sex role attitude, and drug use variables, since those areas represent the major focus of either the Long Form or the Monitoring the Future data collection. The comparisons were based on means of those variables as well as on correlations between them. Secondly, a specific form of response set which appeared in the Long Form data in long item sets towards the later parts of the questionnaire, and which we termed "straight-line" response pattern, was investigated and its effects on means and correlations were determined.

Comparison of the Two Data Sets on Standard Variables

Means and standard deviations for responses of males and females who completed the Long Form or one of the Monitoring the Future questionnaires are presented in Tables 2-2 and 2-3. In the case of variables which are measured in all five standard Monitoring the Future questionnaire forms, the means were calculated by pooling the respondents from the five forms (in these cases, the ranges of means and standard deviations are provided in additional columns). No weights were used for calculating the means for the Long Form respondents, while the Monitoring the Future data were weighted in order to take account of variations in the sizes of samples from one school to another as well as the variations occurring at the earlier stages of sampling (see also Bachman and Johnston, 1978).

Differences between means for the Long Form respondents and the Monitoring the Future sample were evaluated by t-test. A larger number of strong differences between the two groups appeared than would be expected if both were simple random samples from the same universe. The pattern of differences suggests that the two groups of seniors are systematically different, primarily along socio-economic, race and academic lines. Specifically, the Long Form respondents are somewhat more likely to be black, have less educated fathers and mothers, and rate their own academic abilities lower than those in the Monitoring the Future sample. Male Long Form respondents, in addition, are less likely to plan on going to college. On the other hand, only small differences exist for school grades, drug use variables, political orientation, and religious commitment. With regard to specific sex role attitudes, the Long Form respondents reacted more traditionally than the Monitoring the Future sample.

It is possible to approximate the Monitoring the Future sample when analyzing the data from the Long Form data collection; this is done by using a weight variable in order to scale down the proportion of seniors from black and lower socioeconomic background among the Long Form respondents to the proportion observed in the Monitoring the Future sample. Such a weight variable was developed in the following way: Bivariate tables were calculated for race and parental education for both the Long Form and the Monitoring the Future samples of 1977 through 1979. (The three annual samples were used in combination to smooth out any small yearly fluctuations.) The weights were then created for each combination of race and parental education by dividing the Monitoring the Future sample's cell N by the Long Form's cell N, and multiplying this figure by the Long Form's total N divided by the Monitoring the Future sample's total N. This procedure yields a weight for each cell in the Long Form data which adjusts the cell's proportion so as to match the proportion in the national sample. The weights range from .46 to 1.9; the average weight is .98.

31

When comparisons between the Long Form respondents and the Monitoring the Future respondents were repeated using these weights (data not shown), the differences were substantially reduced and all of them fell short of statistical significance. This is of course the case because the racial and socioeconomic imbalances are related to differences in abilities, aspirations, and attitudes.

On a second level of comparison, correlations between demographic characteristics and sex role attitudinal items, as well as correlations among sex role attitudinal items, were compared across samples. The overall distributions of the differences between correlations revealed somewhat larger differences than would be expected by pure chance.[2] A more detailed look at the direction of the largest differences suggests little systematic distortion; i.e., in some instances, the Monitoring the Future correlations are larger; in some instances the Long Form correlations are larger; and in some instances they are of similar strength but in opposite directions. (See also Herzog and Bachman [1979] for a more detailed description of these comparisons.)

Investigations of Response Set

While the comparison of the two data sets revealed rather little evidence of systematic differences across a variety of means and correlations, we did identify one specific difference which appears to be related to the length of the questionnaire used in the Long Form data collection. This difference manifests itself as an increased tendency, towards later parts of the Long Form questionnaire, to use an identical response category for most or all items in the same set. In other words, respondents are increasingly more likely to show some form of position bias in later parts of the questionnaire.

A more detailed account of the form of the position bias and its effects on means and correlations is provided in Appendix A and by Herzog and Bachman (1981). Here, it must suffice to say that the position bias consists of a tendency to respond with the same response category to a number of items included in the same set. This pattern of responding appears to be

---

[2] These correlations were calculated before the weights for the Long Form data were developed and therefore do not involve any weighting procedure for the Long Form data.

restricted to large item sets which are located towards
the end of a long questionnaire; and even among those
sets of items, some show very little of this response
pattern. We suspect that the sets dealing with questions of a very personal and/or interesting subject
matter are less susceptible to this response pattern
than are the ones dealing with issues of little direct
relevance to the respondent's life.

The response pattern described above does have an
effect on mean scores: means are biased towards the
predominant position of the stereotypical response.
There is also an effect on correlations involving questions from the same set of items: due to the operation
of the response bias, pairs of questions show positive
correlations that are higher, and/or negative correlations that are lower, than would be the case without
the influence of the response bias. Correlations involving one item from a set afflicted with substantial
response set and another "non-afflicted" item show min-
imal bias.

ANALYTICAL PROCEDURES AND PRESENTATION OF FINDINGS

At the end of the previous chapter we outlined
the research objectives that are addressed in this
report and the general strategy that is used in analyzing the data. We now specify the analytical procedures
in somewhat more detail and describe the tabular
presentation of the findings.

As we described in the first chapter, our investigations begin with a presentation of sex role attitudes that seniors hold. We then examine the
preferences of division of labor between spouses that
they hold for their future marriage; their plans and
expectations for education and work; and their plans
and expectations for marriage and family formation.

Tabular presentation of data. A standard format
for analyses and data presentation is followed in Chapters 3 through 6. For each of the measurement areas
within a chapter, we provide several standard tables of
data. The first type of table in each case includes
(a) the complete wording of the questionnaire items;
(b) the response distributions for male and female
seniors in the class of 1980; (c) mean values for male
and female seniors for the classes of 1976 through
1980; and (d) correlation coefficients indicating the
strength of sex differences and the strengths of cohort

trends from 1976 through 1980 by sex. The second standard type of tables presents the correlations between each questionnaire item (or index) and a set of standard background factors, as well as the variance accounted for by the entire set of background factors, using combined data from the senior classes of 1976 through 1980. (These background factors are described in Table 2-4.)

The two standard data tables described above make use of data from the large and nationally representative Monitoring the Future project. The remaining tables are based on the special survey of about 1000 seniors in 1978, designed to permit a wider range of correlational analyses. The third type of standard table examines interrelationships involving the items and/or indexes which appear within a particular chapter. The fourth type of standard table, employed in Chapters 4 through 6, presents bivariate and multivariate relational analyses in which background factors, sex role attitudes, and other relevant measures, are examined as predictors (or correlates) of the various plans and attitudes concerning marriage, parenthood, education, and occupation.

Data analysis procedures. The tables described above contain statistics resulting from various analytical techniques which we will now discuss in somewhat more detail. In the first set of tables, which show response distributions for 1980 and means for 1976 through 1980 by sex, we quantified the sex differences and cohort trend differences by using correlation coefficients. The coefficient for sex indicates the strength of the overall sex difference; a positive coefficient indicates higher values among females (males are coded 1, females = 2). The coefficient for cohort trend indicates the strength of the linear trend 1976 through 1980 within each sex; a positive coefficient indicates higher values in more recent years (members of the class of 1976 are coded 1; 1977=2; 1978=3; 1979=4; 1980=5).

The second set of tables shows how each specific questionnaire item is correlated with a standard set of background factors. Since preliminary analyses had indicated relatively few and inconsistent differences when comparing correlations from different graduating classes, the correlations in these tables are based on data that are combined from the classes of 1976 through 1980. The amount of variance that can be explained by this entire set of standard background variables is also included in the tables.

34

Tables of the third type are presented where interrelations between specific items are of interest. Often such a presentation is used to clarify our decisions about forming indexes from various sets of items.

The fourth set of tables focuses on results from multiple regression analyses (although bivariate correlations are also included). Specifically, standardized regression coefficients and the amount of explained variance are presented. The number of regression analyses is determined by the number of independent factors that we chose to investigate; and this number is generally higher in later chapters, because relevant concepts introduced in earlier chapters are incorporated.

In most analyses of the Monitoring the Future data we do not use any statistical significance tests; rather, our interpretation relies exclusively on the strength or importance of the relationships. We chose this strategy because the number of respondents in the Monitoring the Future data is so large that even weak effects are statistically significant, although not necessarily meaningful. On the other hand, the data from the Long Form data collection are based on far fewer respondents; thus measures of statistical significance become more critical in guiding interpretations.

Statistical significance estimates for the Long Form data are somewhat hampered by our difficulties of making reasonable assumptions about design effects[3], short of extensive and costly calculations. By ex-

---

[3]The design effect is a measure of the difference between data from a complex sample as described above and data from a simple random sample. In this complex sample clusters of students attending the same school are deliberately chosen (so as to keep surveying costs within bounds). Since students who attend the same school tend to resemble one another more than two randomly selected students, less unique information is learned from each individual student in a complex sample design than in a simple random sample, in which students would be chosen without regard to the school they attend. This implies that observed values have larger error margins in complex samples than in simple random samples. Traditional tests of statistical significance are based on the assumption of a simple random sample; therefore, test statistics should be adjusted using a design effect estimate when complex samples are being used. This is most easily done by reducing the number of respondents correspondingly.

trapolation from the Monitoring the Future data, on which some design effect calculations had been performed, and by taking differences in cluster size and weighting procedures into account, we can make at least a "semi-educated" guess about the design effect for most of the variables of interest in the Long Form data. We believe that this design effect is no lower than 2, possibly higher. Concretely, a design effect of 2 means that for the purpose of statistical significance calculations we assume that the actual number of respondents of our complex sample is only as effective as a random sample of half that size. Therefore, the significance levels indicated in most Long Form tables assume samples half the size of the actual number of respondents. (This applies to tables where data for males and females are analyzed separately; when they are combined, a design effect of 2.5 is used.)

Although we always present the data separate for male and female seniors and sometimes draw comparative interpretations, we present only standardized measures for the bivariate and multivariate analyses--i.e., correlations and standardized regression coefficients. For many items this approach is unproblematic, since the variances of the response distributions are similar for both sexes. However, there are some notable exceptions. For example, female seniors' responses to sex role attitude questions often show less variance than those of male seniors--generally because the female scores cluster closer to one or the other of the scale limits. We invite the reader to examine the response distributions in the first type of tables, the standard deviations of the background characteristics in Table 2-4, and standard deviations provided for some of the indexes. It should also be noted that the interpretations concerning sex differences in patterns of correlations provided in the text are based on careful examination of standard deviations and unstandardized coefficients, in addition to examination of standardized coefficients.

Table 2-1

Distributions of Long Form Respondents and Monitoring the Future Samples
on Region, Urban Density, and Size of School

	Monitoring the Future National Sample 1976	Long Form Respondents 1978	Monitoring the Future National Sample 1978
Region			
North-East	23%	24%	24%
North-Central	31	33	29
South	31	30	33
West	15	13	14
Urban Density			
Self-Representing (12 Largest) Standard Metropolitan Statistical Areas	25	25	26
Other Standard Metropolitan Statistical Areas	40	43	44
Non-Standard Metropolitan Statistical Areas	35	32	30
School Size			
Less Than 150 Seniors	24	26	22
150-300 Seniors	34	31	29
Over 300 Seniors	42	43	49

Table 2-2

Comparisons Between the Long Form Respondents and the Monitoring the Future 1978 Sample:
Means and Standard Deviations on Major Background, Drug Use, and Sex Role Attitudinal Variables, for Males

| Variable | Long Form Respondents 1978 | | | MtF Sample 1978 | | | t-Ratio | Range of Five MtF Questionnaire Forms | | | |
| | | | | | | | | $\bar{X}$ | | S.D. | |
	N	$\bar{X}$	S.D.	Wtd. N	$\bar{X}$	S.D.		Low	High	Low	High
Race (1=White/2=Black)	400	1.22	0.41	8011	1.11	0.31	6.91	1.09	1.11	0.29	0.32
Marital Status (1=Single, 2=Married, Engaged)	423	1.07	0.25	8680	1.06	0.24	0.51	1.05	1.07	0.22	0.25
Academic Ability (School Ability & Intelligence: 1=Low, 7=High)	414	4.73	0.98	8197	4.92	1.07	-3.46	4.89	4.95	1.04	1.12
# Cigarettes Smoked/Last 30 days (1=Not at all, 7=2 or more packs)	413	1.79	1.35	8610	1.93	1.49	-1.90	1.90	1.98	1.46	1.54
# Drinks/Last 30 days (1=None, 7=40 or more)	386	3.05	1.74	8217	3.09	1.67	-0.38	2.99	3.18	1.60	1.71
# Times Smoked Marijuana-Hashish/Last 30 days (1=None, 7=40 or more)	422	2.29	1.99	8426	2.46	2.07	-1.75	2.42	2.51	2.04	2.11
Father's Education Level (1=Grade school or less, 6=Grad or profssional school)	396	3.15	1.44	8195	3.51	1.44	-4.91	3.48	3.55	1.43	1.45
Mother's Education Level (1=Grade school or less, 6=Grad or professional school)	411	3.08	1.56	8358	3.37	1.18	-4.89	3.32	3.39	1.16	1.20
Mother Worked While R was Young (1=No, 4=Yes, nearly all the time)	429	2.22	1.03	8628	2.11	1.08	2.00	2.08	2.14	1.06	1.09

Table 2-2 (Continued)

Variable	Long Form Respondents 1978			MtF Sample 1978			t-Ratio	Range of Five MtF Questionnaire Forms			
								$\bar{x}$		S.D.	
	N	$\bar{x}$	S.D.	Wtd. N	$\bar{x}$	S.D.		Low	High	Low	High
Political Orientation (1=Very conservative, 6=Radical)	322	3.16	1.16	6583	3.18	1.10	-0.40	3.13	3.22	1.09	1.11
Importance of Religion in R's Life (1=Not important, 4=Very important)	429	2.67	1.01	8576	2.64	1.00	0.73	2.61	2.66	0.98	1.01
R's High School Grades (1=D, 9=A)	427	5.39	1.85	8417	5.42	1.92	-0.33	5.36	5.51	1.91	1.96
Hours/Week Worked During School Year (1=None, 8=30+ hours)	422	4.46	2.51	8259	4.54	2.44	-0.64	4.46	4.63	2.42	2.47
Dating Frequency (1=Never, 6=More than 3/week)	419	3.23	1.49	8103	3.35	1.52	-1.58	3.32	3.38	1.50	1.54
College Plans (1=Definitely won't graduate from 4 year college 4=Definitely will)	415	2.35	1.14	8097	2.56	1.19	-3.51	2.52	2.62	1.18	1.21

Table 2-2 (Continued)

Variable	Long Form Respondents 1978			MtF Sample 1978				Range of Five MtF Questionnaire Forms				
								X̄			S.D.	
	N	X̄	S.D.	Wtd. N	X̄	S.D.	t-Ratio	Low	High	Low	High	
Sex Role Variables												
Married Couple Without Children:												
Husband works full-time, wife does not have job (1=Not acceptable. 4=Desirable)	430	2.55	0.90	1716	2.51	0.86	0.81					
Husband and wife work full-time (1=Not acceptable, 4=Desirable)	428	2.33	1.03	1709	2.43	1.02	-1.85					
Married Couple With Pre-School Children:												
Husband works full-time wife does not have job (1=Not acceptable. 4=Desirable)	430	3.16	0.92	1715	3.19	0.88	-0.59					
Husband and wife both have full-time jobs (1=Not Acceptable, 4=Desirable)	426	1.57	0.94	1709	1.46	0.85	2.31					
Husband has full-time job, wife does not work:												
Wife does all child care (1=Not acceptable. 4=Desirable)	428	2.29	1.03	1712	2.27	1.02	0.47					
Husband and wife share child care equally (1=Not acceptable. 4=Desirable)	426	2.82	0.94	1706	2.94	0.90	-2.38					

Table 2-2 (Continued)

Variable	Long Form Respondents 1978			MtF Sample 1978				Range of Five MtF Questionnaire Forms					
								X̄			S.D.		
	N	X̄	S.D.	Wtd. N	X̄	S.D.	t-Ratio	Low	High		Low	High	
Men and women should be paid equally for equal work (1=Disagree, 5=Agree).	427	4.45	0.92	1709	4.48	1.03	-0.50						
Better if men work outside of home and women take care of home and family (1=Disagree, 5=Agree)	424	3.57	1.17	1698	3.58	1.37	-0.15						
Child suffers with working mother (1=Disagree, 5=Agree)	424	3.70	1.14	1695	3.81	1.33	-1.61						
Working mother can have as warm a relationship with family as non-working mother (1=Disagree, 5=Agree)	425	2.99	1.30	1703	2.87	1.53	1.50						
Fuller lives for people who marry (1=Disagree, 5=Agree)	382	3.36	1.13	1827	2.99	1.43	4.71						
Husband should make all important decisions (1=Disagree, 5=Agree)	383	3.22	1.11	1835	2.79	1.39	5.68						

41

Table 2-3

Comparisons Between the Long Form Respondents and the Monitoring the Future 1978 Sample:
Means and Standard Deviations on Major Background, Drug Use, and Sex Role Attitudinal Variables, for Females

Variable	Long Form Respondents 1978			MtF Sample 1978			t-Ratio	Range of Five MtF Questionnaire Forms			
								$\bar{X}$		S.D.	
	N	$\bar{X}$	S.D.	Wtd. N	$\bar{X}$	S.D.		Low	High	Low	High
Race (1=White/2=Black)	504	1.22	0.42	8589	1.14	0.34	5.20	1.13	1.15	0.33	0.35
Marital Status (1=Single, 2=Married, engaged)	530	1.16	0.83	9190	1.13	0.33	1.78	1.12	1.14	0.32	0.35
Academic Ability (School Ability & Intelligence: 1=Low, 7=High)	511	4.71	1.04	8658	4.82	0.98	-2.54	4.80	4.83	0.98	1.02
# Cigarettes Smoked/Last 30 Days (1=Not at all, 7=2 or more packs)	520	1.94	1.40	9095	1.95	1.42	-0.17	1.93	1.96	1.41	1.46
# Drinks/Last 30 Days (1=None, 7=40 or more)	500	2.65	1.57	8676	2.51	1.47	2.14	2.45	2.56	1.40	1.52
# Times Smoked Marijuana-Hashish/Last 30 Days (1=None, 7=40 or more)	518	2.02	1.72	8953	1.93	1.67	1.10	1.90	1.95	1.63	1.74
Father's Education Level (1=Grade school or less, 6=Grad or professional school)	504	2.98	1.42	8602	3.35	1.46	-5.64	3.28	3.40	1.45	1.48
Mother's Education Level (1=Grade school or less, 6=Grad or professional school)	521	3.00	1.16	8906	3.24	1.21	-4.54	3.20	3.27	1.19	1.24
Mother Worked While R Was Young (1=No, 4=Yes, nearly all the time)	536	2.25	1.12	9153	2.19	1.11	1.11	2.17	2.22	1.09	1.13

Table 2-3 (Continued)

Variable	Long Form Respondents 1978			MtF Sample 1978				Range of Five MtF Questionnaire Forms			
								$\bar{x}$		S.D.	
	N	$\bar{x}$	S.D.	Wtd. N	$\bar{x}$	S.D.	t-Ratio	Low	High	Low	High
Political Orientation (1=Very conservative, 6=Radical)	358	3.21	0.95	6146	3.21	0.95	-0.04	3.17	3.27	0.92	0.96
Importance of Religion in R's Life (1=Not important, 4=Very important)	538	2.89	0.96	9156	2.90	0.94	-0.22	2.87	2.93	0.93	0.96
R's High School Grades (1=D, 9=A)	534	6.18	1.86	8979	6.03	1.84	1.82	5.95	6.06	1.84	1.88
Hours/Week Worked During School Year (1=None, 8=30+ hours)	527	3.96	2.50	8907	3.90	2.32	0.56	3.82	3.98	2.28	2.36
Dating Frequency (1=Never, 6=More than 3/week)	534	3.67	1.67	8813	3.62	1.66	0.69	3.57	3.68	1.63	1.70
College Plans (1=Definitely won't graduate from 4 year college, 4=Definitely will)	527	2.40	1.18	8738	2.48	1.21	-1.48	2.43	2.53	1.19	1.23

Variable	Long Form Respondents 1978			MtF Sample 1978			t-Ratio	Range of Five MtF Questionnaire Forms			
								X̄		S.D.	
	N	X̄	S.D.	Wtd. N	X̄	S.D.		Low	High	Low	High
Sex Role Variables											
Married Couple Without Children:											
Husband works full-time, wife does not have job (1=Not acceptable, 4=Desirable)	534	1.88	0.89	1853	1.92	0.88	-0.83				
Husband and wife work full-time (1=Not acceptable, 4=Desirable)	533	2.94	0.94	1853	2.86	0.94	1.68				
Married Couple With Pre-School Chilren:											
Husband works full-time wife does not have job (1=Not acceptable, 4=Desirable)	534	2.93	0.99	1856	2.98	0.97	-0.96				
Husband and wife both have full-time jobs (1=Not Acceptable, 4=Desirable)	529	1.63	0.93	1851	1.53	0.83	2.52				
Husband has full-time job wife does not work:											
Wife does all child care (1=Not acceptable, 4=Desirable)	535	2.17	0.99	1853	2.10	0.98	1.58				
Husband and wife share child care equally (1=Not acceptable, 4=Desirable)	532	3.08	0.91	1846	3.11	0.88	-0.55				

Table 2-3 (Continued)

Variable	Long Form Respondents 1978			MtF Sample 1978				Range of Five MtF Questionnaire Forms			
	N	X̄	S.D.	Wtd. N	X̄	S.D.	t-Ratio	X̄ Low	X̄ High	S.D. Low	S.D. High
Men and women should be paid equally for equal work (1=Disagree, 5=Agree)	535	4.77	0.63	1916	4.86	0.48	-3.66				
Better if men work outside of home and women take care of home and family (1=Disagree, 5=Agree)	535	2.95	1.36	1907	2.78	1.45	2.31				
Child suffers with working mother (1=Disagree, 5=Agree)	533	3.42	1.30	1902	3.14	1.48	3.90				
Working mother can have as warm a relationship with family as non-working mother (1=Disagree, 5=Agree)	535	3.48	1.34	1915	3.67	1.41	-2.77				
Fuller lives for people who marry (1=Disagree, 5=Agree)	506	3.33	1.27	1753	2.96	1.50	5.07				
Husband should make all important decisions (1=Disagree, 5=Agree)	506	2.55	1.28	1752	1.91	1.22	10.23				

Table 2-4

Description of Variables Measuring Background Characteristics

Background Characteristic	Item or Derivative	Response Categories	Combined Data 1976-1980 Administrations Mean M	F	Standard Deviation M	F
Race	"How do you describe yourself?"	0=White 1=Black 9=Other (was coded as Missing Data for all analyses)	.11	.14	.31	.35
Live with Mother	"Which of the following people live in the same household with you? (Mark ALL that apply)"	1=Mother (or female guardian) 0=(Not Marked)	.92	.93	.27	.26
Live with Father	"Which of the following people live in the same household with you? (Mark ALL that apply)"	1=Father (or male guardian) 0=(Not Marked)	.83	.81	.38	.39
Mother Worked	"Did your mother have a paid job (half-time or more) during the time you were growing up?"	1=No 2=Yes, some of the time 3=Yes, Most of the time 4=Yes, all of the time	2.12	2.19	1.08	1.12
Father's Education Level	"What is the highest level of schooling your father completed?"	1=Completed grade school or less 2=Some high school 3=Completed high school 4=Some college 5=Completed college 6=Graduate or professional school	3.50	3.38	1.45	1.47
Mother's Education Level	"What is the highest level of schooling your mother completed?"	1=Completed grade school or less 2=Some high school 3=Completed high school 4=Some college 5=Completed college 6=Graduate or professional school	3.37	3.27	1.19	1.22
Urbanicity of Residence	A composite variable constructed from sampling information on where the respondent lives now and his/her report on where he/she grew up.	1=On a farm 2=In the country, not on a farm 3=Non-Standard Metropolitan Area, small town or city 4=Non-self-representing Standard Metropolitan Area 5=Self-representing Standard Metropolitan Area	3.71	3.74	1.13	1.09

46

Table 2-4 (Continued)

Background Characteristic	Item or Derivative[1]	Response Categories	Combined Data 1976-1980 Administrations			
			Mean		Standard Deviation	
			M	F	M	F
Academic Ability	A mean of two questions referring to the respondent's self-rated school ability and self-rated intelligence.	1=Far Below Average 7=Far Above Average	4.91	4.84	1.08	.98
Grades	"Which of the following best describes your average grade so far in high school?"	9=A (93-100) 8=A- (90-92) 7=B+ (87-89) . . . 1=D (69 or below)	5.45	6.08	1.93	1.85
College Plans	"How likely is it that you will do each of the following things after high school. . . Graduate from college (four-year program)?"	0=Probably or definitely won't 1=Probably or definitely will	.55	.51	.50	.50
Political Orientation	"How would you describe your political beliefs?"	1=Very Conservative 2=Conservative 3=Moderate 4=Liberal 5=Very liberal 6=Radical	3.19	3.20	1.12	.95
Religious Commitment	A mean of two questions referring to how often the respondent attends religious services and the importance attributed to religion in his/her life.	10=No Commitment 40=High Commitment	27.12	29.70	9.07	8.69
Dating Frequency	"On the average, how often do you go out with a date (or your spouse, if you are married)?"	1=Never 2=Once a month or less 3=2 or 3 times a month 4=Once a week 5=2 or 3 times a week 6=Over 3 times a week	3.35	3.59	1.53	1.67

[1]For more information on these variables, see Bachman, Johnston, and O'Malley, 1981.

47

CHAPTER 3

SEX ROLE ATTITUDES

A rapidly growing literature reports on sex role attitudes of various subgroups of the U.S. population, on the formation of these attitudes, and on their change in recent years. Although the term "sex role attitude" is often left undefined, a range of foci can be distinguished. One focus is on norms about gender differences in roles and behaviors: most notably, men should operate in the public sphere where they hold paid employment; women should remain in the private sphere, attending to home and children. Another focus is on beliefs about personality differences by gender: Men are aggressive and ambitious; women are dependent and emotional. A third focus is on beliefs about stratification by gender: the issue is whether women should have the same opportunities and receive the same rewards as men. In other words, some treatments of sex role attitudes focus on gender differences as such, others on the consequences of such differences. Individuals who subscribe to such differences and differential opportunities and rewards are described as holding "traditional" sex role views, although the term "sexist" has also been used (e.g., Bayer, 1975; Angrist, Mickelsen, and Penna, 1977). The opposite end of the continuum has been termed "egalitarian" (e.g., Mason and Bumpass, 1975; Mason et al., 1976; Thornton and Freedman, 1979), "contemporary" (e.g., Lipman-Blumen, 1972; Vanfossen,1977), "modern" (e.g., Orcutt and Bayer, 1978), or "feminist" (e.g., Parelius, 1975; Mason and Bumpass, 1975). Our own preference is to refer to sex role attitudes as ranging on a continuum from traditional to non-traditional, where "non-traditional" attitudes are those which do not urge differences in roles or opportunities based on gender.

Research in which more than one of those conceptualizations of sex role attitudes was used shows that the support for role differentiation constitutes a different dimension from the support for equal opportunities (e.g., Mason and Bumpass, 1975). There is some evidence to suggest that recently these two dimensions have become more highly interrelated (Mason,

Czajka, and Arber, 1976), suggesting a growing tendency toward ideological consistency in sex role attitudes.

We can draw a fairly clear theoretical distinction between sex role attitudes as general beliefs about women's and men's roles, on one hand, and personal preferences for one's own family and work life, on the other hand. Thus, for example, a woman might strongly reject the notion that "women ought to stay home and leave paid employment to men," but at the same time her own personal preference might be the role of full-time homemaker and mother. The two positions are by no means incompatible, although we would expect general attitudes to be positively associated with personal preferences. In the present chapter we limit our focus to sex role attitudes; later we will examine some of the ways in which such attitudes impact on the "traditionality" of personal plans and preferences.

Sex role attitudes are acquired by the individual during the socialization process. First and foremost, the attitudes prevalent in the parental home and the actual behaviors displayed by parents constitute a critical set of influence factors on the child. For example, paid employment by the mother has been reported to foster non-traditional sex role attitudes (as well as higher than average career aspirations and higher evaluation of female competence) in daughters (Hoffman and Nye, 1974), although the process by which the effect of mothers work gets transmitted is less well understood. The absence of the father has been linked to problems with masculine identification in boys. However, that research is fraught with methodological shortcomings (see, e.g., Safilios-Rothschild, 1979); the most critical one for our purpose is that sex role attitudes are conceptualized in a bipolar form as either masculine or feminine, and intermediate or mixed forms of identification are acknowledged as a failure of developing proper identifications.

More global parameters of the parental home and immediate environment also have been reported to be associated with sex role attitudes and behaviors. Among them, socioeconomic status of the parental family shows some relationships, although the evidence has not accumulated to a consistent pattern of findings. On one hand, support for non-traditional sex role attitudes has always been concentrated among the higher socioeconomic and particularly among the more highly educated adults (Mason and Bumpass, 1975; Mason, Czajka, and Arber, 1976; Thornton and Freedman, 1979) and awareness about distinct sex roles is higher among children from a working class background (Safilios-

Rothschild, 1979). On the other hand, husbands in
higher job echelons and higher income brackets are less
likely to have a working wife (Kreps, 1971); they experience more work demands that interfere with their
involvement in housework and child care (Blood and
Wolfe, 1960); and they have more marital power to
resist such involvement (Ericksen, Yancey, and Ericksen, 1979). These differences suggest that parents in
higher socioeconomic strata portray more traditional
sex roles than parents from lower socioeconomic strata
despite their higher endorsement of non-traditional sex
roles.

Another global parameter--which is to some
degree related to social class--is the racial and eth-
nic setting of the family. Black women on the average
have never assumed as traditional a role as have white
women: they were always more likely to hold paid
employment (Bowen and Finegan, 1969; Sweet, 1973) and
to maintain a strong position in the family (Ericksen,
et al., 1979; Scanzoni, 1971; Willie and Greenblatt,
1978). Therefore, they presumably portray more
egalitarian sex roles to their offsprings.

Other societal institutions are, of course, ex-
erting influence on the formation of sex role attitudes
in addition to parental influence. For example, role
differentiation by sex is an integral part of Judeo-
Christian religions. Although there appears to be some
variation among specific religious denominations, most
of them support the traditional family and its procrea-
tive function, and thereby indirectly discourage change
of the female role. Some research in fact suggests a
relationship between traditional sex role attitudes and
religiosity (Bernard, 1975).

By the same token, notions of male supremacy are
fundamental parts of a patriarchical social structure
(Lipman-Blumen and Tickamyer, 1975), while philosophies
on the left tend to view women's emancipation as a form
of class struggle and thus support their equality.
Liberal political views might therefore be expected to
be related positively to sharing of roles as a means of
achieving equality between the sexes (Hershey and Sullivan, 1977).

The learning of sex role attitudes begins at a
very young age through socialization mechanisms such as
differential parental treatment and reinforcement of
the sexes, observational learning, and cognitive understanding of what it means "to be a man or a woman"
(Maccoby and Jacklin, 1974). Thus notions of what constitutes sex-appropriate behaviors are already present
in quite young children, as demonstrated by Hartley

(1959-1960, 1964). Since learning continues and cognitive capabilities develop throughout childhood into early adolescence, sex role attitudes are postulated to become more established as a child grows older. There is in fact some evidence to suggest that older children are more sex-typed in their behaviors and plans than younger ones (Kagan and Moss, 1962; Maccoby and Jacklin, 1974; Rosen and Aneshensel, 1978).

The cognitive-developmental approach to sex role development (Kohlberg, 1966; Rebecca, Hefner, and Oleshansky, 1976) suggests that such a consolidation of sex-typed behaviors and attitudes only occurs up to a certain developmental stage, i.e., till the conformistic stage is reached. When the individual progresses beyond that stage, sex role attitudes become more differentiated and more flexible, overcoming conformistic and stereotyped attitudes. Since cognitive development is closely related to intelligence, we would expect non-traditional sex role attitudes among adolescents to be related to their intelligence and abilities.

Moreover, the socialization process continues throughout the life span, as Brim (1968) has convincingly argued. Thus, sex role attitudes may be modified according to new experiences. Among adolescents, we would expect that the dating experiences will have an impact on sex role attitudes. Since frequent dating at least among young women probably reflects orientation towards traditional female roles, we would expect it to be related with traditional sex role attitudes. Some evidence is in fact available to support this notion (Scanzoni and Fox, 1980).

In the wake of the women's liberation movement, attitudes about the proper roles of the sexes have been changing rather rapidly, resulting in a climate of increasingly equal opportunities for women and men. There is now widespread support for equality of women in educational opportunities, equal pay for equal work, and equal access to political offices (Bayer, 1975; Ferree, 1974; Mason et al., 1976; Spitze and Huber, 1980; Thornton and Freedman, 1979). Attitudes have also become more favorable towards paid work by married women and even by mothers of young children (Mason et al., 1976; Parelius, 1975).

The measures of sex role attitudes presented here were largely taken from earlier studies, as indicated below. The most common question format is a statement of the way things "should" be, with the respondent asked to indicate extent of agreement or disagreement (including a "neither" category for respondents who have mixed views, are neutral, or simply do not have a clear opinion). Each of these items clearly invite the respondent to prescribe or endorse certain role arrangements for women and/or men. Other items, which also use the agree-disagree response format, are statements of "the way things are" rather than the way they should be. For some such items, it may not be entirely clear whether agreement represents endorsement; nevertheless, we have included them because they have appeared in other studies and because they do show relationships similar to those for the "should" items. In any case, however, these items refer to the general population, as opposed to the respondent's own preferences.

We have found it useful to group our measures of sex role attitudes under the following topics:

-- Equal opportunities for women in the public sphere

-- Preference for patriarchical family

-- Encouraging a daughter's independence

-- Effects of a wife/mother working outside the home

-- Importance of the parent role for males and females

-- Conventional marriage, extramarital sex

In the following sections we explore each of these topics in turn, looking at (1) overall levels of agreement or disagreement, (2) differences between male and female seniors, (3) any evidence of change (trends) during the past five years, and (4) patterns of correlations between sex role attitudes and various dimensions of background and other characteristics.

EQUAL OPPORTUNITIES FOR WOMEN

The four items which are relevant to this topic probe equal opportunities for both sexes in education, occupation and pay. As a convenience to our discussion, and also because it provides a means of reducing the effects of response error and thus sharpening our findings, we have computed an index of attitudes about

equal opportunities (a mean of the four items in Table
3-1.1).[1]

Descriptive Results and Trends

The large majority of high school seniors agree--
or at least agree mostly--that women should have equal
opportunities, as shown on the left-hand side of Table
3-1.1. But within that overall pattern of agreement
there are a number of important differences, having to
do partly with what sort of equality is being considered and partly with who is responding. The most
obvious and also the most important difference involves
gender; a majority of male seniors are in favor of
equality, but support for sexual equality is consistently and substantially higher among female seniors.
The percentage distributions show the gender differences very clearly for seniors in the class of 1980. Our
discussion concentrates on differences in means;
however, the distributions also indicate that there is
often greater diversity (larger variance) in male
responses compared with female responses. The trends
in means, shown in the right-hand side of the table,
indicate that these attitudes have not been changing
very much during the past five years. For each of the
four items in the table, the mean ratings are practically identical for female seniors in the classes of
1976 through 1980. Among male seniors, on the other
hand, a very modest increase in egalitarian views appeared from 1976 through 1980, suggesting a slight nar-
rowing of the gap. Nevertheless, there is quite a long
way to go before the gap is closed; at the rate of
change suggested by these particular data, it would not
disappear until sometime in the next century.

When we look at the four specific items shown in
Table 3-1.1, it is clear that some kinds of equality
are more generally acceptable than others. Practically
no one, male or female, disagrees with the idea that
educational opportunities should be equal between the
sexes; but even in that area some nine percent of
female seniors and 16 percent of male seniors fall
short of unqualified agreement. In the area of work,
the minorities expressing disagreement are larger, and
so are the gender differences: Equal pay for equal work

---

[1]Other indexes are employed throughout this
report whenever several items (a) are clearly related
on conceptual grounds, (b) are intercorrelated and show
basically similar patterns of correlations with other
variables, and (c) happen to appear in the same questionnaire form.

is a proposition which receives full agreement from about nine out of ten female seniors, contrasted with seven of ten male seniors. The departures from agreement are even greater in response to the statement that "women should be considered as seriously as men for jobs as executives or politicians"; less than half of the males fully agree, compared with three quarters of the females. Finally, the statement that "a woman should have exactly the same job opportunities as a man" receives the least unqualified agreement (40 percent among male seniors, 58 percent among females). It is of interest to note that male responses to this latter item are not very different, on the average, from their responses to the preceding item on equal consideration for executive or political jobs. Among females, however, the differences are greater, primarily reflecting a shift from "agree" to "mostly agree." We speculate that for some females, and also a few males, the word "exactly" may represent a bit of a stumbling block. Thus if one holds that even a tiny handful of occupations--e.g., washroom attendant or coach of the women's basketball team--ought to be gender specific, then one might feel constrained to express less than full agreement with the item as stated. (The parallel item on exactly equal educational opportunities seems less problematic.)

Background Characteristics

We discussed earlier a number of dimensions of social background and early experiences which might predict an individual's sex role attitudes. Table 3-2.1 presents, separately for male and female seniors, the ways in which thirteen such dimensions are correlated with attitudes toward equal opportunities for women. Note, however, that Table 3-2.1 does not include any data on trends in correlations, because our preliminary examination of the data did not reveal any clear trends. Given that finding, we judged it useful to present the correlations using combined data from all five senior classes, 1976 through 1980. This produces a fairly high degree of precision; specifically, we estimate that the five percent (two-tailed) confidence intervals for single correlations are smaller than +.03 while those for differences between male and female correlations are smaller than +.04. Thus, even though some of the relationships reported here are relatively small, we have a good deal of confidence in their accuracy.[2]

Perhaps the most general point to be made about the correlations appearing in Table 3-2.1 is that there are some fairly substantial differences between male and female seniors in the extent to which their views about equal opportunities are predictable from the dimensions of background and experience shown in the table. Although the correlations for females are higher, the females also show less variance (i.e., more "uniformity") in their endorsement of equal opportunities, and these offsetting differences mean that the "impact" of background and experience factors (as reflected in unstandardized regression coefficients) appears roughly equal for males and females. Unstandardized measures are generally considered preferable for comparisons under such conditions; however, given that the smaller variances for females in this case are linked to scale limitations (i.e., "ceiling effects"), then one might argue that standardized measures provide a better indication of differences.

Among the most important predictors of support for equal opportunity are those dimensions having to do with academic accomplishment--grades, college plans, and self-concept of academic ability. Related to the seniors' own academic interests and accomplishments are their parents' educational attainments; thus it is not surprising to find these are also positively correlated with support for equal opportunities. Regression analyses, not reported in detail here, support the interpretation that the impact of parents' education occurs indirectly via the seniors' own educational aspirations and accomplishments, since regression coefficients for parental education on attitudes toward equal opportunities are virtually zero, once the seniors' academic plans and accomplishments are controlled.

Several other relationships require only brief mention at this point. There is a slight tendency,

---

[2]The usual estimates of confidence intervals are based on statistical procedures designed for simple random samples. Our complex samples thus had to be adjusted or "discounted" according to design effects discussed and estimated elsewhere. Assuming a single-form design effect of 1.5, and given annual samples of about 1,500 males and females, the five cohorts (1976 through 1980) yield samples of about 7,500 males and 7,500 females per form, each with an "effective N" of about 5,000.

among both male and female seniors, for those with more
urban backgrounds to show higher support for equal
treatment; put differently, it appears that seniors in
rural areas are a bit more traditional than their
counterparts living in the cities. Also, it appears
that support for equal opportunities is somewhat weaker
among those with strong commitment to religion and with
relatively conservative political views. Finally,
black females show a bit less support for equal treatment than do white females, while there are no similar
racial differences among males. This particular racial
difference is somewhat atypical. As will be shown
below, on many other sex role dimensions blacks--both
males and females--are somewhat less traditional than
whites.

PATRIARCHICAL FAMILY STRUCTURE

Two items which have appeared in other studies of
sex role attitudes were included in the present study
as examples of rather strong traditional sex role
stereotypes. Both have to do with views about "ideal"
family arrangements, and agreement with the items could
be characterized as support for a patriarchical type of
family. Specifically, they refer to the two major
dimensions of sex segregation in the nuclear family:
division of labor and division of power. These items,
like those in the previous section, reveal substantial
differences between sex role attitudes of young men and
young women.

Beginning with the more extreme of the two items,
the statement that "The husband should make all the important decisions in the family," (an item which had
been included in previous surveys, for example the 1970
National Fertility Study) we find that there is more
disagreement than agreement among both male and female
seniors (see Table 3-1.2, left-hand panel). All in
all, responses to this item reflect a fairly strong
rejection of male supremacy.

The other item is not stated in terms of how
things "should" be, but rather makes an assertion about
what is "usually better for everyone involved"--in this
case a male achievement role outside the home and a
female role limited to child rearing and homemaking.
The question thus has the difficulty of representing
things as they "usually" are rather than as the
respondent thinks they ought to be. In other words, it
confounds the respondent's perceptions of the statisti-

cal norm with his or her personal attitudes. Moreover, the statement leaves out an important specification: It is phrased as comparison, but the alternative is not defined (i.e., better than what?). In spite of these technical difficulties, the item has some history of use in surveys, and the responses (in Table 3-1.2, left-hand side) help to indicate the reason for its popularity. The gender differences again are substantial, and this time we see that more males agree than disagree, whereas the reverse is true for females. But perhaps more interesting than this difference is the fact that only about half of the females express disagreement, and well over one third indicate agreement. This represents a considerable contrast with the very high rates of female endorsement of the equal opportunity items. Clearly there are some female seniors who favor equal opportunities but nevertheless view the more traditional family arrangement as "usually better for everyone involved." Such views, of course, are not really contradictory even though we describe one as traditional and the other as egalitarian; the former refers to equal opportunities in the public arena, assuming women wish to pursue equal goals as men, while the latter refers to whether women should pursue equal goals in the first place.

Trends

These attitudes concerning the patriarchical family structure have undergone some change during recent years. There has been a gradual decline in the proportion of seniors favoring the traditional male achiever/ female homemaker model. Female seniors in the class of 1976 were split just about evenly on the issue (a mean of 3.05 on a scale of 1 to 5); but in the class of 1980, as noted above, disagreement outweighed agreement (a mean of 2.68). The shift for males was nearly as large (from 3.85 down to 3.51). Also, there has been a very slight decline in support for the idea that the husband should make all the important decisions in the family.

Background Characteristics

The pattern of correlations with background factors shown in Table 3-2.2 is similar in several respects to those involving the equal opportunity views (see Table 3-2.1). Again, academic accomplishments of seniors (and their parents) are positively associated with non-traditional sex role attitudes, though all of the relationships are quite modest in size. Support for patriarchical family arrangements is also slightly associated with political conservatism and religious commitment. Additionally, seniors whose mothers worked outside the home and who have a rural background are a bit below average in agreement with the statement that things work best when the woman stays home. Since the former connection is a fairly obvious one, it is per- haps surprising that the relationship is not larger. As has been pointed out by others (Macke and Morgan, 1978), in evaluating the impact of a mother's work on attitudes and preferences of her children it may be critical to know how the mother felt about her work.

ENCOURAGING A DAUGHTER'S INDEPENDENCE

Since at least a part of the existing differentia- tion of roles and rewards by sex appears to be based on differential socialization practice, a critical dimen- sion of sex role attitudes deals with such practices. One item that asserts that "parents should encourage just as much independence in their daughters as in their sons" (an item from the 1970 National Fertility Study) refers to attitudes about sex role socializa- tion. As indicated in Table 3-1.3, the gender dif- ferences are substantial. While among male seniors slightly more than one third indicate agreement with the statement and another third "mostly agree," among females more than two thirds agree, another 20 percent "mostly agree," and only 5 percent disagree. Once again there is the possibility of various interpreta- tions of the question. One might, in fact, hold the view that walking alone on a dark street (which could be viewed as a sort of "independence") is more dangerous for daughters than for sons, and that inde- pendence therefore should not be fostered equally among both sexes.

Trends and Background Characteristics

As the data in Tables 3-1.3 and 3-2.3 indicate, responses to this item about independence in daughters have not shifted appreciably during the late seventies, nor are they correlated with academic abilities or most other background dimensions. The general tendency for traditional sex role views to be associated with religious commitment and political conservatism is reflected here again, but the effects are not very strong.

As we will show in the next chapter, preferences for paid employment by the wife are critically affected by whether the wife is assumed to have children to care for. This relationship suggest that beliefs about effects of a mother's work on her children are an important aspect of sex role attitudes, in the sense that these beliefs help sustain traditional attitudes about the division of labor between the spouses. Table 3-1.4 presents two items dealing with this issue, one stated in positive, one in negative terms. Both items were included in the 1970 National Fertility Study. While the responses show the now-familiar gender differences, they also show some of the highest levels of female support for traditional sex roles.

Trends in Beliefs about Effects on Children

Slightly more female seniors agree than disagree with the statement that "a preschool child is likely to suffer if the mother works." Among male seniors, agreement exceeds disagreement by a factor of nearly three to one. On the other hand, the assertion that "a working mother can establish just as warm and secure a relationship with her children as a mother who does not work" prompts three times as much agreement as disagreement among females, whereas males divide about equally. These responses of seniors in the class of 1980, while reflecting a good deal of traditionality, are nevertheless somewhat less traditional than responses from the class of 1976. As the table shows, there has been a fairly steady shift in a non-traditional direction for both males and females.

Background Characteristics

Since the above two items are correlated in similar ways to background factors (although the signs are opposite),and since they are appreciably intercorrelated (r = -.48 for males, -.51 for females), an index based on the two items will prove useful as a way of simplifying and sharpening the pattern to be described. These particular sex role views show no appreciable correlation with seniors' (nor parents') academic accomplishments, although there is a very modest tendency for females planning on a college education to be less traditional in their views about working mothers (see Table 3-2.4). Political conservatism and religious commitment continue to correlate with traditionality in these specific indicators of sex role attitudes, and the links are slightly stronger for females than for males.

The strongest predictor of a senior's attitudes about working mothers is his or her own experience while growing up. The more extensively a senior's mother was employed outside the home during that time, the more likely the senior is to hold positive views about working mothers. Thus it appears that most seniors whose mothers worked did not conclude that they "suffered" unduly, or were deprived of "warm and secure relationships" with their mothers.

Another rather strong predictor of views about working mothers is race; blacks are less traditional than whites, and the differences are somewhat larger than the correlation coefficients might imply (because correlations are constrained by the fact that there are many more whites than blacks in our samples). Of course, a majority of black seniors had experienced a mother holding a paid job most or all of the time when they were growing up, compared with only about half as many whites. Accordingly, a part of the racial difference might be attributable directly to this personal experience. But regression analyses (not displayed here) indicate that most of the racial difference remains after taking account of whether the respondent had a working mother, and thus we must conclude that part of the effect of race is due to broader subcultural differences related to sex role attitudes.

Trends in Beliefs about Effects on Marriage

Three more items dealing with different effects of a wife's employment are displayed in Table 3-1.5. Responses to these items indicate that a majority of the seniors agree (or mostly agree) that "having a job gives a wife more of a chance to develop herself as a person"; that a majority disagree (or mostly disagree) with the assertion that "having a job takes away from a woman's relationship with her husband"; and that these majorities are larger among females than among males. Neither of these two items has shown a clear pattern of change during the late seventies.

While the two items described above are stated in terms of the way things "are", the third item in Table 3-1.5 is a statement of what "should" be the case: "if a wife works, her husband should take a greater part in housework and child care." There is a good deal of support for that statement, but not without some reservation on the part of females as well as males. Close to one third of the females and somewhat more of the males mostly agree with the statement; but the "disagree" or "neither" categories are checked by just over one quarter of the males and just under one quarter of the females among seniors in the class of 1980. There has been some movement in seniors' responses to this item during the late seventies; in fact, the mean score for males in the class of 1980 just equals the mean score that females had in the class of 1976 (suggesting that along this dimension males are only four years "behind" females). It may be worth noting that here again we deal with an item that presents some wording problems. The item makes a comparative statement ("a greater part") but the base of the comparison is not specified. For example, many seniors prefer equal sharing of childcare even if only the husband is employed, and such individuals might not fully endorse a "greater" (i.e., more than equal) part in childcare for the husband whose wife is also employed.

Background Characteristics

The correlations with background factors displayed in Table 3-2.5 show a number of weak relationships. There is a slight tendency for the more academically oriented females to be less traditional in their views about working wives. Perhaps more interesting is the fact that, unlike the previously discussed items, views about a working wife's relationship with her husband or "development of herself as a person" are not correlated with race or with the experience of growing up while one's mother was employed. We cannot help speculating that the lack of predictability may be due to the fact that these particular items are somewhat less clear in their meaning than most of the other items reflecting sex role attitudes.

IMPORTANCE OF THE PARENTING ROLE

This section, and especially the next one, present data which are of some relevance to our present discussion, but which do not fall so clearly within our definition of sex role attitudes as the items discussed before, since they do not explicitly refer to the division of labor between the sexes nor to differences in influence and opportunities. In this section we examine the views of high school seniors about the importance, or value, of raising children, and about whether mothers and fathers should spend more time with their children. These items are located in two different questionnaire forms in order that seniors are not tempted either to draw distinctions or to strive for complete consistency in their responses concerning motherhood and fatherhood. (One form contains an item on the importance of fatherhood and an item about whether mothers should spend more time with children. The other form asks the parallel questions about motherhood and about fathers, respectively. A two-item index was computed for each form.)

The responses to the four items on parenting, shown in Table 3-1.6, indicate that a majority of seniors, both male and female, consider parenthood a very fulfilling experience, and feel that most parents should spend more time with their children. Looking more closely at responses to the two items concerning parenthood as a fulfilling experience, we find no difference in male and female seniors' views about the importance of fatherhood; furthermore, female seniors' views about motherhood are essentially the same (on the average) as the views about fatherhood. (Note however, that nearly twice as many female seniors disagree here than in the comparable item regarding fathers, although the percentages are still small). Among male seniors, however, the responses about motherhood are noticeably different; there is less agreement and a large proportion indicating that they neither agree nor disagree. This particular question about motherhood being a "most fulfilling experience" may strike some seniors as being sexist; if so, males may be especially cautious about endorsing such an item.

The items about whether mothers and fathers should spend more time with their children show a consistent gender difference: females are somewhat more likely than males to agree. A different and somewhat larger distinction appears when we contrast the seniors' prescriptions for fathers and for mothers: the statement about fathers spending more time with their children prompts greater agreement than the parallel statement about mothers--and this differential holds equally among male and female seniors. This latter finding may well reflect the opposition to the uneven involvement of both parents in child care, as it exists in a large majority of families today.

Trends

None of these items show a significant trend change over the past five years.

Background Characteristics

The correlational data in Table 3-2.6 indicate that those seniors placing the highest emphasis on parenthood are apt to be high in religious commitment and politically conservative. On the other hand, emphasis on parenthood is not strongly correlated with academic achievements of seniors or their parents, but the small relationships that appear are negative. These findings, interpreted in the light of those reported in the earlier sections, would seem to indicate that agreement with these parenthood items is related, at least somewhat, to the traditional end of the sex-role attitude continuum. But the picture is complicated by several observations which do not fit that generalization. In particular, for three out of four of the items we find that females show higher agreement, on the average, than do males—and these are the first instances reported here in which female seniors appear more "traditional" than males. Additionally, the correlations with race (blacks showing higher agreement with the parenthood items than do whites) are not consistent with the general pattern of blacks appearing less traditional than whites.

In sum, it appears that seniors generally place a high value on parenthood. Although this is in some respects a "traditional" point of view (e.g., linked to strong religious commitment and political conservatism), it is also a view which receives somewhat higher endorsements from females than from males. This more complicated pattern of findings for these items, compared with items presented earlier, confirms our view that the items do not fit altogether well within our definition of sex role attitudes. Although they are related to sex role attitudes in the sense that they deal with one of the major roles which is usually sex-segregated, the relationship is a complex one.

CONVENTIONAL MARRIAGE; EXTRAMARITAL SEX

The final set of items discussed in this chapter fall rather clearly outside our definition of sex role attitudes; moreover, special correlational analyses discussed later reveal that they show no appreciable correlation with the sex role attitudes discussed above. Why then should we include them here at all? The reasons are briefly the following. First, these items deal with marriage, and many of the sex role attitudes discussed earlier are conceptualized within the context of marriage. Furthermore, it is sometimes suggested that the "liberated" female (and perhaps male also) might be less disposed toward conventional marriage. Thus our exploration of these items helps to round out our understanding of high school seniors' views about sex roles and marriage.

Table 3-1.7 presents four items that invite seniors' agreement or disagreement with statements about the viability of conventional marriage, and the advisability of premarital and extramarital sex. The first three items, which appear in the same form, have further been combined to form an index. The first item, which questions marriage as a way of life, prompts disagreement by just over half of the seniors and agreement by about 30 percent, with no appreciable difference between male and female responses. The next item, an assertion that couples should live together before getting married, produces the same levels of disagreement on the part of female seniors, whereas males agree and disagree in roughly equal numbers. The highest proportions of disagreement occur in response to the third item, a statement that "having a close intimate relationship with only one partner is too restrictive for the average person." Here again, the tendency to disagree is somewhat stronger among the females than among the males. The final item asserts that "most people will have fuller and happier lives..." within the framework of conventional marriage. There are no gender differences in responses to this item; seniors divide just about equally into agree and disagree categories, with one in four unwilling to commit to either side.

The picture suggested by the above percentages is that seniors today are not all convinced that conventional marriage is the one best answer for most people (although their own plans and expectations, reported in a later chapter, show that most favor marriage for themselves). Many seniors express at least some reservations about marriage, but relatively few go as far as to agree fully with the statement that "...one questions it as a way of life." Another part of this picture is the fact that higher proportions of female than male seniors express resistance to the ideas that a couple should live together before marriage, and that monogamy "...is too restrictive for the average person." This certainly fits the stereotype of females resisting male suggestions for sexual relationships outside of marriage; however, it must be noted that the differences are not as large as many of the ones reported earlier in this chapter.

Trends

The trend data shown in Table 3-1.7, particularly the index scores based on the first three items, show some convergence of male and female attitudes in this area during the past few years. Interestingly, this has not occurred because females have moved more toward the "male" position. On the contrary, female views on these issues have changed very little since the class of 1976, whereas male seniors have shown a modest increase in support of conventional marriage. As a result, the gap between males and females is only about half as large for the class of 1980 as it was for the class of 1976 (see index mean scores in Table 3-1.7). Thus, during the latter half of the seventies we do not see any evidence of erosion of young people's commitment to marriage; and there may actually be some movement back toward it on the part of young men.

Background Characteristics

The correlates of views on conventional marriage (see Table 3-2.7) are interesting in several respects. Not surprisingly, seniors from intact homes are a bit more positive about conventional marriage than are seniors not living with both parents. Additionally, there is slightly less support for conventional marriage among seniors whose mothers worked outside the home. Religious commitment and political conservatism are both also associated with support for traditional marriage.

Each of the relationships listed above imply that support for conventional marriage belongs toward the traditional end of any sex role attitude continuum, but the picture becomes more complicated when we consider the following observations. Seniors with high grade-point averages and high reported academic ability, who generally tend toward non-traditional sex role attitudes, also show greater than average enthusiasm for conventional marriage. Scanzoni and Fox (1980) have recently pointed to a closely related finding: among teenage women, traditional sex role attitudes are related positively to having had sexual intercourse. As we noted before, we conclude from these findings that views on conventional marriage and extramarital sex should not be conceptualized as sex role attitudes, even though they involve some closely related issues.

INTERRELATIONSHIPS AMONG THE SEX ROLE ATTITUDES

In each of the previous sections we examined the relationships between sex role attitudes and various dimensions of social origin and early experiences. We noted repeatedly that males and--to a lesser extent-- seniors with strong religious commitments and those with politically conservative views scored relatively high on what we labelled the "traditional" end of the attitude in question. These findings alone would lead one to expect some degree of interrelatedness among the various sex role attitude dimensions we have considered here. But there is a more important reason for expecting some interrelatedness: the primary thrust of conceptualization in this area, as implied by such terms as "traditional," or "sexist," or "egalitarian," or "feminist," is that a broad underlying dimension is involved which cuts across a variety of more specific attitudes. In this section we therefore explore the degree of interrelatedness among our measures of sex role attitudes in order to see whether there is evidence for such an underlying dimension of sex role traditionality. Additionally, we undertake the development of a single index to serve as a general-purpose measure of such a dimension.

Since the sex role attitude items appear in several different questionnaire forms in the annual Monitoring the Future surveys, our exploration of interrelationships must rely on a different source of data: responses of approximately 1,000 seniors to the special Long Form questionnaire administered in 1978. The Long Form included all of the sex role items discussed above, plus a number of others. Thus we were able to examine intercorrelations among all of the above items and indexes, and also to develop a new index of sex role traditionality which combines items from several of the different Monitoring the Future questionnaire forms (as well as some items not presently included in the annual surveys).[3]

---

[3]It should be noted that the Long Form versions of the intercorrelations among items, and the correlations between sex role attitudes and various background dimensions, were compared with those from the annual Monitoring the Future samples whenever possible. No important differences in relationships were evident, thus adding to our confidence in employing the Long Form data for correlational analyses.

We have already noted that views about the importance of parenting, and about conventional marriage and
extramarital sex, do not seem to fit very well within
our definition of sex role attitudes--i.e., attitudes
about whether and in what ways roles and opportunities
should be different for males and females. Accordingly, we decided that the items dealing with these topics
(shown in Tables 3-1.6, 3-1.7, 3-2.6 and 3-2.7) should
not be included in a general index of sex role
traditionality, but that two separate indices should be
formed. We also decided to exclude the items dealing
with equality of opportunities for males and females
(shown in Tables 3-1.1 and 3-2.1); but in this case our
reason for exclusion is that the concept of equal opportunity seems sufficiently important to treat it as a
separate dimension rather than lumping it together with
attitudes about sex role responsibilities, etc. The
remaining eight items shown in Tables 3-1.2 through
3-1.5 and 3-2.2 through 3-2.5 seemed appropriate for
inclusion in a general index of sex role
traditionality.

An examination of the intercorrelations among the
eight items originally presented in Tables 3-1.2
through 3-1.5 (all items coded so that a high score indicated a traditional response) revealed thirteen correlations in the range of .05 to .19, nine correlations
in the range from .20 to .39, and six correlations of
.40 or higher. The above findings, based on the total
Long Form sample, were fairly closely replicated among
both the male and female subsamples.

We extended the above form of analysis to include
another eight items which were available in the Long
Form but which had not been repeated throughout all of
the annual Monitoring the Future data collections (and
thus were not included in the analysis presented earlier in the chapter). These items, which are listed as
the last eight entries in Table 3-3, were judged to be
appropriate indicators of the general concept of sex
role traditionality. Intercorrelations among these
eight items (when coded so that high scores indicated
traditional views) were all positive, with thirteen in
the range of .20 to .39 and the remaining fifteen lower
than .20. Again, analyses for male and female subsamples showed similar relationships. Furthermore, we
found that this set of items showed consistently positive correlations with the first set of eight items:
two correlations above .40, twenty-two in the range of
.20 to .39, thirty-nine in the range of .00 to .19, and
one negative (-.02).

We thus proceeded to compute three indices, one
for each set of eight items and one for the full set of

sixteen items. The indices were formed as means of the relevant items. The two eight-item indexes correlated .60 for the total sample, .57 for the females, and .48 for the males. The tendency for males to show slightly lower correlations than females has been noted earlier in this chapter (based on the annual Monitoring the Future samples), and we will return to that issue a bit later; for the present, however, the important finding is that for both males and females it appears that the two sets of eight items overlap considerably, and thus may usefully be combined in a single index of sex role traditionality.

The middle three columns of Table 3-3 display (for males, females, and the total sample) the correlations between the overall index of sex role traditionality and all items and indexes described earlier in this chapter. These columns thus include the correlations between the overall index and each of its sixteen ingredient items. The two weakest item-index correlations involve the item stating that "if a wife works, her husband should take a greater part in housework and childcare" (r=.20 for total sample), and the item stating that "parents should encourage just as much independence in their daughters as in their sons" (r=.29 for the total sample). The remaining item-index correlations range from .38 to .68, with most lying in a range from .46 to .58. We consider this reasonably good empirical support for our a priori decision to develop the index based on these sixteen items.

Turning now to the remaining items and indexes in Table 3-3, as they relate to the overall index of sex role traditionality, we find that there is a substantial correlation with the items and index dealing with support for equal opportunities for women. As expected, the more traditional individuals are less likely to favor equal opportunities for women, and this shows up a bit more strongly for the total sample (r = -.45) than for either sex. The picture is not as straightforward for the items and index dealing with the importance of parenting. Little relationship exists between this index and overall sex role traditionality for the total sample (r = .08) or for males (r = .08), whereas for females the two dimensions are positively associated (r = .23). An examination of the individual items indicates that neither item having to do with fatherhood shows much of a relationship with sex role traditionality, but the two items about motherhood do, especially among females. The clearest illustration is the item which states that "most mothers should spend more time with their children than they do now;" among females this is strongly associated with sex role traditionality (r = .40), but among males

69

the relationship is only moderate (r = .20). The index dealing with support for traditional marriage actually shows a slight negative relationship with sex role traditionality (r = -.15 for the total sample), although the single item (not part of the index) asserting that marriage leads to fuller lives shows a slight positive relationship with overall sex role traditionality (r = .15 for the total sample).

The remaining correlations in Table 3-3 involve the two indexes showing (a) support for equal opportunities for women, and (b) the importance of parenting. The two indexes show little correlation with each other (r = .08 for the total sample), or with the index of support for traditional marriage (total sample correlations of .09 and .05). In fact, the index of the importance of parenting shows rather little relationship with practically all of the items (other than its four ingredients); two exceptions involve positive correlations with the statement that most people have fuller lives if they are married (r = .30 for the total sample), and with the statement that husbands with working wives should help more with housework and childcare (r = .32, total sample, for agreement with that statement). But it is certainly not surprising that an index reflecting the importance of parenting would correlate with the two specific items noted above; the more important finding, which dovetails with our earlier observations about the items on parenting, is that this dimension seems quite separate and distinct from the dimensions having to do with traditionality or feminism or sexism or equal rights.

A few comments are in order concerning the extent to which patterns of correlation are similar for male seniors and female seniors. The most important observation is that the relationships are, on the whole, quite similar. Although the mean scores are in many cases distinctly different for males and females, the patterns of interrelationship are not. To the extent that there are differences in patterns of correlation, there is a tendency for female correlations to be slightly stronger than those for males. Given the fact that there are appreciable gender differences in many of the mean scores, the correlations based on the total sample (males plus females) tend often to be slightly stronger than for either gender alone, because the gender differences usually show females as less traditional than males (except for those items having to do with importance of parenting and support for traditional marriage). Each of the above observations can be checked in Table 3-3, but it should be noted that they also hold true for the inter-item correla-

70

tions not shown in that table. Thus we conclude that the interrelationships among sex role attitudes do show a moderate degree of consistency among females; and the patterns of consistency are similar and nearly as strong for males, although males show a greater overall tendency toward traditionality in sex role attitudes.

SUMMARY

For the purpose of this study, sex role attitudes are conceptualized as opinions and beliefs about the ways that family and work roles do, and should, differ by gender. A number of questions in the annual Monitoring the Future questionnaires refer to these issues. Some of the questions probe the gender or role difference directly, others assess attitudes towards one particular role, such as parenting. Many of these questions show reasonably high interrelations. They also show similar patterns of relationship to gender, academic accomplishments, religiosity, and political orientation. Specifically, young men, seniors with strong religious commitment, those with politically conservative views, and those with relatively low academic abilities tend to score relatively high on what we labelled measures of traditional views with regard to equal opportunities, patriarchical family structure, socialization of independence in daughters, and effects of wife's work on herself, her children, and her marriage. Based on this evidence, an index of "traditional sex role attitudes" was formed, including all these items except the four items referring to equality of opportunities for the sexes. For conceptual reasons, these latter items were included into a separate index.

Four items referring to the parenting role and four items referring to the concept of conventional marriage and extramarital sex showed little intercorrelation with the remaining items, and showed different patterns of relationships with the standard set of background factors. Therefore, they were formed into two separate indices.

The items that are most central to our definition of sex role attitudes--opinions about division of paid work and housework and the effects of mother's work on her children--have undergone some change in the non-traditional direction during the last five years. These changes have occurred at about an equal pace for

71

both sexes, leaving the substantial gender differences
on these items largely unchanged.

Table 3-1.1

Attitudes About Equal Opportunities for Women: Distributions and Trends

The next questions ask your opinions about a number of difficult topics. How much do you agree or disagree with each statement below?

| | | 1980 Percentage Distributions | | | | | 1976-1980 Trends and Sex Differences | | | | | | |
| | | Dis-agree (1) | Mostly dis-agree (2) | Neither agree (3) | Mostly agree (4) | Agree (5) | Means | | | | | Zero-order correlation coefficients[1] | |
							1976	1977	1978	1979	1980	Trend	Sex
Men & women should be paid the same money if they do the same work	M:	4.1	2.4	3.3	20.9	69.2	4.54	4.55	4.48	4.54	4.49	-.02	.23
	F:	0.4	0.5	0.6	9.3	89.3	4.89	4.86	4.86	4.86	4.87	-.01	
Women should be considered as seriously as men for jobs as executives or politicians	M:	9.8	6.8	8.7	28.0	46.7	3.80	3.90	3.96	4.03	3.95	.04	.30
	F:	2.2	1.4	2.3	19.2	74.9	4.55	4.64	4.60	4.65	4.63	.03	
A woman should have exactly the same job opportunities as a man	M:	13.5	9.7	6.8	29.7	40.2	3.56	3.65	3.67	3.70	3.74	.04	.25
	F:	4.2	3.5	4.3	30.3	57.6	4.29	4.28	4.30	4.30	4.34	.01	
A woman should have exactly the same educational opportunities as a man	M:	1.8	0.8	1.4	12.1	83.8	4.74	4.74	4.73	4.75	4.76	.01	.11
	F:	0.3	0.6	0.7	8.0	90.5	4.88	4.88	4.86	4.87	4.88	.00	
Equal Opportunity Index (Above 4 Items)	M:						4.16	4.21	4.21	4.26	4.23	.03	.32
	F:						4.65	4.67	4.66	4.67	4.68	.02	

[1]For an explanation of these coefficients, see Chapter 2.

Table 3-1.2

Attitudes About Patriarchical Family Structure: Distributions and Trends

		1980 Percentage Distributions					1976-1980 Trends and Sex Differences						
							Means					Zero-order correlation coefficients[1]	
		Dis-agree (1)	Mostly dis-agree (2)	Neither agree (3)	Mostly agree (4)	Agree (5)	1976	1977	1978	1979	1980	Trend	Sex
It is usually better for everyone involved if the man is the achiever outside the home and the woman takes care of the home and family	M:	13.7	10.5	16.6	29.4	29.4	3.85	3.72	3.59	3.59	3.51	-.09	-.28
	F:	30.3	19.6	14.0	24.3	11.8	3.05	2.90	2.79	2.76	2.68	-.08	
The husband should make all the important decisions in the family	M:	26.2	21.6	22.6	17.8	11.8	2.82	2.86	2.79	2.75	2.68	-.04	-.30
	F:	52.4	20.9	10.5	11.4	4.8	2.03	1.98	1.91	1.89	1.95	-.03	

[1]For an explanation of these coefficients, see Chapter 2.

74

Table 3-1.3

Attitudes About Encouraging a Daughter's Independence: Distributions and Trends

	1980 Percentage Distributions					1976-1980 Trends and Sex Differences						
						Means					Zero-order correlation coefficients[1]	
	Dis- agree (1)	Mostly dis- agree (2)	Neither agree (3)	Mostly agree (4)	Agree (5)	1976	1977	1978	1979	1980	Trend	Sex
Parents should encourage just as much independence in their daughters as M:	7.6	9.6	13.1	32.0	37.7	3.72	3.68	3.76	3.74	3.83	.03	
in their sons F:	1.7	3.2	3.9	19.6	71.6	4.50	4.44	4.49	4.50	4.56	.03	.32

[1] For an explanation of these coefficients, see Chapter 2.

Table 3-1.4

Attitudes About Effects of Working Mother on Children: Distributions and Trends

| | | 1980 Percentage Distributions | | | | | 1976-1980 Trends and Sex Differences | | | | | | |
| | | Dis-agree (1) | Mostly dis-agree (2) | Neither agree (3) | Mostly agree (4) | Agree (5) | Means | | | | | Zero-order correlation coefficients[1] | |
							1976	1977	1978	1979	1980	Trend	Sex
A preschool child is likely to suffer if the mother works	M:	11.9	10.6	14.1	23.7	39.7	3.97	3.89	3.81	3.83	3.69	-.07	
	F:	18.2	21.1	15.4	24.4	20.9	3.30	3.28	3.14	3.16	3.09	-.05	-.23
A working mother can establish just as warm and secure a relationship with her children as a mother who does not work	M:	22.9	22.8	10.1	21.0	23.2	2.74	2.78	2.87	2.86	2.99	.05	
	F:	8.4	14.5	7.7	31.2	38.1	3.50	3.59	3.67	3.74	3.76	.07	.27
Working Mother Index (Above 2 items)[2]	M:						3.62	3.56	3.47	3.48	3.35	-.07	
	F:						2.90	2.85	2.74	2.71	2.66	-.07	-.28

[1]For an explanation of these coefficients, see Chapter 2.

[2]The second item was reversed before inclusion in the index.

Table 3-1.5

Attitudes About Effects of Working Wife on Marriage: Distributions and Trends

	1980 Percentage Distributions					1976-1980 Trends and Sex Differences						
	Dis-agree (1)	Mostly dis-agree (2)	Neither agree (3)	Mostly agree (4)	Agree (5)	Means					Zero-order correlation coefficients[1]	
						1976	1977	1978	1979	1980	Trend	Sex
Having a job takes away from a woman's relationship with her husband M:	37.7	30.0	14.3	11.6	6.4	2.29	2.27	2.20	2.29	2.19	-.02	
F:	56.9	24.4	8.8	7.0	2.8	1.67	1.70	1.66	1.72	1.74	.02	-.23
Having a job gives a wife more of a chance to develop herself as a person M:	5.0	5.3	11.6	37.7	40.4	3.90	3.95	4.01	3.97	4.03	.04	
F:	2.9	2.5	5.3	25.7	63.6	4.37	4.44	4.46	4.44	4.45	.02	.22
If a wife works, her husband should take a greater part in housework & childcare M:	7.1	7.7	12.8	40.7	31.7	3.66	3.70	3.77	3.80	3.82	.05	
F:	5.5	6.4	11.5	33.5	43.1	3.82	3.98	3.97	4.02	4.02	.05	.09

[1]For an explanation of these coefficients, see Chapter 2.

Table 3-1.6

Attitudes About Importance of the Parenting Role: Distributions and Trends

| | 1980 Percentage Distributions | | | | | 1976-1980 Trends and Sex Differences | | | | | | |
| | Dis-agree (1) | Mostly dis-agree (2) | Neither agree (3) | Mostly agree (4) | Agree (5) | Means | | | | | Zero-order correlation coefficients[1] | |
						1976	1977	1978	1979	1980	Trend	Sex
Being a father & raising children is one of the most fulfilling experiences a man can have M:	6.2	4.8	17.5	33.9	37.5	3.90	3.86	3.89	3.97	3.92	.02	
F:	4.2	4.0	20.6	33.0	38.3	3.88	3.81	3.86	3.95	3.97	.04	-.01
Most mothers should spend more time with their children than they do now M:	4.6	9.3	31.4	29.7	25.0	3.68	3.69	3.68	3.68	3.61	-.02	
F:	3.6	8.8	19.1	30.9	37.5	3.87	3.85	3.92	3.90	3.90	.01	.10
Being a mother & raising children is one of the most fulfilling experiences a woman can have M:	4.3	5.1	38.4	24.7	27.5	3.64	3.62	3.63	3.63	3.66	.01	
F:	7.0	8.6	14.7	28.8	40.9	3.77	3.72	3.74	3.74	3.88	.03	.06
Most fathers should spend more time with their children than they do now M:	1.9	3.1	15.8	35.0	44.2	4.19	4.19	4.25	4.23	4.17	.00	
F:	1.0	2.3	12.8	32.3	51.7	4.36	4.40	4.32	4.33	4.31	-.03	.08

[1]For an explanation of these coefficients, see Chapter 2.

Table 3-1.7

Attitudes About Conventional Marriage and Extramarital Sex: Distributions and Trends

		1980 Percentage Distributions					1976-1980 Trends and Sex Differences						Zero-order correlation coefficients[1]	
		Dis- agree (1)	Mostly dis- agree (2)	Neither (3)	Mostly agree (4)	Agree (5)	Means						Trend	Sex
							1976	1977	1978	1979	1980		Trend	Sex
How much do you agree or disagree with each statement below?														
One sees so few good or happy marriages that one questions it as a way of life	M:	31.7	22.4	19.2	17.0	9.6	2.69	2.60	2.63	2.61	2.51		-.04	.00
	F:	31.3	20.6	15.8	19.9	12.5	2.59	2.66	2.62	2.56	2.62		-.01	
It is usually a good idea for a couple to live together before getting married in order to find out whether they really get along	M:	26.3	13.6	18.7	21.1	20.2	3.17	3.11	3.15	3.04	2.95		-.05	-.17
	F:	36.0	16.5	14.5	17.9	15.1	2.59	2.59	2.60	2.47	2.59		-.02	
Having a close intimate relationship with only one partner is too restrictive for the average person	M:	34.4	24.9	16.9	16.0	7.8	2.69	2.53	2.51	2.44	2.38		-.08	-.13
	F:	48.0	21.7	11.6	11.7	7.0	2.17	2.27	2.16	2.07	2.08		-.04	
Most people will have fuller & happier lives if they choose legal marriage rather than staying single, or just living with someone	M:	20.5	13.9	26.9	16.8	22.0	3.04	2.92	2.99	3.13	3.06		.03	.01
	F:	22.4	14.9	22.4	15.2	25.3	2.90	3.00	2.96	3.03	3.06		.03	
Traditional Marriage Index (First 3 items above)	M:						3.15	3.25	3.24	3.30	3.39		.07	.14
	F:						3.55	3.49	3.54	3.64	3.57		.03	

[1] For an explanation of these coefficients, see Chapter 2.

Table 3-2.1

Attitudes About Equal Opportunities for Women: Effects of Background Characteristics[1]

		Zero-Order Correlation Coefficients													Multiple Correlation Coefficients
		Race	Live with Mother	Live with Father	Mother Worked	Father Educ.	Mother Educ.	Urbani-city	Acad. Abil.	Grades	Coll. Plans	Polit. Orient.	Relig. Commit.	Dating Freq.	
Woman should be paid same if do same work	M:	.00	.05	.01	.03	.02	.03	.03	.06	.06	.05	.04	-.01	-.02	.09
	F:	-.09	.03	.05	.00	.07	.05	.03	.07	.08	.08	.05	-.04	.01	.14
Woman should be considered as seriously for executive or politician	M:	.02	.04	-.01	.04	.05	.05	.05	.08	.08	.08	.06	-.04	-.04	.14
	F:	-.02	.03	.01	.04	.09	.11	.06	.14	.11	.13	.14	-.10	.00	.24
Woman should have same job opportunities	M:	-.01	.04	.01	.03	.06	.03	.06	.07	.10	.11	.06	-.05	-.04	.16
	F:	-.05	.02	.01	.02	.10	.10	.09	.11	.10	.14	.13	-.11	-.02	.24
Woman should have same educational opportunities	M:	-.04	.05	.02	.00	.04	.02	.05	.05	.05	.07	.03	.00	-.01	.09
	F:	-.12	.04	.07	-.01	.11	.10	.02	.13	.14	.13	.04	-.02	-.01	.21
Equal Opportunity Index (Above 4 items)	M:	.00	.06	.01	.04	.06	.05	.07	.09	.10	.11	.07	-.04	-.04	.17
	F:	-.09	.04	.03	.02	.13	.13	.08	.17	.15	.18	.14	-.11	-.01	.30

[1]For description of background characteristics refer to Table 2-4.

Table 3-2.2

Attitudes About Patriarchical Family Structure: Effects of Background Characteristics[1]

							Zero-Order Correlation Coefficients								Multiple Correlation Coefficients
		Race	Live with Mother	Live with Father	Mother Worked	Father Educ.	Mother Educ.	Urbani-city	Acad. Ability	Grades	Coll. Plans	Polit. Orient.	Relig. Commit.	Dating Freq.	
Better if man works outside home and woman cares for home	M:	-.03	.00	.02	-.10	-.07	-.09	-.08	-.10	-.09	-.11	-.11	.10	.04	.23
	F:	.00	-.02	.00	-.07	-.09	-.10	-.11	-.12	-.09	-.16	-.16	.15	.06	.29
Husband should make important decisions in family	M:	.00	-.03	-.02	-.03	-.08	-.08	-.03	-.11	-.13	-.12	-.10	.05	.03	.19
	F:	.04	-.03	.00	.01	-.05	-.07	-.03	-.11	-.09	-.11	-.14	.15	.03	.24

[1]For description of background characteristics refer to Table 2-4.

Table 3-2.3

Attitudes About Encouraging a Daughter's Independence: Effects of Background Characteristics[1]

							Zero-Order Correlation Coefficients							Multiple Correlation Coefficients
	Race	Live with Mother Father	Live with Father	Mother Worked	Father Educ.	Mother Educ.	Urbani-city	Acad. Ability	Grades	Coll. Plans	Polit. Orient.	Relig. Commit.	Dating Freq.	
Parents should encourage as much independence in daughter as in M:	.01	.00	.01	.02	.03	.03	-.02	.05	.05	.03	.05	-.03	-.04	.10
son F:	-.06	.01	.03	-.02	.04	.05	.01	.05	.04	.05	.10	-.09	-.01	.15

[1]For description of background characteristics refer to Table 2-4.

Table 3-2.4

Attitudes About Effects of Working Mother on Children: Effects of Background Characteristics[1]

									Zero-Order Correlation Coefficients							Multiple Correlation Coefficients
		Race	Live with Mother	Live with Father	Mother Worked	Father Educ.	Mother Educ.	Urbani-city	Acad. Ability	Grades	Coll. Plans	Polit. Orient.	Relig. Commit.	Dating Freq.	
Preschool child likely to suffer if mother works	M:	-.18	.02	.08	-.18	.03	-.02	-.02	.03	.02	-.02	-.08	.10	.03	.26
	F:	-.14	.03	.05	-.18	-.01	-.04	-.03	-.01	.01	-.07	-.11	.12	.03	.27
Working woman as warm relationship as non-working mother	M:	.13	-.03	-.08	.18	-.01	.01	.01	-.01	-.01	.02	.07	-.09	-.02	.23
	F:	.10	-.01	-.02	.15	.01	.03	.02	.03	.01	.08	.13	-.11	-.03	.25
Working Mother Index (Above 2 items)[2]	M:	-.18	.03	.09	-.21	-.02	-.02	-.02	.02	.01	-.02	-.09	.11	.03	.28
	F:	-.14	.02	.04	-.19	-.01	-.04	-.03	-.02	.00	-.09	-.14	.14	.04	.30

[1]For description of background characteristics refer to Table 2-4.

[2]The second item was reversed before inclusion in the index.

Table 3-2.5

Attitudes About Effects of Working Wife on Marriage: Effects of Background Characteristics[1]

		Zero-Order Correlation Coefficients													Multiple Correlation Coefficients
		Race	Live with Mother	Live with Father	Mother Worked	Father Educ.	Mother Educ.	Urbani-city	Acad. Ability	Grades	Coll. Plans	Polit. Orient.	Relig. Commit.	Dating Freq.	
Wife having job interfers with relationship with husband	M:	-.06	.00	.03	-.08	-.04	-.05	-.02	-.03	-.05	-.07	-.03	-.01	-.01	.12
	F:	.00	-.02	-.01	-.02	-.06	-.09	-.03	-.09	-.08	-.09	-.08	.05	-.02	.15
Wife having job gives chance for self-development	M:	.05	.00	-.04	.07	.03	.02	.00	.03	.04	.05	.04	-.05	-.02	.11
	F:	-.02	.04	.01	.05	.03	.03	.01	.07	.07	.06	.10	-.08	.01	.16
If wife works, husband should help with housework and childcare	M:	.04	.00	-.02	.04	-.02	.01	.00	.07	.04	.04	.02	.01	-.02	.09
	F:	.02	.02	-.01	.00	.06	.05	.01	.13	.10	.13	.07	-.03	-.05	.18

[1]For description of background characteristics refer to Table 2-4.

84

Table 3-2.6

Attitudes About the Importance of the Parenting Role: Effects of Background Characteristics[1]

		Zero-Order Correlation Coefficients													Multiple Correlation Coefficients
		Race	Live with Mother	Live with Father	Mother Worked	Father Educ.	Mother Educ.	Urbani- city	Acad. Ability	Grades	Coll. Plans	Polit. Orient.	Relig. Commit.	Dating Freq.	
Being father and raising children one of most fulfilling ex- perience man can have	M:	.05	.01	-.01	-.01	-.03	-.03	-.02	-.01	.00	.00	-.07	.17	.04	.19
	F:	.05	.00	.00	.00	-.05	-.03	-.06	.01	-.01	.00	-.10	.13	.01	.17
Most mothers should spend more time with children	M:	.10	-.02	-.01	.01	-.09	-.06	-.08	-.05	-.05	-.07	-.10	.14	.02	.21
	F:	.13	-.06	-.05	.01	-.13	-.14	-.09	-.09	-.07	-.12	-.14	.19	.02	.30
Being mother and raising children one of most fulfilling ex- perience woman can have	M:	.12	-.03	-.03	.01	-.08	-.09	-.05	-.05	-.06	-.06	-.10	.15	.05	.23
	F:	.10	-.02	.00	.02	-.13	-.09	-.06	-.09	-.05	-.11	-.14	.21	.07	.30
Most fathers should spend more time with children	M:	.10	.00	-.03	.03	-.06	-.05	-.04	.02	.01	.01	-.02	.10	.00	.14
	F:	.10	-.05	-.08	.02	-.07	-.06	-.05	.01	.00	-.02	-.05	.08	.00	.15

[1]For description of background characteristics refer to Table 2-4.

Table 3-2.7

Attitudes About Conventional Marriage and Extramarital Sex: Effects of Background Characteristics[1]

			Zero-Order Correlation Coefficients												Multiple Correlation Coefficients
		Race	Live with Mother	Live with Father	Mother Worked	Mother Educ.	Father Educ.	Urbani-city	Acad. Ability	Grades	Coll. Plans	Polit. Orient.	Relig. Commit.	Dating Freq.	
So few good marriages, one questions it as way of life	M:	.15	-.06	-.10	.06	-.10	-.09	-.02	-.15	-.16	-.13	.07	-.14	-.04	.27
	F:	.19	-.05	-.14	.10	-.12	-.12	.00	-.12	-.14	-.06	.10	-.11	-.04	.29
Good idea to live together before getting married	M:	.08	-.05	-.08	.06	.01	.01	.12	-.08	-.14	-.07	.16	-.37	.02	.42
	F:	.05	-.05	-.11	.09	-.03	-.01	.11	-.10	-.16	-.08	.23	-.40	.13	.46
Only one partner too restrictive	M:	.10	-.05	-.04	.07	-.06	-.04	-.03	-.11	-.11	-.07	.07	-.09	-.02	.19
	F:	.11	-.02	-.03	.04	-.04	-.05	.01	-.11	-.11	.00	.10	-.08	-.05	.20
Have happier life if choose marriage over living together or staying single	M:	-.03	.02	.06	-.05	-.01	-.02	-.11	.05	.08	.04	-.20	.30	-.02	.35
	F:	-.03	.00	.07	-.05	.01	.00	-.09	.05	.09	.01	-.18	.30	-.03	.34
Traditional Marriage Index (First 3 items above)	M:	-.15	.08	.10	-.09	.07	.06	-.04	.15	.19	.12	-.14	.29	.01	.38
	F:	-.17	.06	.14	-.11	.09	.09	-.06	.16	.20	.07	-.21	.29	-.02	.42

[1]For description of background characteristics refer to Table 2-4.

Table 3-3

Sex Role Attitudes: Interrelationships between Indices
and Single Variables

	High Tradi-tionality Score[1]	Equal Opportunities Index			Sex Role Traditionality			Importance of Parenting		
		M	F	Total	M	F	Total	M	F	Total
Mean		4.22	4.62	4.43	3.01	2.50	2.73	3.62	3.86	3.74
Standard Deviation		.79	.56	.72	.52	.63	.63	.70	.73	.74
Product-Moment Correlations:[2]										
Women should be paid same if do same work[3]	Disagree	-.72	-.62	-.70	.19	.22	.26	.00	-.03	-.06
Women should be considered as seriously for executive or politician[3]	Disagree	-.85	-.77	-.84	.36	.33	.40	-.01	.00	-.05
Women should have same job opportunities[3]	Disagree	-.79	-.81	-.81	.36	.37	.41	.00	.07	.01
Women should have same educational opportunities[3]	Disagree	-.73	-.70	-.74	.19	.11	.18	-.02	-.07	-.07
Equal Opportunity Index (Above 4 items)					-.37	-.42	-.45	.12	-.08	.08
Husband should make important decisions in family[4]	Agree	-.17	-.34	-.29	.46	.65	.62	.16	.20	.13
Better if man works outside home & woman cares for home[4]	Agree	-.08	-.31	-.25	.59	.70	.68	.11	.25	.14
Parents should encourage as much independence in daughter as in son[4]	Disagree	-.09	-.13	-.16	.20	.25	.29	-.09	-.17	-.18
Preschool child likely to suffer if mother works[4]	Agree	.03	-.07	-.03	.48	.54	.51	.19	.28	.21
Working woman as close to child as non-working mother[4]	Disagree	-.14	-.09	-.16	.43	.46	.47	.12	.11	.08
Working Mother Index (Above 2 items)		-.07	-.09	-.11	.56	.58	.58	.17	.24	.17

Table 3-3 (Cont.)

	High Traditionality Score[1]	Equal Opportunities Index			Sex Role Traditionality			Importance of Parenting		
		M	F	Total	M	F	Total	M	F	Total
Wife having job interferes with relationship with husband[4]	Agree	-.10	-.27	-.25	.38	.51	.52	.08	.09	.02
Wife having job gives chance for self-development[4]	Disagree	-.12	-.17	-.20	.21	.37	.38	-.17	-.18	-.22
If wife works, husband should help with housework & childcare[4]	Disagree	-.11	-.12	-.14	.19	.19	.20	-.34	-.30	-.32
Being father & raising children one of most fulfilling experience man can have[5]	Agree	.10	.04	.09	-.03	-.03	-.07	.68	.68	.69
Most mothers should spend more time with children[5]	Agree	.01	-.10	-.03	.20	.40	.27	.65	.70	.68
Being mother & raising children one of most fulfilling experience woman can have[5]	Agree	.05	-.15	.02	.12	.23	.09	.70	.75	.75
Most fathers should spend more time with children[5]	Agree	.15	-.01	.12	-.08	-.01	-.11	.66	.65	.66
Importance of Parenting (Above 4 items)		.12	-.08	.08	.08	.23	.08	--	--	--
Have happier life if choose marriage over living together or staying single	Agree	.00	-.08	-.04	.15	.16	.15	.33	.29	.30
So few good marriages, one questions it as way of life	Disagree	.08	.07	.07	-.15	-.16	-.14	-.06	-.08	-.08
Good idea to live together before getting married	Disagree	-.01	-.06	.00	.04	.04	-.01	.15	.06	.10
Only one partner too restrictive	Disagree	.06	.10	.13	-.13	-.13	-.18	.03	.07	.08
Traditional Marriage Index (Above 3 items)	--	.05	.05	.09	-.10	-.11	-.15	.06	.02	.05

Table 3-3 (Cont.)

High Tradi-tionality Score[1]		Equal Opportunities Index			Sex Role Traditionality			Importance of Parenting		
		M	F	Total	M	F	Total	M	F	Total
More important for wife to help with husband's career[4]	Agree	-.21	-.23	-.24	.53	.59	.58	.10	.27	.17
If wife makes more money than husband, marriage headed for trouble[4]	Agree	-.18	-.15	-.19	.45	.50	.47	.08	.13	.09
Most women happier if stay at home[4]	Agree	-.19	-.22	-.25	.51	.58	.58	.15	.27	.17
House husband not right[4]	Agree	-.08	-.16	-.12	.49	.46	.46	.13	.20	.14
Parents should allow boys to cry as often as girls[4]	Disagree	-.21	-.22	-.26	.38	.35	.42	-.01	.04	-.02
Parents should not allow boys to fight more than girls[4]	Disagree	-.25	-.23	-.27	.37	.34	.39	-.07	.10	-.01
If one partner smarter, better if it's husband[4]	Agree	-.13	-.27	-.24	.55	.61	.61	.07	.10	.04
Fathers main responsibility to family is paycheck[4]	Agree	-.13	-.25	-.24	.49	.55	.55	.14	.19	.12

[1]Item scoring was reversed, when necessary, so that high scores are assigned to more "traditional" views.

[2]Based on Long Form sample of 434 males and 538 female seniors surveyed in 1978.

[3]This is one of the items included in the Index of Support for Equal Opportunities for Women. Since there are only four items in the index, there is a strong part-whole effect in the item-index correlations.

[4]This is one of the items included in the Index of Sex Role Traditionality. Since there are sixteen items in the index, the part-whole effect on an item-index correlation is moderate.

[5]This is one of the items included in the Index of Importance of Parenting. Since there are only four items in the index, there is a strong part-whole effect in the item-index correlations.

89

CHAPTER 4

PERSONAL PREFERENCES FOR THE DIVISION OF LABOR IN THE FAMILY

The term "sex role" is used to denote a wide range of normative and behavioral differences between the sexes. Among the core differences are those involving the division of work and family responsibilities between husband and wife. Historically, this division of responsibilities emerged during industrialization, when production was moved out of the home and into the factories. While women stayed home and attended to children and housework, men followed the opportunities for paid work and began to specialize more exclusively in production. This pattern was described by Parsons and Bales (1955) as the basic role structure of the family, according to which the husband is the task-oriented leader and the wife the emotional caretaker of the family members.

Young and Willmott (1973) have argued that this role structure is not inherent in the family per se but rather reflects the effect of certain historical constellations. These authors describe a more integrated pattern of work between husband and wife for the pre-industrialized society, in which both partners were involved in productive as well as maintenance tasks. The historical relativity of sex-segregated role structure is further underscored by recent changes in sex roles. Most notable among these is the increasing number of gainfully employed married women (Treiman and Terrell, 1975a; U.S. Bureau of the Census, 1976). During the 1950's and the 1960's this increase consisted primarily of middle-aged women without children at home; in the seventies the large part was accounted for by younger women with preschool children (Bednarzik and Klein, 1977; Farkas, 1977). While much of the earlier research suggested that the wife's participation in the work force is associated with increased involvement of the husband in housework and child care (Blood and Hamblin, 1958; Blood and Wolfe, 1960; Holmstrom, 1972; Weil, 1961), more recent studies relying on the time budget method for assessing housework and child care have called this conclusion into question (Meissner, Humphreys, Meis, and Scheu, 1975; Robinson, 1977).

These studies tend to show that there is very little difference between the involvement of husbands of working and non-working wives. Whatever the exact level of change in the husband's role may turn out to be, it is clear that it is much less extensive than the change in the wife's role.

In discussing these various forms of division of family responsibilities, it appears useful to view the family as a unit faced with a set of tasks all of which are relevant for maintaining the physical and psychological well-being of its members (Ericksen, Yancey, and Ericksen, 1979; Pleck, 1977). Historically, different solutions for allocation of these tasks have emerged, some of them more sex-segregated, some more shared. At present, we seem to be witnessing a trend towards sharing of duties between husband and wife, although the trend is more adequately described as reflecting some involvement of each spouse in the other's sphere rather than equal sharing of major tasks (Young and Willmott, 1973). Furthermore, the degree of sharing is more pronounced for the work role than for the family roles.

As mentioned before, these trends toward more egalitarian division of labor appear to be paralleled by attitudinal changes among the adult population (Mason, Czajka, and Arber, 1976; Thornton and Freedman, 1979). But what are the attitudes of young people who have not yet entered marital and parental roles? With what expectations do they approach these roles? And how flexible are their expectations? This latter point is particularly critical in a time of change when partners are more likely to bring different expectations into their marriage, and flexibility may critically facilitate their negotiation process. The evidence on all these questions is incomplete and inconsistent; some investigators have observed trends towards egalitarian attitudes among college students (Bayer, 1975; Parelius, 1975), but others have reported considerable conservatism among high school students, and in some instances also among college students (Angrist, Mickelsen, and Penna, 1977; Christensen, 1961; Dunn, 1960; Nelson and Goldman, 1969; Osmond and Martin, 1975; Payne, 1956). Many of the latter studies, however, suffer from methodological limitations such as old and possibly obsolete data, use of local samples of students, or question formats not detailed enough to enable a careful analysis of the range of possible attitudes.

Naturally, the attitudes of individuals are likely to vary, apart from the aggregate changes over time. According to a socialization perspective, the social environment encountered during childhood and adolescence constitutes an important influence on subsequent expectations and aspirations. As noted before, black women traditionally have been involved in the labor force at higher percentages than have white women, and the presence of preschool children has not served as much as a barrier to their employment as it has in the white community. Also, black couples are reported as more egalitarian in the division of housework (Ericksen, Yancey, and Ericksen, 1979; but for a contrasting finding see Blood and Wolfe, 1960) and in decision making (Scanzoni, 1971; Willie and Greenblatt, 1978). Thus, we might predict black adolescents to be more supportive of shared family responsibilities than whites.

As suggested earlier, middle-class adults are more likely to support non-traditional sex role attitudes than working class adults, while at the same time, displaying in their actual behaviors more traditional sex roles. However, in a study of approximately 250 couples, upper- and middle-class respondents reported considerable sharing of roles and decision-making, while lower-class respondents described more sex-segregated patterns (Rainwater, 1965). In sum, it is not entirely clear how a family of higher socioeconomic level differs from the lower level family regarding the sex role attitudes it is most likely to foster.

The sex-role relevant climate of a family can be specified better if direct measures of the hypothesized mediators are available. One such example is the model set by a working mother. As reviewed by Hoffman and Nye (1974), effects on daughters of having had a working mother include higher than average career aspirations, non-traditional sex role concepts, greater approval of employment by mothers of young children, and a higher evaluation of female competence. Although some have suggested that the effect of a mother's work may interact with her own orientations towards her work and with the nature of her relationship with her offspring (Macke and Morgan, 1978; Safilios-Rothschild, 1979), we have no measures available in the Monitoring the Future data to test any interactions of that sort.

Of course, sex role attitudes are related to factors other than family background. The adolescent's own educational plans are likely to be important correlates also. Since educational aspirations are correlated with parental education (Alexander and Eckland, 1974; Hout and Morgan, 1975; Sewell and Shah, 1967), their effects reflect to some degree the influence of parental education on sex role attitudes; but they also

stand for the kind of peer subgroup an adolescent is
likely to be involved with, the kind of educational experiences he or she is likely to be exposed to in high
school, and the kind of future work and family roles he
or she envisages. Educational plans might thus be
predicted to be related to sex role attitudes and
preferences for the division of labor.

We might also expect preferences for the division of labor to be related to academic abilities, and
religious and political orientation by virtue of their
relationship with sex role attitudes.

In this chapter we (a) describe in detail seniors'
preferences for the division of labor between husband
and wife, including the flexibility inherent in the
various alternatives, (b) assess changes in these
preferences over recent years, and (c) explore potential correlates. We also (d) examine the interrelationships between the variables and form a limited
set of indices for use in subsequent analyses. We
finally (e) investigate the impact of sex role attitudes on preferences for the division of labor.

Question Content and Format

In several respects, the items used in the
Monitoring the Future study to measure preferences are
more detailed than the measures contained in most surveys. First, using a scale ranging from "not at all
acceptable" to "desirable," seniors rate each of five
different ways a particular family task might be appor-
tioned between the spouses. The apportionments range
from traditionally sex-segregated to completely shared
to segregated in a sex-reversed sense. This format al-
lows each respondent to express the latitude of his or
her acceptance across the range of arrangements, in addition to indicating his or her preferred arrangement.
These ratings are furthermore made separately for each
of three major tasks--paid employment, child care, and
housework. The three tasks cover the major responsibilities of a couple towards its family of procreation, and the separate assessments of each of the tasks
will enable examination of these various aspects of the
female and the male role. Finally, critical family
circumstances, such as whether the wife holds paid
employment or the couple has young children, are
specified, i.e., the respondent is asked to imagine
himself or herself in each of the specific family
situations. This has the effect of making the measures
more specific and thereby more reliable, since
preferences are likely to be contingent upon the situation that the respondents assume to exist. Of course,

these contingencies are not entirely independent of each other; i.e., intended labor force participation affects intended family size (Waite and Stolzenberg, 1976). But scenarios as broadly defined as these will apply to large parts of the adult population at some point during their life span (Glick, 1977) and thus may justifiably be specified as general contingencies.

This question format results in a set of five or six items for each task and family situation, that are rated on a four-point scale: "Not at all acceptable," "Somewhat acceptable," "Acceptable," and "Desirable." The full questions are given in Tables 4-1.1 through 4-1.5.

Data Presentation

A graphic display was developed to summarize the data in a quickly apprehendable form. These graphs are based on data collected in 1979. The actual response distributions of the 1980 data are given in Tables 4-1.1 through 4-1.5, as are trends between 1976 and 1980. Since this kind of figure has not been introduced before and will be used throughout this entire section, it will be useful to outline some of its key features, using Figure 4-1 as an example.

1. The different possible divisions of labor are arrayed as a rough continuum across the bottom of the figure, ranging from a high degree of labor specialization of the traditional type (on the left), to an egalitarian sharing of labor, to a high degree of labor specialization of a sex-reversed type (on the right). (One other possible arrangement, both partners working half-time, did not fit neatly on the continuum and is not included in the figures.)

2. The bottom set of profile lines in Figure 4-1 shows the percentages of males (solid line) and females (dashed line) who rated each arrangement as desirable.

3. The next set of lines shows the percentage who rate each arrangement as at least acceptable--i.e., as either desirable or acceptable.

4. The top set of lines indicates the percentage who rate each arrangement as at least somewhat acceptable.

5. The distance between the top set of lines and 100 percent represents those who rate the alternative as not at all acceptable. (This is the case because

missing data cases were excluded from the percentage calculations.)

DIVISION OF PAID WORK

It is clear from Figure 4-1 that the two most widely accepted types of working arrangement for a couple without children is for the husband to work full-time while the wife is employed either full-time or half-time. These two alternatives receive the largest proportions of "desirable" and "acceptable" ratings by both males and females. It is interesting to note that the least problematic alternative for both sexes--i.e. the one that only about 3 percent rate "not at all acceptable"--involves the husband working full-time and the wife working half-time. While for many this is not their first choice, this compromise between traditionality and egalitarianism presumably comes close enough to be acceptable or at least somewhat acceptable to almost everyone. In contrast, the completely shared arrangement with both partners working full-time is not universally acceptable; about 20 percent of the males and 12 percent of the females rate it as unacceptable.

The most traditional arrangement, i.e., in which the husband is employed full-time while the wife is not employed, is considered desirable by only about 13 percent of the males and 4 percent of the females. The sex differences are most striking in the proportions who find this alternative not at all acceptable--39 percent of the females feel they could not accept this arrangement compared with only 16 percent of the males.

The right-hand portion of Figure 4-1 shows what might be termed sex role reversal--wife employed full-time with husband employed only half-time or not at all. It is very clear from the figure that this is not a popular notion among high school seniors. Large majorities of both males and females rate these arrangements as unacceptable. It may not be surprising that fully 83 percent of males rule out an arrangement in which they would not be employed at all (with a full-time working wife); however, it is interesting to note that just as many females (85%) would be unwilling to tolerate an unemployed husband. In other words, only 15 percent of the female seniors would consider it even marginally acceptable to work full-time and "support" a spouse with no job, whereas fully 84 percent of male seniors would find it at least marginally acceptable to

have a wife with no employment outside the home.
Clearly, when it comes to employment versus non-
employment, the sex role prescriptions for males are
much more narrowly constrained than those for females.

Preferences for the woman's work arrangement are
most dramatically affected by the existence of pre-
school children in the family, as the answers to a
second set of questions (Figure 4-2) illustrate. Among
the five alternatives for the division of paid work,
the arrangement which is clearly preferred above all
others is that the husband work full-time and the wife
not hold a paid job. Thirty-nine percent of the
seniors rate this arrangement as desirable and only 8
percent consider it as not at all acceptable.

Any arrangement in which the wife would work full-
time, on the other hand, finds little acceptance;
sixty-three percent or more judge each of these alternatives as not acceptable. Moreover, only 14 percent
think it desirable for the wife to work half-time if
the husband is working. A large majority of them feel,
however, that they could at least accept this latter
arrangement. This finding suggests that it is half-
time work by the mother of young children which is becoming the widely accepted non-traditional option.

Interestingly, the profile lines show that the acceptability of a wife's working does not vary with the
extent to which her husband works, i.e., there appears
to be little weight given to the fact that a husband
who is not employed could take on some of the child
care responsibilities his working wife cannot manage.
The overriding consideration underlying these ratings
appears to be the rejection of a husband who does not
work.

Trends

Tables 4-1.1 through 4-1.2 present mean values for
1976 through 1980 on the variables dealing with the
division of paid work between husband and wife. As
evidenced in these values, preferences have been shift-
ing away from the working husband and towards a working
couple. Although the trends are not at all strong,
they are consistent in direction over what must be considered a very short historical period in which to observe social change.

At the same time, little systematic change has occurred in preferences for sex-reversed arrangements.
The idea of a husband working less than full-time while

his wife works full-time is almost as strongly rejected in 1980 as it was in 1976.

These trends in preferences for work outside the home are quite similar for the two sexes; thus, there is no substantial closing or widening of the sex gap on these issues.

Background Characteristics

Although Tables 4-2.1 and 4-2.2 do not reveal very many strong relationships, clear effects of race on the preference for employment of mothers of young children are noted. More specifically, blacks look more favorably upon such employment; about half of the black seniors find a full-time working mother of young children at least somewhat acceptable, while only about one quarter of the white seniors express the same preferences. Another clear correlate of these preferences is reflected in the level of work involvement by the respondent's mother; respondents who were raised by a working mother tend to feel more positive about employment by a mother of young children. Based on regression results not reported here, the two variables, race and working mother, have largely independent effects on preferences for paid employment.

These two variables are much less clearly related to preferences for paid employment by a wife without children, although blacks are again less likely to favor none or half-time employment by such a wife than are whites.

Self-reported ability, college plans, and political orientation show generally weaker effects on preferences for paid employment of wives than race and working mother, but most of the relationships are in the expected direction; i.e., respondents with higher ability, college plans, and a more liberal political orientation are a bit more likely to prefer employment by a wife, whether with or without children. A curious exception is observed for males' preferences concerning paid employment of mothers. In this case, males' abilities and their educational aspirations are negatively related to acceptance of employment.

This latter observation points to an interesting interaction of sex with ability and educational plans. Female seniors' preferences for the wife's employment if no children are assumed to be present are positively related to abilities and educational plans--probably reflecting effects of career aspirations--but less of a relationship is found for the situation where children are present. In other words, only when no children are present do higher career aspirations among young women translate into a preference for working. Among male seniors, on the other hand, abilities and educational plans are related only to preferences for paid employment of wives with children, while little relationship is noticeable for employment of wives without children. In this case, however, the relationship is actually negative. We interpret this finding as reflecting the more able males' greater sensitivity to the welfare of children, a concern which is not counterbalanced by their higher tendency towards a career, as in the case of females. On the contrary, by assuming a more traditional attitude they may be protecting their own occupational strivings from being curtailed by child care duties. Note that this interaction is not just an artifact of sex differences in variance, since little variance differences are observed for the responses to the questions on division of labor and the questions on abilities.

DIVISION OF CHILDCARE AND HOUSEWORK

Two questions directly dealing with child care were included in the set of division-of-labor questions. Consider first the preferences for child care arrangements for a couple in which only the husband is employed, as shown in Figure 4-3. In this particular family situation, equal responsibility for child care is the most often desired alternative (35%) and is rejected by almost none (6%). The mother handling all of the child care responsibilities is judged as desirable by only a few (11%) and as unacceptable by a goodly number (31%). These findings may seem somewhat surprising in that they suggest that the husband should share child care responsibilities equally with his wife, in addition to having a full-time job. However, it may be that "child care" is understood in less inclusive terms by many seniors than the entire range of chores of keeping children fed, dressed, changed, and supervised. Respondents may be thinking primarily in terms of time spent in active interaction with children or of the time when both parents can be home. If this were the case, the equally shared involvement of a full-time employed husband and non-employed wife might seem more understandable. Ex post facto, we can only suggest that the dimension of child care as used in this set of questions may be somewhat less precise in its meaning than the dimension of paid employment. Altogether, however, it appears safe to conclude from these data that seniors do not believe that a father is relieved of child care responsibilities by virtue of being the sole breadwinner in the family.

Consider next the situation of the working couple, as shown in Figure 4-4. Since this situation deals with the division of child care on evenings and on weekends only, a substantial involvement of a working parent is more feasible than where day-to-day child care is concerned. The difference in the preferences for equal division between this and the previous set of questions may thus partly reflect a difference in feasibility rather than in actual preference; therefore, a direct comparison between the two sets of items is not attempted. The preference for equal division of child care is even more strong in this situation, probably reflecting the effect of an equity norm. In contrast, all the remaining alternatives defining an unequal share of child care are rated desirable by only a small minority that in no case exceeds 10 percent, though more rate them as at least somewhat acceptable. Note, however, that among the unequal arrangements, somewhat higher percentages of seniors are tolerant of a division in which the wife has a disproportionate responsibility for the children than one in which the husband does.

In contrast to division of child care, arrangements for the division of housework were rated only for a couple in which both partners are working full-time.'

The general pattern of views about a working couple sharing housework is fairly similar to the pattern of views about a working couple sharing child care (Figure 4-5). The equal division of housework is clearly the preferred arrangement, and females favor it more strongly than males. However, where housework is concerned, there is not as strong a preference for an equal division as there is in the case of child care. It may be that seniors perceive the equal contribution of both partners as less critical for the outcome of housework than for the outcome of child care.

'A set of questions on housework for a couple in which only the husband works was included in the Long Form questionnaire and will be included in analysis reported below.

Trends

Rather little systematic change has occurred in preferences for housework and child care (Tables 4-1.3 through 4-1.5), although whatever trends there are point again in an egalitarian direction: equal sharing of housework and child care has become slightly more acceptable or desirable to seniors when they think about their prospective marriages.

Background Characteristics

The pattern of correlates for the preferences for division of housework and child care (see Tables 4-2.3 through 4-2.5) can be summarized rather briefly. The most consistent correlates of equal involvement are grades, self-reported academic abilities, and college plans. In addition, seniors with a more liberal-radical political orientation or with less religious commitment also tend to favor shared division of duties. While some of the sex difference in correlational strength is real, some must be attributed to variance differences between the sexes. In sum, the pattern seems to parallel the correlations observed for division of paid work between a husband and wife without children.

INTERRELATIONSHIPS BETWEEN PREFERENCES: A SET OF INDICES

In addition to the analyses reported above we have conducted extensive investigations on the intraindividual patterning of these ratings (Herzog, Bachman, and Johnston, 1979). These investigations have convinced us that the respondents are in fact using the set of variables for each specific duty and family situation in a systematic and logical fashion. The most typical respondent rates one arrangement as desirable, and rates the next most similar arrangements (those adjacent on the continuum) as acceptable or somewhat acceptable. It thus appears that the set of variables is used more or less like a scale ranging from an entirely sex-segregated over a somewhat shared to an entirely egalitarian arrangement.

It seems, therefore, that a composite index ranging from a sex-segregated to a shared arrangement for each family duty and family situation might capture the major information contained in these ratings.

101

Since the two sex-reversed arrangements are rated as acceptable or desirable by extremely few seniors and since they would complicate the unidimensionality of the scale, they were not included in the indices to be presented below.

The indices are based upon the six sets of three questions referring to division of paid work, child care, and housework. In order to capture each respondent's "central" tendency for each set of questions, the three items in each set are assigned continuous values starting with "1" for the most traditional or sex-segregated arrangement and ending with "3" for the shared or egalitarian arrangement. These values are then multiplied by the degree of acceptability assigned to each (i.e., not at all acceptable = 0, somewhat acceptable = 1, acceptable = 2, and desirable = 3). When the sum of these multiplied values is divided by the sum of the acceptability ratings (ranging from 0 to 9), values ranging between 1 and 3 result, which represent the respondent's location on the dimension from traditional to shared division of labor independent of his/her general level of acceptability of all the arrangements. Respondents who had either rated all of the arrangements as "not at all acceptable" (i.e., sum of acceptability ratings = 0) or all of them as "desirable" (i.e., sum of ratings = 9) were deleted from the index, since those respondents did not, in fact, make a choice. (Only one to three percent of all the respondents were excluded on this basis.)

Means for the six indices as well as item-index correlations based on the Long Form data are given in Table 4-3. They suggest that the indices reflect quite closely the patterns of results observed by more detailed analyses. In particular, they replicate the findings reported earlier of (a) a shift toward more traditional attitudes on division of paid work when preschool children are added to the family situation, and (b) consistently more conservative attitudes of the male than the female seniors.

The six indices relate quite predictably to their components (as this was built into their construction). They are negatively correlated with the traditional/conservative items and positively with the egalitarian items. Most interestingly, half-time work by a wife relates negatively (in the case of female respondents) or not at all (in the case of males) to the index on division of paid work when the questions deal with a couple having no children, but positively when the questions concern parents of preschool children. In other words, half-time work by the wife is part of the liberal orientation when she has children but part of the conservative orientation when she doesn't.

As shown in Table 4-3, the six indices are also related in a systematic fashion to each other. The two indices on division of paid work are correlated at approximately .35, but at lower levels to the four indices of division of housework and child care, which in turn are highly related among each other. This finding implies that despite the overall shifts in preferences that occur according to the family situation that is assumed, general orientations about the division of labor among the couple persist within duties outside the home and within duties inside the home. At the same time, there is much less carry-over between duties within and duties outside of the home.

In order to facilitate multivariate analyses in later chapters, we have combined the two indices referring to division of paid work into one overall index and the four indices referring to division of housework and child care into another overall index. These two indices--labeled as "Division of Paid Work" and "Division of Home Duties"--are also included in the table.

THE EFFECT OF SEX ROLE ATTITUDES ON PREFERENCES FOR DIVISION OF LABOR

As suggested by the previous sets of analyses, the background factors do not provide much insight into why young people prefer different arrangements for the division of labor in their own prospective families. Most likely, these preferences are more influenced by general attitudes about the roles of the sexes than by the background characteristics examined before. We therefore examine next the effect of the sex role attitudes, described in the previous chapter, on preferences for the division of labor. The analyses reported in this section are based exclusively on the Long Form data since they utilize variables which were contained in different questionnaire forms in the Monitoring the Future study.

Among the sex role attitude indices, the index of traditional sex role attitudes is quite strongly related to preferences for the division of labor; the average correlations between the traditional sex role index and the six division of labor indices is $r = -.34$ for females, $r = -.27$ for males. This relationship was, of course, expected since the index of traditional sex role attitudes is composed of items dealing largely with the definition of the roles of husband and wife. Interestingly, the personal preferences regarding child care and housework are further related to the attitudes about equal opportunities for women, although these correlations are weaker than the previous ones (i.e., average correlation coefficient for females is $r = .21$, for males $r = .22$). In other words, young men and women who support egalitarian treatment of the sexes in the public arena appear more likely to prefer egalitarian arrangements for taking care of their duties at home.

Since the two sex role attitude indices--traditional sex role attitudes and equal opportunities--are negatively related to each other, as demonstrated in the previous chapter, it is likely that their relationships with division of labor preferences are somewhat overlapping. This possibility needs to be tested in a multivariate analysis in which both of these attitudes are simultaneously used as predictors of any division of labor preference. Moreover, the relationships may also be influenced by one or more prior causal factors that are shared.

In order to explore these several possibilities, a number of multiple regression analyses were performed predicting separately to each index of preferences for division of labor. A first set of regression analyses includes as predictors only the background factors that were already discussed in this chapter. In fact, we included only a subset of these background factors, the ones that produced bivariate correlations of .10 or higher (for males and/or females) in the Monitoring the

Future analyses.[2] This set of regressions serves to
check effects of background factors in the Long Form
data and to incorporate them into a multivariate
framework.

A second set of regressions includes as predictors
the three sex role attitude indices, in addition to the
background factors included in the previous regression
equations. These latter regression analyses permit us
to examine the effects of each of the three sex role
attitude indices, after the effects of the background
factors and the other two sex role indices have been
controlled. The standardized regression coefficients
from these analyses and the proportion of variance explained[3]--along with bivariate coefficients--are
presented in Tables 4-4.1 through 4-4.5.[4]

While traditional sex role attitudes retain a
strong and statistically significant[5] effect on
preferences for the division of labor after controls
have been implemented, this is not the case for the attitudes about equal opportunities for women. The coefficients associated with the latter index are reduced

----

[2]One other restriction in the use of background
factors as predictors should be noted here. If we had
used any combination of the Academic Ability measure,
Grades, and College Plans as joint predictors, the
results could have been misleading. Since these three
variables are highly intercorrelated, the multiple
regression procedure might have "split up" their shared
predictive value with the result that three small
separate "effects" would appear rather than one larger
relationship. In order to deal with this problem, we
built a variable termed "Academic Ability Composite,"
which is a mean of Grades and Academic Ability (with
both variables standardized). Also, whenever the College Plans variable was included among the predictors
it was added as a separate step so that the impact of
the Academic Ability Composite could be examined independent of College Plans.

[3]The proportion of variance explained by the
predictors was corrected for degrees of freedom.

[4]Only five indices for division-of-labor
preferences were examined, since relevant Monitoring
the Future data were available for only those five indices.

[5]The significance calculations are based on an
estimated design effect of 2. For rationale see Chapter 2.

substantially when controls are introduced. Thus attitudes about equality of opportunities explain little if anything more about preferences than is already explained by the index of traditional sex role attitudes and relevant background factors.

The third sex role attitude index--importance of parenting--relates negatively to preferences for paid work, and positively to preferences for equal sharing of child care. None of these relationships is very strong, however.

In sum, the data from the Long Form suggest that young men's and women's attitudes about family and work roles and the ways that those roles should be divided up between the sexes are directly and consistently related to the preferences that these young people have formed with respect to their own divisions of labor when they are married.

SUMMARY

Several general themes seem to emerge from the data as discussed above.

A Preference for Egalitarianism Within Limits

The first three alternatives which respondents rated for each family situation can be regarded as spanning the range from traditionally sex-segregated to shared arrangements. From this perspective high school seniors appear quite open to sharing family responsibilities between the partners. Specifically, most of them would accept or even desire that a wife participate full-time or half-time in paid employment if she has no children; and even assuming the presence of young children, quite a few seniors rate half-time work by the mother as at least acceptable. The seniors react in an even more egalitarian fashion where child care and household duties are concerned. This focus is particularly clear for the family situation where the wife is assumed to have a full-time job, but it is also evident for child care when the mother has no outside employment. Moreover, these preferences reflect some small but significant shifts towards shared arrangements since 1976. For paid work in particular, the largest shifts are in the direction of both spouses working full-time, where a couple without children is concerned, and in the direction of half-time work by the wife, where pre-school children are present.

Although we have identified considerable support for egalitarian arrangements, we must add that the data by no means reflect a complete abandonment of the sex-segregated role distinctions. Most notably, the acceptable options for paid work of wives without children include non-employment and half-time employment, as well as full-time employment. In other words, there are still many seniors who prefer a wife who works half-time or not at all over one who holds a full-time job. Moreover, if the couple is assumed to have pre-school children, the wife is very clearly the one who is expected to drop out of the labor force or to change to part-time work in order to attend to the children. Although the preferences for child care exhibit a strong focus on the egalitarian alternative, considerable numbers of seniors would still find it at least somewhat acceptable if the wife were responsible for all or most of the child care.

Some apparent contradictions in the data further suggest that what appears to be a preference for egalitarianism may actually hide a more subtle form of traditionalism. Consider the following juxtaposition of findings: if the preferences of most seniors for an equal division of child care is taken as a valid finding, not just a wording artifact, then it seems inconsistent with the finding that most prefer the woman to stay home with her young children. If half of the child care really were to be done by the husband, the wife would be freed for paid work. It would then appear inconsistent that a husband should still have to work full-time, since the wife's economic contribution could presumably lighten his obligation. Further, having only a part-time job would free the husband to do his share of the child care.

We offer the following interpretation of these apparent contradictions: there is, on one hand, a tendency towards sharing of duties between marital partners; on the other hand, however, the final responsibility is still seen as resting with the one partner who traditionally held that particular duty. Thus, a husband's help in child care is very welcome even to a point of equal involvement with the wife; but the final responsibility still rests with the wife, and it is the wife who will be blamed if any insufficiencies with regard to child care would develop (Kellerman and Katz, 1978). By the same token, the involvement of a woman in paid work is widely accepted; but it is still the husband who is likely to be held accountable if economic support for the family is not adequate.

Small Children Change Things--For the Wife

The presence of preschool children drastically affects the preference pattern for women's work. For the
couple with no children, half-time or full-time work
for the wife seems acceptable or even desirable to a
considerable proportion of seniors. On the other hand,
when a couple has one or more pre-school children,
having the wife refrain from working seems desirable to
almost half of the seniors and is at least somewhat acceptable to virtually all of them. In clear contrast
to the effect on women's work patterns, preferences for
men's work are very little affected by the presence of
young children. In each case, less than full-time
employment meets with little acceptance.

Overall, the findings are impressive in their
strength and quality; despite the observed tendencies
toward shared responsibilities (including more equal
sharing of child care), the arrival of children affects
only the preference pattern for the wife's work.
Moreover, these views are shared by male and female
seniors, pointing to a general agreement about the differential modifiability of work patterns with the ad-
vent of children.

More Flexibility for the Wife than the Husband

Viewed from a slightly different angle, preferences regarding the male and the female work roles differ
greatly in latitude or flexibility. We have noted
before that for childless wives, full-time, half-time,
or no employment are all rated at least somewhat acceptable by over 72 percent of the seniors. For wives
with young children the alternatives are more limited;
no employment or half-time employment are the only
widely accepted arrangements. However, a completely
different picture emerges for the husband. In his
case, only full-time work is preferred, while acceptability (in terms of at least "somewhat acceptable")
infrequently exceeds 40 percent for all the part-time
alternatives. Overall, there is an impressive lack of
flexibility in the way the husband's employment responsibilities are viewed by both male and female seniors.
Also, and this is particularly remarkable in this age
of changing sex roles, no significant change in
preferences regarding the husband's role has been
registered during the last five years.

Little Interest in Sex Role Reversal

In general, we have found few seniors who rate sex role reversed arrangements as desirable or even acceptable--a pattern which has not changed appreciably from 1976 to 1980. Substantial majorities of the seniors would find it unacceptable for the husband of a childless couple to work half-time (62%) or not work at all (84%), even if his wife worked full-time and thereby contributed considerably to their economic support. Similarly, for a couple with preschool children, the great majority reject the option of the husband working less than the wife, even though it might reasonably be argued that the children would benefit from having their father spend more time at home. Furthermore, sex role reversal is no more welcome where child care and housework are concerned; over half of both male and female seniors reject as unacceptable any situation in which the husband does more than an equal share under any of the circumstances covered in the questionnaire, and fewer than 3 percent rate any such situation as desirable.

Sex Differences in Preference Patterns

As shown in the figures and quantitatively summarized in Tables 4-1.1 through 4-1.5, sex differences that are notable are quite consistent. Fewer female than male seniors are traditional in their preferences concerning particular arrangements for allocating various types of family responsibilities between themselves and their future husbands while more females than males favor egalitarian arrangements.

The consistent tendency for males to be somewhat more conservative, on the average, confirms other reports of more traditional sex role attitudes in males than in females (Angrist, Mickelsen, and Penna, 1977; Osmond and Martin, 1975). Nevertheless, it seems to us that the level of sex differences observed in our data are not pronounced enough to predict widespread and fundamental disagreement between the sexes about the proper roles for husbands and wives, especially when we consider that most respondents report that several different arrangements would be at least somewhat acceptable.

Other Correlates of Preference Patterns

Above average support for working wives as well as equally shared child care and housework is evident among female respondents who report high academic ability, those with college plans, and those with liberal political beliefs. Although the relationships are not strong, they are consistent with hypotheses formulated on the basis of previous research.

In contrast to the females, young men show somewhat less clear patterns of correlation. This suggests that men's abilities, attitudes, and ideologies bear a less uniform relationship to their preferences for the division of tasks between spouses. It appears indeed quite plausible that sex role preferences would be less well linked with men's attitudinal structure and with their life styles, since variation in sex role definition has less bearing on men's lives or, at least, such bearing is less commonly recognized by the seniors.

Two unique and reasonably strong predictors are observed where the division of paid work for a couple with young children is concerned: respondents who are black and respondents who have had a working mother themselves are more likely to respond positively to the employment of a mother with young children. Thus, while personal ambitions and attitudes appear to influence intentions for labor force participation among young women, the presumed presence of preschool children in their future family weakens the effect of those very variables and equalizes intended labor force participation. The only variables which noticeably increase preferences for a working wife under the latter circumstances deal with directly relevant experiences-- the examples of working mothers or otherwise self-supporting women, which abound in the black community. Interestingly, the example of the working mother has a positive effect on the preferences of young men as well as young women. This finding suggests that the effect should be understood in a broad sense as displaying a viable lifestyle or as a setting of norms rather than in the more narrow sense of providing a model for the same-sexed child.

In addition to background factors, preferences are very clearly influenced by traditional sex role attitudes. Young men and women with traditional attitudes are more likely than those with non-traditional views to prefer sex-segregated arrangements for their own marriages.

Table 4-1.1

Preferred Division of Paid Work of a Couple without Children: Distributions and Trends

		1980 Percentage Distributions				1976-1980 Trends and Sex Differences						
		Not at all ac-ceptable (1)	Somewhat accept-able (2)	Accept-able (3)	Desir-able (4)	Means					Zero-order correlation coefficients[2]	
						1976	1977	1978	1979	1980	Trend	Sex
Imagine you are married and have no children. How would you feel about each of the following working arrangements?												
Husband works full-time Wife doesn't work	M:	16.0	30.8	40.6	12.6	2.55	2.54	2.51	2.49	2.50	-.02	-.31
	F:	38.6	34.8	22.5	4.1	1.98	1.96	1.92	1.89	1.92	-.03	
Husband works full-time Wife works about half-time	M:	2.5	18.2	60.7	18.5	2.93	2.99	2.93	2.96	2.95	.00	-.07
	F:	4.5	24.2	52.5	18.9	2.89	2.84	2.85	2.82	2.86	-.02	
Both work full-time	M:	19.4	22.9	40.9	16.9	2.39	2.43	2.43	2.50	2.55	.05	.19
	F:	11.6	16.9	46.0	25.6	2.75	2.80	2.86	2.95	2.86	.05	
Both work about half-time	M:	47.1	27.9	17.4	7.5	1.83	1.81	1.78	1.72	1.85	.00	.01
	F:	48.5	28.6	16.2	6.7	1.89	1.80	1.85	1.78	1.81	-.03	
Husband works about half-time Wife works full-time	M:	64.6	18.5	12.1	4.4	1.47	1.49	1.51	1.45	1.56	.02	.03
	F:	59.5	25.5	13.3	1.6	1.52	1.57	1.55	1.52	1.57	.01	
Husband doesn't work Wife works full-time	M:	83.0	7.6	4.7	4.8	1.27	1.29	1.30	1.23	1.31	.00	-.04
	F:	84.6	9.8	3.8	1.7	1.23	1.23	1.23	1.19	1.23	-.01	
Index[1] (first 3 items above)	M:					1.95	1.96	1.96	1.99	2.00	.06	.32
	F:					2.19	2.21	2.24	2.26	2.23	.05	

[1]For description of the index formation, see text.

[2]For an explanation of these coefficients, see Chapter 2.

111

Table 4-1.2

Preferred Division of Paid Work of a Couple with Preschool Children: Distributions and Trends

| | | 1980 Percentage Distributions | | | | 1976-1980 Trends and Sex Differences | | | | | | |
		Not at all acceptable (1)	Somewhat acceptable (2)	Acceptable (3)	Desirable (4)	Means 1976	1977	1978	1979	1980	Zero-order correlation coefficients[2] Trend	Sex
Imagine you are married and have one or more pre-school children. How would you feel about each of the following working arrangements?												
Husband works full-time	M:	6.8	12.8	36.1	44.3	3.32	3.26	3.19	3.18	3.18	-.06	
Wife doesn't work	F:	10.4	17.9	37.6	34.2	3.12	3.02	2.98	2.99	2.96	-.05	-.12
Husband works full-time	M:	14.7	29.6	44.9	10.8	2.32	2.38	2.47	2.50	2.52	.08	
Wife works about half-time	F:	8.2	27.4	48.9	15.4	2.56	2.64	2.68	2.73	2.72	.06	.13
Both work full-time	M:	65.4	17.3	11.0	6.2	1.42	1.43	1.46	1.50	1.58	.06	
	F:	61.6	20.1	13.2	5.2	1.44	1.53	1.53	1.53	1.62	.06	.03
Both work about half-time	M:	51.8	28.6	13.6	6.0	1.68	1.66	1.67	1.64	1.74	.02	
	F:	49.8	29.9	15.9	4.3	1.76	1.74	1.79	1.72	1.75	-.01	.04
Husband works about half-time	M:	72.2	17.1	7.8	2.8	1.32	1.36	1.38	1.34	1.41	.03	
Wife works full-time	F:	71.7	18.7	7.7	1.9	1.31	1.35	1.36	1.38	1.40	.04	.00
Husband doesn't work	M:	79.6	9.3	7.4	3.7	1.29	1.32	1.28	1.27	1.35	.02	
Wife works full-time	F:	81.2	10.2	5.9	2.7	1.27	1.26	1.26	1.27	1.30	.01	-.02
Index[1]	M:					1.46	1.49	1.52	1.54	1.57	.09	
(first 3 items above)	F:					1.56	1.60	1.62	1.62	1.66	.08	.12

[1]For description of the index formation, see text.

[2]For an explanation of these coefficients, see Chapter 2.

Table 4-1.3

Preferred Division of Child Care When the Husband Works: Distributions and Trends

Imagine you are married and have one or more pre-school children. Imagine also that the husband is working full-time and the wife does not have a job outside the home. How would you feel about each of these arrangements for the day-to-day care of the children?

| | | 1980 Percentage Distributions | | | | 1976-1980 Trends and Sex Differences | | | | | | | |
| | | Not at all acceptable (1) | Somewhat acceptable (2) | Accept-able (3) | Desir-able (4) | Means | | | | | Zero-order correlation coefficients[2] | |
						1976	1977	1978	1979	1980	Trend	Sex
Wife does all child care	M:	26.9	29.7	28.6	14.8	2.35	2.37	2.27	2.32	2.31	-.02	
	F:	35.4	30.8	26.5	7.2	2.13	2.08	2.10	2.08	2.05	-.02	-.12
Wife does most of it	M:	6.6	29.7	45.0	18.7	2.78	2.74	2.75	2.74	2.76	-.01	
	F:	9.5	30.0	44.6	15.9	2.76	2.71	2.69	2.73	2.67	-.03	-.03
Both do it equally	M:	6.9	22.4	40.8	30.0	2.86	2.92	2.94	2.94	2.94	.03	
	F:	5.2	18.6	37.2	39.1	3.04	3.09	3.11	3.14	3.10	.02	.10
Husband does most of it	M:	51.6	36.4	9.3	2.7	1.55	1.58	1.55	1.59	1.63	.03	
	F:	58.5	32.3	7.1	2.1	1.42	1.49	1.49	1.52	1.53	.05	-.06
Husband does all of it	M:	86.5	8.3	2.4	2.9	1.19	1.21	1.19	1.19	1.22	.01	
	F:	90.0	7.3	1.4	1.3	1.12	1.14	1.15	1.12	1.14	.01	-.06
Index[1] (first 3 items above)	M:					2.15	2.16	2.19	2.17	2.18	.02	
	F:					2.23	2.26	2.26	2.27	2.27	.04	.11

[1]For description of the index formation, see text.

[2]For an explanation of these coefficients, see Chapter 2.

113

Table 4-1.4

Preferred Division of Child Care When Both Spouses Work: Distributions and Trends

		1980 Percentage Distributions				1976-1980 Trends and Sex Differences						
		Not at all ac- ceptable (1)	Somewhat accept- able (2)	Accept- able (3)	Desir- able (4)	Means					Zero-order correlation coefficients[3]	
						1976[1]	1977	1978	1979	1980	Trend	Sex
Imagine you are married and have one or more pre-school children and both you and your spouse work full-time. How would you feel about each of these arrangements for the day-to-day care of the children) after working hours and on weekends?												
Wife does all child care	M:	57.2	25.7	9.9	7.2		1.65	1.71	1.70	1.67	.01	
	F:	70.7	18.0	9.4	1.9		1.42	1.47	1.36	1.43	-.01	-.16
Wife does most of it	M:	17.7	44.1	21.3	6.9		2.04	2.09	2.03	2.07	.01	
	F:	32.1	42.9	20.6	4.4		1.91	2.02	1.89	1.97	.00	-.06
Both do it equally	M:	4.8	17.2	37.8	40.3		2.94	3.10	3.05	3.14	.06	
	F:	1.4	8.7	24.1	65.8		3.32	3.43	3.35	3.54	.08	.21
Husband does most of it	M:	50.9	35.6	11.0	2.5		1.57	1.58	1.59	1.65	.04	
	F:	52.7	36.6	9.1	1.6		1.49	1.53	1.50	1.60	.04	-.05
Husband does all of it	M:	83.2	10.6	4.0	2.2		1.28	1.24	1.27	1.25	-.01	
	F:	85.6	9.2	3.6	1.6		1.18	1.19	1.18	1.21	.01	-.06
Index[2] (first 3 items above)	M:						2.45	2.47	2.47	2.48	.02	
	F:						2.61	2.59	2.63	2.62	.02	.17

[1] Items not included in 1976 survey instrument.

[2] For description of index formation, see text.

[3] For an explanation of these coefficients, see Chapter 2.

114

Table 4-1.5

Preferred Division of Housework When Both Spouses Work: Distributions and Trends

| | | 1980 Percentage Distributions | | | | 1976-1980 Trends and Sex Differences | | | | | | |
| | | | | | | Means | | | | | Zero-order correlation coefficients [3] | |
		Not at all acceptable (1)	Somewhat acceptable (2)	Acceptable (3)	Desirable (4)	1976[1]	1977	1978	1979	1980	Trend	Sex
Imagine both you and your spouse are working full-time. How would you feel about each of these arrangements for doing things like cooking, cleaning and laundry?												
Wife does all cooking cleaning and laundry	M:	39.3	29.5	20.2	11.0		2.07	2.11	2.02	2.03	-.02	
	F:	56.5	23.4	16.0	4.0		1.73	1.78	1.71	1.68	-.03	-.17
Wife does most of it	M:	20.2	37.0	31.6	11.5		2.32	2.36	2.26	2.35	.00	
	F:	26.7	38.4	26.8	8.1		2.12	2.22	2.10	2.16	.00	-.09
Both do it equally	M:	8.2	24.8	37.4	29.6		2.73	2.88	2.86	2.88	.05	
	F:	4.1	11.9	27.9	56.1		3.17	3.27	3.15	3.36	.06	.21
Husband does most of it	M:	61.2	29.0	7.8	2.0		1.48	1.48	1.48	1.51	.01	
	F:	60.4	29.5	7.8	2.3		1.48	1.44	1.45	1.52	.02	-.01
Husband does all of it	M:	88.1	6.8	3.5	1.7		1.23	1.20	1.24	1.19	-.02	
	F:	86.7	8.3	2.8	2.2		1.17	1.17	1.19	1.21	.02	-0.3
<u>Index</u>[2] (first 3 items above)	M:						2.25	2.28	2.32	2.29	.03	
	F:						2.45	2.44	2.45	2.49	.04	.19

[1] Items not included in 1976 survey instrument.

[2] For description of index formation, see text.

[3] For an explanation of these coefficients, see Chapter 2.

115

Table 4-2.1

Preferred Division of Paid Work of a Couple Without Children: Effects of Background Characteristics

		Zero-Order Correlation Coefficients													Multiple Correlation Coefficients
		Race	Live with Mother	Live with Father	Mother Worked	Father Educ.	Mother Educ.	Urbani- city	Acad. Ability	Grades	Coll. Plans	Polit. Orient	Relig. Commit	Dating Freq.	
Married, no child:															
Husband work FT wife not	M:	-.15	.04	.05	-.10	-.01	-.03	-.07	.03	.04	-.03	-.07	.08	.01	.21
	F:	-.08	.00	.04	-.10	-.05	-.07	-.08	-.07	-.04	-.11	-.10	.07	.01	.21
Husband work FT wife half-time	M:	-.14	.05	.06	-.01	.06	.06	.05	.13	.09	.08	-.01	.00	.00	.18
	F:	-.18	.04	.07	-.09	.02	.01	-.05	-.02	.03	-.05	-.08	.05	.05	.21
Both work FT	M:	.05	.02	.00	.09	.06	.08	.05	.06	.07	.10	.09	-.06	-.01	.19
	F:	-.07	.02	.01	.07	.07	.09	.02	.19	.16	.14	.07	-.06	-.01	.25
Index (3 items above)	M:	.13	.00	-.02	.12	.05	.08	.08	.04	.04	.10	.10	-.07	-.01	.24
	F:	.05	.01	-.03	.12	.08	.10	.08	.16	.10	.17	.12	-.08	-.03	.27

Table 4-2.2

Preferred Division of Paid Work of a Couple with Preschool Children: Effects of Background Characteristics

		Zero-Order Correlation Coefficients													Multiple Correlation Coefficients
	Race	Live with Mother	Live with Father	Mother Worked	Father Educ.	Mother Educ.	Urbani-city	Acad. Ability	Grades	Coll. Plans	Polit. Orient	Relig. Commit	Dating Freq.	
Marr. with pre-school child:														
Husband work FT wife not M:	-.27	.09	.11	-.17	.09	.07	.04	.17	.16	.11	-.04	.06	-.01	.33
F:	-.29	.07	.12	-.18	.06	.04	-.03	.07	.10	-.02	-.10	.09	.02	.34
Husband work FT wife half-time M:	.04	.00	-.02	.14	.02	.06	-.02	.02	.03	.04	.03	-.04	.00	.16
F:	-.02	-.01	-.01	.09	-.01	.01	-.04	.02	.02	.03	.02	-.04	.01	.12
Both work FT M:	.19	-.06	-.08	.17	-.06	-.05	-.10	-.13	-.08	-.08	.02	-.03	.03	.27
F:	.22	-.06	-.08	.17	-.09	-.05	-.05	-.03	-.05	.00	.03	-.03	.00	.27
Index (3 items above) M:	.25	-.07	-.09	.22	-.06	-.03	-.09	-.13	-.09	-.06	-.04	-.04	.02	.33
F:	.29	-.06	-.11	.22	-.07	-.04	-.02	-.02	-.06	.03	.07	-.07	-.01	.35

Table 4-2.3

Preferred Division of Child Care When the Husband Works: Effects of Background Characteristics

							Zero-Order Correlation Coefficients									Multiple Correlation Coefficients
		Race	Live with Mother	Live with Father	Mother Worked	Father Educ.	Mother Educ.	Urbani-city	Acad. Ability	Grades	Coll. Plans	Polit. Orient	Relig. Commit	Dating Freq.	
Husband work FT wife not:															
Wife does all childcare	M:	.01	.00	-.02	-.01	-.03	-.04	-.02	-.04	-.05	-.06	.00	-.04	.01	.07
	F:	.05	-.03	-.03	-.01	-.08	-.09	-.05	-.08	-.06	-.09	-.08	-.03	.03	.15
Wife does most of it	M:	-.10	.05	.04	-.04	.07	.05	.01	.11	.07	.04	-.02	-.03	.00	.15
	F:	-.13	.02	.06	-.06	.06	.03	-.03	.10	.09	.04	-.07	.05	.04	.18
Both do it equally	M:	-.08	.03	.02	.00	.05	.06	.03	.06	.06	.07	.04	.05	.00	.13
	F:	-.10	.03	.04	.00	.03	.04	.02	.06	.06	.03	.03	-.05	-.01	.12
Index (3 items above)	M:	-.05	.01	.03	.01	.05	.07	.04	.06	.06	.08	.02	.05	-.01	.11
	F:	-.07	.02	.03	.00	.08	.09	.05	.07	.06	.08	.07	-.05	-.04	.15

Table 4-2.4

Preferred Division of Child Care when Both Spouses Work: Effects of Background Characteristics[1]

| | | Zero-Order Correlation Coefficients | | | | | | | | | | | | | Multiple Correlation Coefficients |
	Race	Live with Mother	Live with Father	Mother Worked	Father Educ.	Mother Educ.	Urbanicity	Acad. Ability	Grades	Coll. Plans	Polit. Orient	Relig. Commit	Dating Freq.	
Both work FT:														
Wife does all childcare M:	.00	-.03	.01	-.01	-.05	-.02	-.07	-.10	-.09	-.08	-.03	-.04	-.01	.13
F:	.06	-.06	-.05	.02	-.11	-.09	-.06	-.17	-.14	-.14	-.08	.07	.02	.23
Wife does most of it M:	-.02	-.02	.02	-.03	.01	.00	-.04	.00	-.01	-.01	-.03	-.01	-.04	.06
F:	.03	-.03	-.01	.00	-.05	-.04	-.08	-.04	.00	-.07	-.11	.11	.02	.17
Both do it equally M:	-.04	.06	.04	.01	.07	.06	.05	.14	.13	.11	.02	.02	.02	.17
F:	-.08	.06	.03	-.01	.13	.11	.03	.16	.13	.15	.10	-.02	-.01	.23
Index (3 items above) M:	-.01	.03	-.01	.02	.06	.04	.07	.11	.10	.09	.04	.03	.03	.15
F:	-.07	.06	.04	-.02	.12	.10	.07	.16	.12	.15	.13	-.09	-.03	.26

[1] Since this item set was not included in 1976 questionnaires, data shown represent 1977-1980 surveys.

Table 4-2.5

Preferred Division of Housework When Both Spouses Work: Effects of Background Characteristics[1]

			Zero-Order Correlation Coefficients											Multiple Correlation Coefficients
	Race	Live with Mother	Live with Father	Mother Worked	Father Educ.	Mother Educ.	Urbani-city	Acad. Ability	Grades	Coll. Plans	Polit. Orient	Relig. Commit	Dating Freq.	
Both work FT:														
Wife does all housework M:	-.03	.01	.04	-.05	-.04	-.04	-.05	-.10	-.10	-.07	-.03	-.01	-.01	.13
F:	.04	-.05	-.03	.03	-.15	-.13	-.12	-.18	-.16	-.22	-.14	.09	.06	.32
Wife does most of it M:	-.04	.02	.05	-.06	.00	.00	-.03	.02	.00	-.02	-.03	.01	.01	.08
F:	-.01	-.02	.01	.01	-.07	-.05	-.12	-.02	.01	-.10	-.15	.14	.07	.24
Both do it equally M:	-.02	.02	.02	.05	.01	.04	.05	.07	.06	.07	.04	-.02	.02	.11
F:	.00	.03	-.01	.02	.10	.09	.07	.11	.06	.13	.11	-.07	-.07	.21
Index (3 items above) M:	.01	.00	-.02	.06	.02	.04	.07	.09	.08	.08	.05	-.02	.01	.14
F:	-.02	.04	.01	-.01	.15	.13	.12	.17	.12	.20	.17	-.12	-.09	.32

[1]Since this item set was not included in 1976 questionnaires, data shown represent 1977-1980 surveys.

Table 4-3

Preferred Division of Labor in the Family: Interrelationships
Between Indices and Single Variables[1]

	Index Div.paid Work no child.		Index Div.paid Work presch.ch.		Index Div.paid Work combined		Index Div. Childcare, Husband wk.		Index Div. Childcare, Couple wk.		Index Div. Housework, Husband wk.		Index Div. Housework, Couple wk.		Index Home Duties Combined	
	M	F	M	F	M	F	M	F	M	F	M	F	M	F	M	F
Mean	1.92	2.26	1.53	1.62	1.73	1.94	2.19	2.26	2.29	2.53	2.01	2.01	2.20	2.40	2.18	2.30
Stand. Deviation	.38	.37	.40	.43	.32	.33	.42	.38	.43	.40	.42	.41	.43	.42	.31	.30
Product-Moment Correlations:																
Div.Paid Work																
No children:																
Hb.full,wf.not	-.69	-.77	-.27	-.16	-.58	-.55	-.05	-.16	-.07	-.13	-.08	-.10	-.05	-.20	-.11	-.21
Hb.full,wf.half	.15	-.55	-.07	-.24	.03	-.47	.08	-.11	.03	-.06	.02	-.07	.03	-.13	.03	-.13
Both full	.81	.70	.27	.30	.65	.60	-.02	-.10	.09	.17	.01	.08	.03	.14	.04	.16
Index (3 items)	.37	.35	.37	.33	.82	.78	.01	.16	.13	.16	.05	.11	.07	.21	.10	.22
Presch. child:																
Hb.full,wf.not	-.22	-.35	-.67	-.71	-.57	-.66	-.04	-.08	.01	-.04	-.11	-.16	.02	-.10	-.07	-.12
Hb.full,wf.half	.25	.09	.56	.35	.50	.29	-.03	-.10	-.03	.00	.00	-.02	-.08	.00	-.03	-.06
Both full	.25	.22	.82	.83	.66	.67	-.09	-.02	-.10	-.01	-.04	.12	-.11	.02	-.12	.03
Index (3 items)	.37	.33	.83	.84	.83	.84	-.06	-.02	-.02	-.02	-.01	.11	-.09	.04	-.05	.02
Div.Childcare																
Hb.works:																
Wf.all childc.	-.06	-.17	-.01	-.01	-.04	-.09	-.82	-.82	-.27	-.26	-.40	-.30	-.24	-.23	-.58	-.54
Wf.most	-.05	-.12	-.10	-.11	-.04	-.14	-.45	-.48	-.12	-.18	-.21	-.26	-.07	-.18	-.31	-.36
Both equally	-.04	.04	-.15	-.05	-.12	-.02	.69	.64	.18	.19	.37	.39	.17	.21	.46	.47
Index (3 items)	.01	.16	-.06	-.02	-.04	.08	.29	.34	.29	.34	.48	.46	.27	.32	.68	.69
Couple works:																
Wf.all childc.	-.07	-.13	.04	.00	-.02	-.07	-.26	-.30	-.82	-.87	-.28	-.23	-.58	-.62	-.67	-.68
Wf.most	-.07	-.16	-.02	-.04	-.06	-.12	-.22	-.28	-.63	-.73	-.20	-.26	-.43	-.55	-.52	-.60
Both equally	.10	.13	-.01	-.11	-.06	-.01	.18	.17	.67	.64	.25	.22	.40	.49	.52	.54
Index (3 items)	.13	.16	-.02	-.02	.07	.07	.29	.34	.67	.64	.25	.30	.49	.52	.68	.69
Div.of Housewk.																
Hb.works:																
Wf.all housewk.	-.10	-.14	-.03	-.13	-.08	-.17	-.45	-.39	-.30	-.27	-.80	-.76	-.38	-.36	-.65	-.60
Wf.most	-.03	-.11	-.09	-.17	-.07	-.18	-.13	-.16	-.13	-.13	-.33	-.34	-.17	-.20	-.28	-.27
Both equally	.03	.09	.01	.06	.02	.09	.34	.36	.24	.15	.74	.79	.32	.22	.55	.51
Index (3 items)	.05	.11	.01	.11	.04	.13	.48	.46	.34	.30	.80	.79	.43	.39	.75	.72
Couple works:																
Wf.all housewk.	-.06	-.18	.07	-.06	.00	-.14	-.26	-.25	-.48	-.60	-.33	-.29	-.82	-.88	-.66	-.69
Wf.most	-.01	-.15	-.01	-.10	-.01	-.15	-.22	-.24	-.38	-.49	-.29	-.34	-.60	-.72	-.54	-.61
Both equally	.09	.13	-.03	-.08	-.03	.02	.20	.22	.48	.52	.36	.33	.71	.72	.60	.64
Index (3 items)	.07	.21	-.09	.04	-.01	.14	.27	.32	.64	.70	.43	.39	.82	.82	.79	.82

[1]Based on 434 males and 538 females surveyed in 1978 as part of the Long Form sample.

Table 4-4.1

Preferred Division of Paid Work of a Couple Without Children: Effects of Predictors

		Bivariate Coefficients[1]		Multivariate Coefficients[2]			
Race	M: F:	.08 .07		.09 .07		.11 .11	
Working Mother	M: F:	.05 .07		.06 .07		.06 .00	
Mother's Education	M: F:	.07 .01		.03 -.01		.04 -.05	
Acad. Ability Comp.	M: F:	.14* .13*		.15* .13*		.12 .02	
Political Orientation	M: F:	.11 .06		.09 .06		.06 .00	
Trad. Sex Role Attitudes	M: F:	-.19* -.40*				-.12 -.42*	
Equal Opp. Attitudes	M: F:	.12 .12				.08 -.04	
Parenting Attitudes	M: F:	-.13 -.14*				-.13 -.07	
R (adj.)	M: F:			.15 .10		.23 .39	
R² (adj.)	M: F:			.02 .01		.05 .15	

Note: *p < .05

[1] Entries are zero-order correlation coefficients.

[2] Entries are standardized regression coefficients.

Table 4-4.2

Preferred Division of Paid Work of a Couple With Preschool Children: Effects of Predictors

		Bivariate Coefficients[1]		Multivariate Coefficients[2]			
Race	M: F:	.23* -.12	.30*	.19* -.02	.26*	.19* -.01	.30*
Live with Father	M: F:	-.12	-.12	-.02	-.04	-.01	-.03
Mother Worked	M: F:	.26*	.27*	.22*	.24*	.20*	.20*
Acad. Ability Comp.	M: F:	-.11	-.02	-.05	-.02	-.07	-.08
Trad. Sex Role Attitudes	M: F:	-.18*	-.22*			-.23*	-.25*
Equal Opp. Attitudes	M: F:	-.09	-.02			-.12	-.09
Parenting Attitudes	M: F:	-.10	-.19*			-.07	-.18*
R (adj.)	M: F:			.30	.36	.37	.47
R² (adj.)	M: F:			.09	.13	.14	.22

Note: *p < .05

[1] Entries are zero-order correlation coefficients.

[2] Entries are standardized regression coefficients.

Table 4-4.3

Preferred Division of Child Care When the Husband Works: Effects of Predictors

		Bivariate Coefficients[1]	Multivariate Coefficients[2]
Trad. Sex Role Attitudes	M:	-.25*	-.22*
	F:	-.32*	-.32*
Equal Opp. Attitudes	M:	.18*	.10
	F:	.13*	.00
Parenting Attitudes	M:	.07	.08
	F:	-.09	-.02
R (adj.)	M:		.25
	F:		.30
R² (adj.)	M:		.06
	F:		.09

Note: *p < .05

[1]Entries are zero-order correlation coefficients.

[2]Entries are standardized regression coefficients.

Table 4-4.4

Preferred Division of Child Care When Both Spouses Work: Effects of Predictors

		Bivariate Coefficients[1]	Multivariate Coefficients[2]	
Father's Education	M:	.12	.07	.07
	F:	.09	.01	.01
Mother's Education	M:	.10	.01	.00
	F:	.12	.07	.01
Acad. Ability Comp.	M:	.24*	.23*	.15*
	F:	.23*	.22*	.11
Political Orientation	M:	-.13	-.14*	-.13
	F:	.08	.10	.05
Trad. Sex Role Attitudes	M:	-.31*		-.25*
	F:	-.41*		-.35*
Equal Opp. Attitudes	M:	.24*		.09
	F:	.26*		.10
Parenting Attitudes	M:	.14		.11
	F:	.03		.13*
R (adj.)	M:		.25	.38
	F:		.23	.43
R² (adj.)	M:		.06	.14
	F:		.05	.18

Note: *p < .05

[1]Entries are zero-order correlation coefficients.

[2]Entries are standardized regression coefficients.

125

Table 4-4.5

Preferred Division of Housework When Both Spouses Work: Effects of Predictors

		Bivariate Coefficients[1]	Multivariate Coefficients[2]	
Fathers' Education	M:	.06	.03	.03
	F:	.12	.04	.04
Mother's Education	M:	.05	-.02	-.03
	F:	.14*	.09	.02
Urbanicity	M:	.06	.06	.07
	F:	-.09	-.10	-.06
Acad. Ability Comp.	M:	.23*	.24*	.15*
	F:	.24*	.24*	.12
Political Orientation	M:	-.13	-.15*	-.14*
	F:	.09	.08	.05
Religious Commitment	M:	.01	-.03	-.01
	F:	-.07	-.10	-.05
Trad. Sex Role Attitudes	M:	-.35*		-.29*
	F:	-.42*		-.34*
Equal Opp. Attitudes	M:	.25*		.10
	F:	.27*		.09
Parenting Attitudes	M:	.09		.07
	F:	-.01		.09
R (adj.)	M:		.22	.39
	F:		.27	.43
R² (adj.)	M:		.05	.15
	F:		.07	.19

Note: *p < .05

[1]Entries are zero-order correlations coefficients.

[2]Entries are standardized regression coefficients.

126

Figure 4-1

Preferred Division of Paid Work (No Children)

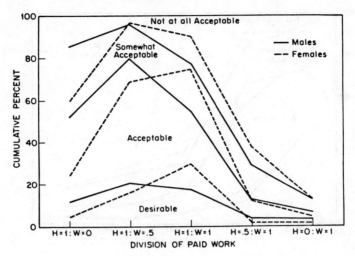

Note: The bottom lines trace the percentages of males and females who rate each arrangement as desirable, the intermediate lines the cumulative percentages who rate each arrangement as either desirable or acceptable, the top lines the cumulative percentages who rate each arrangement as either desirable, acceptable, or somewhat acceptable. 1979 data is displayed.

Figure 4-2

Preferred Division of Paid Work (Preschool Children)

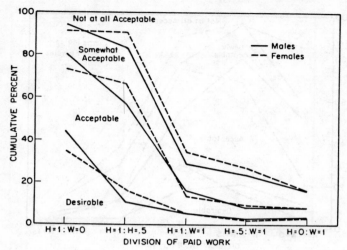

Note: The bottom lines trace the percentages of males and females who rate each arrangement as desirable, the intermediate lines the cumulative percentages who rate each arrangement as either desirable or acceptable, the top lines the cumulative percentages who rate each arrangement as either desirable, acceptable, or somewhat acceptable. 1979 data is displayed.

Figure 4-3

Preferred Division of Child Care (Husband Works Full-Time)

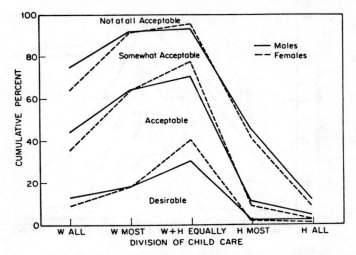

Note: The bottom lines trace the percentages of males and females who rate
each arrangement as desirable, the intermediate lines the cumulative
percentages who rate each arrangement as either desirable or acceptable, the
top lines the cumulative percentages who rate each arrangement as either
desirable, acceptable, or somewhat acceptable. 1979 data is displayed.

129

Figure 4-4

Preferred Division of Child Care (Husband and Wife Work Full-Time)

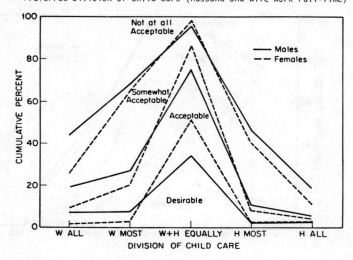

Note: The bottom lines trace the percentages of males and females who rate
each arrangement as desirable, the intermediate lines the cumulative
percentages who rate each arrangement as either desirable or acceptable, the
top lines the cumulative percentages who rate each arrangement as either
desirable, acceptable, or somewhat acceptable. 1979 data is displayed.

130

Figure 4-5

Preferred Division of Housework (Husband and Wife Work Full-Time)

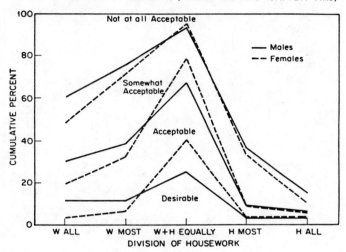

Note: The bottom lines trace the percentages of males and females who rate each arrangement as desirable, the intermediate lines the cumulative percentages who rate each arrangement as either desirable or acceptable, the top lines the cumulative percentages who rate each arrangement as either desirable, acceptable, or somewhat acceptable. 1979 data is displayed.

CHAPTER 5

EDUCATIONAL AND OCCUPATIONAL PLANS

While recent trends show increasing support for
husband's and wives' sharing of family and work roles
and for sex equality in education, occupation, and
public office (Bayer, 1975; Ferree, 1974; Mason and
Bumpass, 1975; Mason, Czajka, and Arber, 1976;
Parelius, 1975; Spitze and Huber, 1980; Thornton and
Freedman, 1979; Chapter 3 and 4 of this report), and
while women have certainly established their place in
the work force in terms of numbers (Smith, 1979), the
basic sex differentiation persists. Women still hold
primary responsibility for child rearing and are expected to modify their labor force participation accordingly, while men are chiefly responsible for
economic support of the family and encounter widespread
disapproval when attempting to modify their full-time
work involvement (Young and Willmott, 1973; Chapter 4).
Also, once women are employed, they differ substantially from employed men in terms of earnings (Featherman
and Hauser, 1976; Treiman and Terrell, 1975b),
authority on the job (Wolf and Fligstein, 1979), and
specific occupational categories and industries that
they have entered (Blau and Hendricks, 1979; Davis,
1980; Fuchs, 1971; Oppenheimer, 1968; Rosenfeld and
Sorenson, 1979; U.S.Department of Labor, 1975a). Altogether, female workers are concentrated in relatively
few occupations that employ mostly women (i.e., clerical, sales, service, and a few professional jobs such
as elementary and secondary school teacher, nurse, social worker, or librarian), while this is less the case
for male workers. Such sex segregation in the labor
force is recognized as a significant factor in the continuing wage differentials between the sexes (Blau and
Jusenius, 1976; Fuchs, 1971; Oaxaca, 1973).

Given the saliency of the roles of wife, mother,
and homemaker for young women, and given the establish-
ment of these basic role priorities as early as elementary school (Hartley, 1959-1960), they are likely to
have a profound impact on the development of occupational aspirations among young women and thereby
contribute to the perpetuation of existing sex differences in the labor force. Several hypotheses have

been specified about the particular process that is involved here.

It has been suggested that work plays a less pivotal role in young women's thinking about their future: Young women expect to spend less time than men over their entire lifetime in paid work and actually seem to underestimate their lifetime work involvement (Jusenius and Sandell, 1974, cited in U.S. Department of Labor, 1977). They also tend to pay less attention to various gains from their future work since they will presumably obtain important pay-offs such as economic support, standard of living, and social prestige indirectly through their husband's work activities (Lipman-Blumen, 1972; Turner, 1964). Thus young women as well as young men tend to view female employment as of more marginal significance than male employment, as not being critical for the family's survival, even though it may afford them some luxuries or prove helpful in case of economic hardship.

Under these circumstances it would appear logical that young women, on the average, plan their future careers less carefully, get less counseling on the issue, get insufficient education, look for short-term returns (Psathas, 1968), forego on-the-job training for somewhat higher starting salaries (Shapiro and Carr, 1978), and frequently interrupt their early career for family responsibilities. In the language of the economic model of human capital, women invest less in human capital and/or lose their investment when they interrupt their career at an early point; and their lesser investment presumably attenuates later returns in form of prestige and income.

Although some data suggest that women are about equally likely to graduate from high school and college as young men (U. S. Department of Education, 1980), they may fail to choose an appropriate type of education and training. For example, girls seem to be less likely to take courses in mathematics, and that prevents them later from enrolling in various scientific fields. In connection with the uncertainty attached to marital and family roles, it has been suggested that women tend to "hedge" their career preparations (Theodore, 1971) which is supposed to express itself in their choice of general educational curricula and in a reluctance to make educational and occupational commitments. In some sense, the career hedging is likely to continue even after choosing a particular marital partner, since the husband's career development almost always gets first attention and often introduces constraints in the form of geographical moves or rigid and demanding time schedules that require increased flexibility on the part of the wife.

It has also been suggested that in making specific occupational choices women seek to satisfy typically female needs. For example, many of the jobs predominantly held by women such as nursing, teaching, clerical, and service work represent an extension of the traditional female role, in that they involve help to others and attendance to domestic duties, which are also predominant features of the traditional female role (Bernard, 1971; Oppenheimer, 1968). Related to this argument is the notion of women's indirect achievement strivings, i.e. women's expectation to achieve economic well-being and status through their husband's achievements rather than through their own job, while regarding their own job exclusively for its potential to exercise skills and abilities (Lipman-Blumen, 1972; Turner, 1964). Such an orientation would imply that women are less likely to emphasize the economic function of a job and related characteristics than men, while they are more attuned to characteristics dealing with self-actualization. Finally, it has been suggested that traditional female occupations appeal to women because of assumed flexibility in work schedules and occupational commitment which makes these occupations appear more compatible with family responsibilities (Kreps, 1971).

Occupational choices are, of course, guided not only by preferences and interests but also by what is perceived as realistic opportunities for successful competition and performance. With regard to women's occupational choices, such an "expectancy-value" approach implies that traditionally female occupations are chosen by a majority of women not only because they are believed to satisfy some uniquely female needs and values, but also because they are assumed--rightly or wrongly--to provide opportunities for women and be commensurate with women's abilities and personalities (Laws, 1976). Therefore, investigations of women's occupational aspirations need to include measures of their perceptions of existing opportunities in various fields and measures of self-perceived competence, along with measures of occupational values.

Aside from factors that refer to the difference in perspectives between young men and women, there are a number of general socialization factors and personal characteristics that have been studied as part of the research efforts focused on status attainment. In that research tradition, parental education and socioeconomic status of the family of origin have been identified as critical predictors of educational and

occupational plans of young people (Alexander and Eckland, 1974; Hout and Morgan, 1975; Marini and Greenberger, 1978a, b; Rosen and Aneshensel, 1978; Sewell
and Shah, 1968). Moreover, some studies have suggested
that the effect of same-sex parent may be stronger than
the effect of the opposite-sex parent (e.g., Aneshensel
and Rosen, 1980). A more specific socialization factor
refers to having had the experience of a working
mother. This experience appears to foster occupational
plans in daughters (Rosen and Aneshensel, 1978; Tangri,
1972), although the mechanism by which this effect gets
transmitted is not well-understood.

Young people's abilities represent another major
factor in determining plans. Such abilities are often
conceptualized as partial mediators of parental education and socioeconomic status on offspring's plans, and
research has tended to support this view (Alexander and
Eckland, 1974; Hout and Morgan, 1975; Marini and Greenberger, 1978a,b; Rosen and Aneshensel, 1978; Sewell and
Hauser, 1975; Sewell and Shah, 1968). Interestingly,
these rather limited models of the formation of plans
have not revealed any substantial differences in this
process for the two sexes, which is rather puzzling in
light of the substantial differences in the labor
force. As has been noted by some, a critical shortcom-
ing of the status attainment literature is the dis-
regard of sex role-related variables of the sort that
we have discussed above (Alexander and Eckland, 1974;
Marini, 1980; Sewell and Shah, 1967). For example,
young women who hold more traditional views about sex
roles may view paid work as more marginal where their
plans for the future are concerned than young women who
hold less traditional views. The few studies that have
addressed this issue provide some suggestive evidence
that sex role attitudes do affect occupational plans
(Aneshensel and Rosen, 1980; Gaskell, 1977-78; McLaughlin, 1974) as well as educational plans (Aneshensel and
Rosen, 1980; Gaskell, 1977-78).

In the wake of the rather marked changes in attitudes towards women's work and family roles that have
taken place recently, it is possible that occupational
plans also have changed. However, little specific
knowledge is available. Among the relevant studies,
Garrison (1979) reports an increase in aspirations
towards higher level professional jobs between 1970 and
1976 among female high school seniors in the State of
Virginia. No such increase was observed for male
seniors, which resulted in a net closing of the sex gap
on these aspirations. Lueptow (1980) reports on a number of occupational values among high school seniors in
Wisconsin over a ten-year span from 1964 to 1975. He
observed several trends: importance of money, interper-

sonal contacts, leadership, adventure, and autonomy increased; importance of security and being able to use one's abilities declined. These trends were similar for both sexes, although there were some overall differences in level--males attributed higher importance to money, status, autonomy, and authority, while females attributed higher importance to interpersonal contacts and altruistic concerns.

We turn now to reporting our own findings on high school seniors' plans for the future. We begin with educational plans, which can be treated fairly briefly. Views about future work are multidimensional. We have found it useful to treat each of the following topics separately: the role of paid work; occupational values; perceptions about potential for success; preferences for various work settings; and specific occupational plans (type of job expected at age 30).

EDUCATIONAL PLANS

Four types of after-high school education were probed in the Monitoring the Future questionnaires as to the likelihood with which the respondent expects to pursue any of them. As Table 5-1.1 shows, more than half of the respondents expect that they "definitely" or "probably" will attend a four-year college program. This is by far the most popular choice among the seniors. Furthermore, more than half of those seniors plan on continuing with graduate or professional schools.

There is only a tiny difference in the proportions of males and females planning to complete college. Young men are a bit more likely to plan on attending graduate school than are young women, but the difference is still small.

Less popular types of education show a slightly stronger sex difference. Young men are more likely than young women to plan on attending a vocational or technical school (i.e., 29% of the males and 25% of the females). On the other hand, young women are somewhat more likely to plan on a two-year college education. These sex differences are consistent with the notion of career hedging; vocational and technical schools are more specified and focused, while two-year college programs provide a more general and more flexible curriculum.

137

Trends

College and graduate school plans have become slightly more frequent over the last five years. Interestingly, while the plans of young women have steadily changed over that period, the plans of young men show a very substantial change only in the last year, with comparatively little change in the years before. We certainly need to watch these trends over a longer period of time in order to determine the reliability of the sudden change in males' plans. A possible interpretation of such a change, if found to be reliable, is that it reflects a reaction to the recent economic recession. The continuous trend among females, on the other hand, more likely reflects long-term changes in women's self-concepts and their outlook on life.

Background Characteristics

Educational plans are, of course, very strongly influenced by abilities and by parents' educational attainments: Able seniors from educated backgrounds are more likely than less able seniors from less educated backgrounds to plan for college and graduate school (Table 5-2.1). The reverse holds for vocational and technical schools: More able seniors from better educated backgrounds are less likely to aspire to these schools than less able seniors from less educated backgrounds. Although not presented here, multivariate analyses show that the effect of parental education is largely mediated through abilities. Also, while parental education appears to affect educational plans of both sexes in similar ways, the effect of abilities is a trifle stronger on males' than on females' educational plans.

Another predictor of seniors' educational plans is the urban character of their residence. Seniors who live in more urban settings are more likely to plan on entering college and graduate school, and somewhat less likely to plan on vocational or technical training.

Race and dating frequency are related to some educational plans for female but less for male seniors. Young black women are more likely than white women to aspire to a college and graduate education. Also, women who report dating more frequently are less inclined towards college and graduate education. Neither of these sex differences in correlations is due to variance differences.

Sex Roles and Educational Plans

As far as the background factors are concerned, the findings from the Long Form data in most respects replicate the findings from the Monitoring the Future data that were just reported. (In the Monitoring the Future data, the link between self-reported academic ability and educational aspirations is slightly stronger for males than for females. The Long Form data exaggerate this sex differential, and thus must be interpreted with some caution.)

As for the central focus of this report, significant bivariate effects of traditional sex role attitudes and preferences for the division of labor in the family on educational plans are present. However, these effects are partly explainable in terms of their relationships with abilities, since the effects are reduced substantially in multiple regression analyses (see Tables 5-3.1 and 5-3.2).

THE ROLE OF PAID WORK

Contrary to predictions based on the literature, it is quite clear from the data that young women expect work to play a major role in their lives, and in this regard they appear not at all different from young men. When asked about the "kind of work you will be doing when you are 30 years old," an overwhelming majority (about 92 percent in 1980) of young women mark a particular occupational category, rather than the category "full-time homemaker or housewife" which was explicitly included as response alternative (Table 5-1.6). Moreover, when asked to rate a set of general life values, young women judge "success in work" equally important as do young men (Table 5-1.2). Finally, young women appear to plan on devoting similar attention and effort to their future work as do young men. They agree to a similar extent with the statement: "I want to do the best in my job, even if this sometimes means working overtime," and they agree even less than men with the statement that "working is nothing more than making a living." Moreover, they are equally likely to indicate that they would continue working, even if they did not need to do so for financial reasons (Table 5-1.2). The latter items indicate in more subjective terms the centrality that work assumes within the projected life space of the seniors and its significance beyond a simple economic necessity. The lack of consistent sex differences suggest that the sexes do not differ critically in the role they assign to paid work within their future life.

On the other hand, we notice several indications that the centrality of the work role <u>relative to marital and family roles</u> must be lower for young women than men. For example, women attribute higher importance to the value of a good marriage and family life than young men, and they think more often about whether they would want to have any children of their own (Table 5-1.2). This suggests that marital and parental roles have an increased saliency and importance for young women. Put in a different way, young women on the average attach distinctly higher importance to family and marital roles than to work roles, whereas for young men there is little average difference in importance. We therefore suspect that the anticipation of and the planning for marital and family roles are more likely to conflict with preparation and plans for the work role among young women than men.

In fact, differences between the sexes in orientation towards work do appear when work is explicitly pitted against family responsibilities, i.e., when the centrality of the work role is evaluated relative to family roles. For example, a set of questions discussed earlier (Chapter 4) includes seniors' preferences for their own and their prospective spouse's employment when they assume that they would have pre-school children. Note that in these comparisons sex differences are revealed in the difference between projected roles for husband and wife. The data suggest that young women (as well as men) view women's work involvement as somewhat more variable than men's, and that the rearing of children is a major factor in modifying expectations for women's labor force participation. But even when seniors are asked to imagine marriage without children, full-time work is still less likely to be fully endorsed for the wife than for the husband.

Trends

In the two previous chapters we have noted high school seniors' increasing acceptance of paid work by a wife and a mother. We have also noted their increasingly positive personal preferences for a working wife and even a working mother in their own prospective marriage. However, the overall role of work described here does not show any systematic change since 1976. Specifically, little change has occurred for any of the four items included in the centrality index, for the importance rating of steady work as life value, or for the willingness to continue working without economic necessity. On the other hand, the percentage of female seniors who choose full-time housewife as their occupation at age 30 has declined continuously. Separate analyses for college-bound and non-college-bound youth (not reported here in detail) indicate that the latter decline has occurred almost exclusively for the non-college-bound--a shift from 22 percent in 1976 to 13 percent in 1979 (Bachman and Johnston, 1979).'

Background Characteristics

The centrality attributed to work is positively related to abilities and educational plans: seniors of both sexes with higher abilities and more ambitious plans expect their work to be more central (see Table 5-2.2). This relationship shows up clearly only for the two items in the index that measure centrality negatively, i.e. by disagreement with work defined solely in economic terms. This means that more able seniors are less likely to assign work a purely economic role within their life but--presumably--expect their work also to fulfill non-economic needs. Interestingly, abilities and educational aspirations are at least as critical in determining centrality of work among young women as among young men.

Similarly, the only predictors of female expectations to be working at the age of 30 that exceed correlations of .10 are abilities (r = .11) and, more importantly, college plans (r =.21).

Sex Role Attitudes and the Role of Work

In order to turn our attention to the effect of sex role attitudes on the anticipated role of work, we have to switch to Long Form data, upon which the following analyses and comments are based. We are particularly interested in what these sex role attitudes can explain above what is already explained by abilities. Secondly, we are interested in what specific preferences and educational plans can contribute above what is already explained by sex role attitudes. To this end we conducted a series of multiple regression analyses. In the first analysis only background factors that showed a substantial effect (i.e., product-moment correlations of .10 or more) in the

---

'For the class of 1981, the proportion of non-college bound women expecting to be full-time homemakers at age 30 was only about 9 percent.

Monitoring the Future analyses are included as predictors of the expected centrality of work. In the second analysis the three sex role attitude indices are included along with the background factors. In the third analysis indices of preferences for division of labor in the family are added to the previously included predictors. In the next analysis college plans are included as predictors, but since we do not postulate a causal direction between plans and preferences (see Chapter 1), college plans are included only in combination with relevant background characteristics and with sex role attitudes, but not with division of labor indices. Finally, all predictors discussed thus far are included simultaneously in a regression analysis predicting the anticipated role of work.

The simple distinction of whether a young woman plans to work at all when she is 30 years old is a basic indicator of the role that she expects work to play in her adult life. At the same time, this question is a very crude indicator, since it only dichotomizes plans, while not providing for any finer distinctions. This is particularly critical in this case, since the distribution on that question is very skewed; less than 10 percent of the young women plan on being full-time homemakers at that point in their lives. This skewed dichotomized distribution and the implied restriction of the upper bound on correlation and regression coefficients have to be kept in mind when evaluating the following findings. (Note also that this variable showed no variation among males and thus was only analyzed for females.)

This indicator of the role of work is related quite strongly to traditional sex role attitudes and, more weakly, to the importance of parenting (see Table 5-3.3). Young women who plan on being full-time homemakers are more traditional in their sex role attitudes and attribute higher importance to parenting than their female classmates who plan on working. Moreover, the future full-time homemakers are more likely to prefer that they as wives do most or all of the housework in their future marriage. (The relationship for division of paid work is of course tautological, and is therefore not interpreted.) Finally, they are less likely to aspire to a college education, which replicates what was already noted in the Monitoring the Future analysis.

The effect of traditional sex role attitudes remains strong when the other sex role attitudes, preferences for division of labor, and college plans are simultaneously included in the multiple regression equation. This suggests that traditional sex role attitudes exert an effect that is largely independent of these other variables. On the other hand, attitudes towards parenting and preferences for the division of home duties achieve substantial bivariate relationships with plans to be a housewife only because they are related to traditional sex role attitudes, but do not achieve an independent effect.

The four-item index (Table 5-3.4) provides a more differentiated assessment of the centrality that a senior assigns to the work role within his or her future life, as can be gathered from the more even distributions of the responses to the ingredient items.

As we concluded from the Monitoring the Future analyses, ability variables are critical predictors of expected centrality of work and do not seem to affect work orientation any differently among women than among men. This finding is replicated in the Long Form data.

Traditional sex role attitudes (as reflected in the index) and preferences for the division of labor in the family, however, relate in different ways to centrality of work for the two sexes. These variables are substantially related to the anticipated centrality of work among women, while little or no such effect is apparent among young men. (None of these sex differences are substantially altered when unstandardized coefficients are compared.) Since the sex role liberal women are also the women who are academically more competent, as was noted before, it is incumbent on us to examine the effect of the index of traditional sex role attitudes after controlling on this background factor. As the relevant multivariate analysis shows, the large part of the effect is in fact independent of abilities: when the sex role attitude variables are included in a multiple regression simultaneously with academic abilities, the effects of traditional sex role index and academic ability are both reduced only modestly. When the division of labor preferences are also included in the multiple regression, the effect of the traditional sex role index is further reduced, due to the overlapping effects of the two sets of variables.

College plans relate quite strongly to the anticipated centrality of the work role for both males and females. While this relationship seems largely independent of sex role attitudes and preferences for the division of labor, part of the relationship is due to the overlap with academic abilities; college plans apparently mediate some of the effect of academic abilities.

OCCUPATIONAL VALUES

An important role in plans for specific occupations and eventual occupational attainments is played by occupational values. The Monitoring the Future questionnaire contains an extensive set of 23 occupational values that were rated by the seniors on a four-point Likert-type scale as to their importance for their future work. The questions are based on items used in the Quality of Work Surveys (Quinn and Staines, 1979) and in the study "Youth and the Meaning of Work" (Gottlieb, 1973); some of them were modified for the inclusion into the Monitoring the Future instrument. The questions are given in Table 5-1.3. For ease of discussion the 23 items are organized into seven groups, and seven indices are formed. The rationale of this organization is discussed in the next section.

Interrelationships Among Occupational Values and the Formation of a Set of Indices

The 23 items measuring occupational values tend to be positively interrelated, although some of them at very low strength. The positive interrelationship reflects most likely a method artifact, since all variables used the same response scale. (This effect is even stronger for the Long Form data, as discussed in Chapter 2 and in Appendix A.) Otherwise, the low or non-existent relationship among some of the items suggest that these ratings of occupational values capture a multidimensional concept. In order to examine the different dimensions more closely and, hopefully, arrive at a small number of indices, we conducted exploratory factor analyses for males as well as for females.

Since the Kaiser criterion suggested that five factors be extracted for males but six for females, we extracted six factors for both sexes to facilitate comparison. The six factors accounted for 34 percent of the variance in males' ratings and 35 percent in females' ratings. The loadings of the separate items on the orthogonally rotated factors were quite similar for the two sexes, suggesting essentially similar factors.

Based on these loadings as well as on conceptual grounds seven groups of items were defined that may be labeled as follows:

144

--   Importance of material rewards and status (4 items)

--   Importance of stability and security (2 items)

--   Importance of responsibility (2 items)

--   Importance of ease of pace on and off the job (4 items)

--   Importance of stimulation and mastery (7 items)

--   Importance of interpersonal contact (2 items)

--   Importance of altruistic concerns (2 items)

Not all of these groups include items that are equally coherent. The group of items that refer to stimulation and mastery is conceptually somewhat less coherent, a fact which is also reflected in the results of the factor analysis showing that these items load less highly on the relevant factor and less consistently across the sexes.

In order to facilitate the following discussion and further analysis, indices were formed as averages across items in each of the groups listed above. The groups of items are shown in Table 5-4.1; also presented are correlations of each item with each of the seven indices. The correlations show, of course, that the items load highly on their respective indices. The correlations also show that the indices are not orthogonal; many of the items show some degree of correlation with indices for which they are not ingredients.

Descriptive Results

The importance that respondents attribute to the sets of occupational values included in the Monitoring the Future questionnaire clearly varies across items and indices (see Table 5-1.3). In general, values referring to the tangible rewards of a job--income, potential for advancement, and job security--and values related to the dimension of stimulation and mastery-- interesting work, potential for learning, use of skills, seeing results of one's work, and the value of being able to be oneself--are rated as most important. Much less importance is attributed to the easy pace on and off the job, as represented by amount of vacation, easy pace, and lack of supervision.

While values referring to interpersonal contact
and altruism are rated by young women as at least as
important as stimulation and tangible rewards, these
values are less important to young men. These sex differences are the strongest in the entire set of values,
only approached by the sex difference on the values of
stimulation and mastery. Again, young women are attributing much higher importance to these latter occupational values. Both of these sex differences are
of course entirely consistent with the traditional
female role, according to which women fulfill a nur-
turant and other-oriented function in the family and,
if employed, are more concerned than men about the
self-actualizing potential of their work.

Sex differences on other values, although less
pronounced, are also in accordance with the traditional
female role. Specifically, the lower importance attributed by females to status and money received from a
job is consistent with the notion that a woman's
employment is not essential for the economic survival
of the family and for its representation in the social
world. In the same vein, young women's lesser attention to the responsibility required by a job is probably best understood by their lesser career commitment.

On the other hand, results on the importance of
an easy pace on the job are inconsistent with our expectations. Young women do not attribute more importance to these factors than do young men. Rather,
young women attribute less importance to the amount of
vacation and leisure time, in spite of the fact that
full-time working wives are under the permanent pres-
sure of insufficient time (Meissner et al., 1975), and
the availability of additional time could presumably
ease the strain of combining work and family responsibilities. Of course, it is possible that women actually hold more dedicated and responsible attitudes
towards their work than men do, and that such attitudes
are expressed in the lesser importance that women attach to the ease of pace both on and off the job. An
alternative explanation of this unexpected sex difference refers to women's higher propensity to answer
in "socially desirable" terms (Bush, Simmons, Hutchinson, and Blyth, 1977-78). Perhaps women believe that
expressing a desire for lots of free time creates the
impression of a lack of social responsibility on their
part and their tendency to give the socially
desirable--i.e., the responsible answer--counteracts
their "real" preferences for more free time. Still
another alternative interpretation, more substantive
than methodological, should also be considered. It is
possible that young women still in high school, and
thus lacking most relevant experiences, are not suffi-

ciently aware of the enormous and often conflicting time demands incurred under the multiple roles of spouse, parent, housewife and worker.

Trends

Values referring to status and money have increased in importance over the last few years, a trend which probably reflects recent changes in economic outlook. The effects are not strong; but considering the short time period over which they can be observed, they are remarkably consistent. Aside from these cohort trends, very little change in occupational values has occurred over the last five senior cohorts.

Background Characteristics

While altruistic and interpersonal values are regarded as more important by female than male seniors, these specific values do not vary much by background characteristics within sex (Table 5-2.3). The only characteristic that is related to altruistic and-- albeit weakly--to interpersonal values is religiosity: Both female and male seniors who consider themselves religious attribute higher importance to altruistic and interpersonal values in their future work.

Emphasis on material rewards and status show substantial differences by race, as well as some interaction between race and sex. In general, blacks score substantially higher than whites in concerns about making money, gaining status, and having the possibility for advancement. Among blacks these concerns do not differ appreciably by sex; however, among whites the females consistently score somewhat lower than the males. This may be related to the fact that black women in recent decades have not experienced the same sex role differentiation that white women have, but participated equally with black men in the pursuit of paid work and thereby economic support of their families. Thus the role models may be somewhat different for black versus white females.

A slightly different pattern is shown by the item about having a job people can respect; black females show the highest average score, followed by black males, and then by white females and males. In other words, the race differences remain intact for this item, but the sex differences shift somewhat in the direction of higher female concerns when the issue is job respect.

Young people of lesser abilities and lesser college orientation are also more likely to be concerned about making money in a job than are their more able counterparts, although they are not different in their concerns for status, respect, and possibilities for advancement. Again, these differences are somewhat stronger for young women than men.

On the other hand, seniors of higher abilities and with college plans are above average in stressing the importance of the responsibilities that a job requires, having difficult problems to solve, and being involved in decision making.

The ease of pace on the job--but not the amount of free time off the job--is also related to abilities and college plans among young women: Female seniors of higher abilities and more ambitious educational plans are less concerned than less able and less ambitious seniors about having an easy time on their future job.

In sum, while occupational values appear not to be extensively influenced by background variables, abilities and educational aspirations as well as race appear to account for some variation, among females more so than among males. Specifically, female seniors who report themselves as less able academically and less ambitious educationally have a quite different orientation towards their future jobs than their more able and ambitious classmates. The former are more concerned about making money and about having an easy time on the job; and at the same time, they are less concerned about the responsibility that is bestowed on them in a particular job. Black female seniors differ from white female seniors in that they are more concerned about a number of status and money-related characteristics of the job. While college plans/ abilities and race are to a certain extent related to each other, their effects on occupational values are largely independent, as shown by the results of multiple regression analyses not reported here. The overall higher relevance of these predictors for females is reflected in the generally somewhat higher amount of variance accounted for in their occupational values.

PERCEPTIONS ABOUT POTENTIAL FOR SUCCESS

As noted above, occupational plans are influenced not only by which work-values young people deem important, but also by which work they believe they will be able to perform--their expectations for success. Two major groups of factors must be distinguished in the assessment of success expectations; one refers to personal characteristics, the other to societal characteristics. Personal characteristics refer to a host of qualifications for any given type of work, such as abilities, educational credentials, experience, and personality characteristics. Particularly relevant for women's occupational aspirations is the notion that women tend to trust their skills and abilities less than men and are altogether somewhat less confident in their self-assessment. This sex difference has been linked to the sex role orientations and has in fact been proposed as the mechanism by which sex role attitudes mediate sex differences in educational and occupational ambitions (Spenner and Featherman, 1978): When females step out of the traditional female role definition and into the male role of work and competition they hold lower expectancies for success. By the same token, the more traditional women will be more thoroughly affected by such sex role values than the less traditional women.

Societal characteristics, on the other hand, refer to perceived opportunities in the labor market, which of course vary according to economic cycles, general developmental level of a given society, and the like. Of particular importance for understanding women's occupational aspirations are perceptions about existing sex discrimination in various fields.

Unfortunately, the measures of these concepts that are available in the Monitoring the Future study have their limitations. In keeping with the multipurpose design of the study, the measures probe perceived personal competence and perceived societal opportunities in rather global ways. Therefore, we cannot always differentiate these perceptions with respect to a specific occupational field.

Turning to the data, we find rather little evidence of sex differences in perceived competencies. Although fewer than half of either sex rate themselves as "average" or lower in academic ability or intelligence, the proportion of females rating themselves above average in intelligence is slightly (about 6%) smaller than the proportion of males. (This is in spite of the fact that females report higher grade point averages). Females also average a little bit lower than males on one question about their expectations that they will be competent as workers; however, responses to a parallel question indicates that they

feel equally well "prepared" for being a worker as
young men (Table 5-1.4).

Young women perceive considerable sex discrimination existing in all the areas that were probed
in the Monitoring the Future questions, except in the
area of getting a college education (see Table 5-1.4).
Specifically, they perceive a lot of discrimination in
becoming elected to political office, in getting into
executive positions in business, and generally into
positions of leadership. Although these examples
reflect fairly extreme choices and may therefore not be
representative of the large majority of jobs women
might aspire to, young women also perceive a considerable degree of sex discrimination in more average
choices such a getting top professional jobs, skilled
labor jobs, and equal pay for equal work. Between
twenty-five and forty percent of the young women
believe that "a good deal" or "a great deal" of discrimination against women is practiced in these latter
settings. As might be expected, male seniors are less
likely than females to perceive "a great deal" of discrimination against women; nevertheless large
majorities of males acknowledge at least "some" discrimination in most of the above areas.

In conclusion, it seems not surprising that we
observe so much sex segregation in occupational plans,
since in addition to their different values discussed
before, young women also perceive external barriers to
their successful competition in many occupational,
educational and public service fields. Moreover, about
a quarter of young women agree with the statement that
their sex will prevent them "somewhat" from getting the
work they would like to have (Table 5-1.4). That the
latter figure is not higher, considering the substantial sex discrimination that is perceived in the labor
market, suggests that young women may have already adjusted their occupational plans to some extent. Planning largely for typically female occupations, they do
not expect sex to represent a hindrance.

Among both female and male respondents these
perceptions of sex discrimination in various areas are
highly interrelated. With one exception, all correlations are higher than $r = .24$; and the average intercorrelation is $r = .42$ for females and $r = .41$ for
males. This suggests that the various perceptions are
all part of one general underlying perception of sex
discrimination. Therefore one single index was formed
by averaging across the seven items; one item was allowed to be missing.

Trends

On the bright side, young women's (as well as young men's) perceptions of existing sex discrimination have changed by a small but systematic amount over the last five years. The seniors in 1980 perceived significantly less existing discrimination than the high school senior cohort of 1976. If we assume that such perceptions have some effect on the seniors' own plans, then this is another indication in support of the prediction that the next decade will see some young women moving away from the traditional female jobs and moving increasingly into male-dominated fields.

Self-reported competencies in various roles also show a slight but steady increase, which might indicate that young people enter the work role with somewhat more confidence than they used to.

Background Characteristics

Perceptions about sex discrimination vary little by background factors (see Table 5-2.4). Exceptions are the sex differences noted above and a slightly higher perception of sex discrimination voiced by the women of a more liberal political orientation.

Confidence in future competence as a worker cannot be explained much better by the factors at our disposition, except for academic abilities which leads to higher confidence, especially among females (although it should be noted that this is a positive correlation between self-ratings).

Sex Role Attitudes and Success Expectations

Overall, the predictors that were examined in the Long Form data also explain little about the perceptions of discrimination among young men and women (see Table 5-3.5). There is some hint in the data that non-traditional or egalitarian attitudes and preferences are related to perceived discrimination, but the coefficients are very weak.

PREFERENCES FOR VARIOUS WORK SETTINGS

Working in a large corporation, in a small business, on one's own, or with a small group of partners

are all rated as acceptable by a majority of the
seniors and are clearly preferred over work in the
military, in a police department, in a school, or in a
government agency, as shown in Table 5-1.5. Of course,
the widely accepted work settings are phrased in very
general terms and thus are unlikely to meet widespread
opposition. In other words, a large corporation, and
even more a small business, can encompass almost any
type of product or service, management style, and
general philosophy; and thus they are not so likely to
be opposed on any of those grounds. Nevertheless, it
is interesting that self-employment also finds
widespread acceptance. It would appear that work on
one's own would be rejected by many more, namely those
who look for a stable, predictable, and secure work environment.

In addition, self-employment displays one of the
largest sex differences, and the only one (other than
military service) in which men show distinctly stronger
preferences than women. Women, on the other hand, are
more inclined towards school and social service settings than men. These latter differences are, of
course, consistent with the traditional roles of the
sexes.

Trends

Over the last few years preferences for working
in large corporations have increased, while preferences
for social service, military, and police work have all
declined. Some of these trends are probably reflective
of trends towards traditional careers, as noted by
other scholars (e.g., Yankelovich, 1974).

An additional trend occurs only for young women
and is most readily interpreted as another indicator of
women slowly adopting traditionally male employment
preferences: young women have become significantly more
accepting of self-employment since 1976. As a result
the sex difference on self-employment preference has
declined substantially.

Background Characteristics

Abilities and educational aspirations are clearly related to preferences for certain work places (see
Table 5-2.5). Most importantly, able and college-bound
seniors are much more likely to rate a school as a
desirable work place than their less able and less ambitious classmates. They are also more inclined toward
a government agency and a small group of partners as an

ideal work place. These settings are, of course, typical for professional jobs. The effects of the three
indicators--self-rated abilities, grades, and college
plans--are overlapping, as shown in the results of the
multiple regression analyses. By the same token, the
effect of parental education on the desire to work with
a small group of partners is partly mediated by
respondents' abilities and college plans.

Religious commitment shows a slight positive
relationship with preferences for a school or a social
service agency as an ideal work setting. These are
settings that are designed to help and nurture others,
which in turn is an important mandate of many
religions.

Finally, young blacks differ from young whites
in their preferences for several of the work settings.
They are more likely to desire work in a large corporation, in a government agency, or in the military service, but less likely to desire work in a small business. Young black men are also more inclined towards
work in a school and a social service organization.
These race differences probably reflect the formation
of occupational plans according to the existing occupational and opportunity structure.

OCCUPATIONAL PLANS

Actual occupational plans were measured by the
question, "What kind of work do you think you will be
doing when you are 30 years old?" A forced choice format, the question provides 14 occupational categories
and a category of "full-time homemaker," each including
in addition a few concrete examples of occupations
within that category. In response to this question
young women and men name very different occupations
(Table 5-1.6) which parallel the existing occupational
segregation in the labor force. The job categories
that are most frequently chosen by young women are:
"professional without doctoral degree," "clerical," and
"professional with doctoral degree." "Service worker"
or "manager/administrator" jobs are chosen less frequently but still by approximately five percent of all
women. Among young men the most popular choices are:
"professional" and "craftsman." Less popular but still
chosen by at least five percent of the men are "operative or semiskilled worker," "owner of small business,"
and "manager/administrator." In sum, while the

popularity of professional and managerial choices is common to both sexes, remaining categories are not.

A convenient summary measure of the overall level of sex segregation is the index of segregation (Duncan and Duncan, 1955). Defined as one-half of the sum of the absolute differences between male and female percentages across occupational categories, the index can be interpreted as the percentage of men (or women) who would have to change occupations in order to achieve equal occupational distributions for the two sexes. This index of segregation indicates a considerable degree of sex segregation in occupational aspirations; namely, about a third to half of the young men would have to change their occupational categories in order to achieve occupational distributions equal to those of young women.

When the question on occupational aspirations was developed, the categories had been specified such that they could be used as a prestige measure on at least an ordinal level of scaling. To achieve this goal the Census prestige ratings of the occupations included in the major categories were examined for homogeneity (U.S. Bureau of the Census, 1971). Upon this exploration some categories were found too heterogeneous and were therefore redefined. Specifically, the category of "professionals" was divided into "professionals without doctoral degree" and "professionals with doctoral degree;" "sales personnel" was divided into "sales representatives" and "sales clerks in a retail store." In addition, a category "owner of small business" was added. (Of course, the category of homemaker/housewife has to be deleted, when the question is used as a single continuum measuring prestige of aspired occupation.)

When this prestige scale is used, the overall prestige level of occupations aspired by young women and young men are very similar. This similarity has also been noted by others reporting on aspirations (Gottfredson, 1978; Marini, 1978) and on the distribution of actual occupations in the adult labor force (Featherman and Hauser, 1976; McClendon, 1976). The similarity in average occupational prestige of males and females has usually been attributed to the fact that women are more likely to aspire to or hold middle-range jobs, while men are more likely to aspire to or hold jobs that are either high or low in prestige (Marini, 1978). In other words, women's jobs vary less in prestige than men's jobs. However, on the prestige scale utilized here young women actually show a slightly higher variance than young men (Standard deviation for males is 3.4, for females 4.1). This is most likely due to the gross categories utilized in the relevant question and the somewhat arbitrary decision to consider the intervals between the categories as equal.

It should be noted, of course, that average prestige level of seniors' aspired occupation is considerably higher than the average prestige level of the adult labor force, as can be shown when average prestige levels are calculated for any national sample of job holders, using roughly the same occupational categories. If we discount the unlikely explanation that the average prestige level of occupations will dramatically rise during the next few decades, then many of the job choices stated by the seniors represent overaspirations. (For a similar view see Marini, 1978.)

Trends

A slight increase in the prestige level of the planned occupations is noticeable over the five years from 1976 to 1980 (see Table 5-1.7). Interestingly, the pattern of the trends closely resembles the patterns observed for educational plans; i.e., young women display a steady increase in prestige over the five years, while young men show a quite substantial increase particularly since 1979. (We must note, however, that all of these shifts are quite subtle).

The index of sex segregation shows a decline over these five years which signals a decline of sex segregation in young people's occupational plans.

Background Characteristics

The prestige level of aspired occupations is very clearly related to self-rated academic abilities and educational plans among both sexes, as well as in somewhat weaker form to parental education and to urbanicity (Table 5-2.6). In addition, the effect of ability is stronger for male than female seniors. Although this sex difference is somewhat reduced when unstandardized coefficients are examined, a sex differential nevertheless remains. Moreover, the effect of college plans is stronger among females than males, when unstandardized coefficients are used.

Since these predictors are interrelated, their effects are overlapping, and therefore they need to be examined in a multivariate analysis. In fact, the effects of parental education and urbanicity seem largely mediated through self-reported academic abilities and, more importantly, through college plans (based on multiple regression results not reported here in detail). Regression analyses further indicate that the entire set of predictors accounts for approximately 37 percent of males',and 32 percent of the females' variance in occupational aspirations.

As noted before, the literature on status attainment confirms the effects of abilities and socioeconomic status (operationalized either as parental education or parental occupation) on occupational aspirations, and also suggests that socioeconomic status is largely mediated through abilities (Hout and Morgan, 1975; Marini and Greenberger, 1978b; Rosen and Aneshensel, 1978; Sewell and Hauser, 1975; Sewell and Shah, 1968). On the other hand, some of these studies have suggested that occupational aspirations of females cannot be explained as well as those of males by these predictors. Our data, as noted above, suggest less of a sex difference among high school seniors in the late 1970's.

Interrelationships Between Occupational
Plans and Other Relevant Variables

So far, we have discussed occupational plans, occupational values, perceptions of opportunities, the significance of the work role, and how these characteristics differ by sex. We have also examined how they relate to a set of demographic and personal characteristics, and whether they have been changing through the most recent five years. One of our underlying assumptions is that the sex segregation in specific occupational plans and preferences has to do with sex differences in more general occupational values, perceptions of opportunities, and overall orientation towards work. We will now examine these hypothesized relationships directly, using two different approaches. In this section we will examine respondents reporting different occupational plans and see what we can learn about how they differ in terms of their sex role attitudes, their preferences, and their college plans. These analyses are performed in bivariate form and do not assume linear relationships. The specific analytical technique is analysis of variance. In the next section, we will examine the factors that affect occupational plans simultaneously, by using multivariate analysis techniques, in particular a series of regression analyses. In addition to the prestige of the planned occupation we will also predict to a few major occupational categories that were recoded into dummy variables for that purpose.

In Table 5-4.3 the occupational aspirations are displayed by category, and mean values on ratings of occupational value indices, perceptions, and orientation towards the work role are shown for each category. In order to highlight the major features of a table of this kind, those values that are substantively important (i.e., they deviate more than one quarter of the overall standard deviation from the overall mean) and that are judged as statistically significant at the one percent-level (i.e., they are significantly different from the remainder[2]) were marked with an asterisk. In addition, we report Eta values to indicate overall strength of relationship, with the full set of occupational categories, and r values to indicate linear relationship with status of aspired occupation.

Since occupational categories are sex-segregated and thus some categories contain very few respondents, we will use only the Monitoring the Future data which contain large enough numbers of respondents. This data set, however, puts more severe restrictions on the variables that may be analyzed. We are able to include in these analyses all occupational value indices; a few single sex role variables referring to the importance of parenting (but not the entire index) and effect of a wife's work (but not the full sex role index); two of the six division-of-labor indices, referring to child care and housework when both spouses are working; and one variable probing anticipated problems in the job search due to one's sex. Since the sex role items show very little variation across occupational categories, they are not included in Table 5-4.3.

As a perusal of the table reveals, only a few significant and important deviations from the overall mean are observed. A specific instance of this general lack of differentiation is presented by the following observation. Young women aspiring to jobs which would be considered as traditionally female, such as clerical, service worker, sales clerk, and professional without a doctoral degree, are in general not any more likely than the average young woman to attribute high importance to altruistic and interpersonal occupational values. There is a tendency among the women who aspire

_____

[2]Since these tests amount to repeated tests on the same data, we adopted the more stringent significance level of .01. The effective N used for the significance calculations was estimated at 2/3 of the actual N in order to take account of a design effect of about 1.5 (which we estimated to be appropriate for these particular analyses carried out for males and females separately using Monitoring the Future data).

157

to such traditionally male jobs as operative, craftsman, and laborer to be less concerned about altruistic and interpersonal values than the average female; however, none of the deviations attains statistical significance due to the small numbers of young women with these aspirations, and caution in interpreting these observations is indicated.

A few deviations from the overall means are noteworthy. Women planning for professional jobs—particularly for professional jobs requiring a doctoral degree—are more concerned about their participation in decision-making and the challenge of having hard problems to solve than the average young woman, while women heading for service and sales jobs—and less clearly for laborer and operative jobs—are less concerned about these aspects of their preferred work. This pattern is correlated with the prestige ordering of the occupational aspirations, as reflected in the almost linear nature of the relationship (r=.19; Eta=.23).

Interestingly, women planning to be clericals are more concerned with status and job stability than the average young woman; women planning to be farmers are less concerned with status and money. These latter women are also less concerned with interpersonal contacts on the job.

Some of these patterns are replicated for occupational aspirations among young men. For example, those young men who aspire to be clericals are more concerned about status, income and job stability than the average young man; those who aspire to become farmers are less concerned with these values; moreover, the latter are less concerned with interpersonal aspects of the job. Also, males' preferences for responsibility in decision-making and problem-solving are related to the prestige of their aspired occupations (r=.16; Eta=.21).

The biggest difference between the sexes lies in service, protective service, and sales jobs, which are related to increased importance attributed to interpersonal values among young men, while little or no such relationship is found among women.

With respect to the perception that one's sex might present a handicap in the job search, the young women who plan on sex-atypical careers such as craftsman, policeman, manager, or professional with a doctoral degree do indeed anticipate more problems than the average woman. However, young men who head for more typically female occupations do not anticipate any problems due to their sex.

Finally, female respondents' preferences for division of labor vary somewhat by their occupational plans: girls heading for sales clerk and military jobs are more traditional than the mean; girls heading for professional jobs that require a doctorate are less traditional; but no such differentiation is apparent among males.

In sum, the data do not reveal strong relationships between occupational plans, and occupational values and perceptions. There are at least two explanations for this finding. First, it is possible that the occupational categories used here are too broad--including too heterogeneous a group of occupations--to result in very sharp differentiations in values and perceptions between the young people who aspire to them. Secondly, it is conceivable that the results are real and not just an artifact of the type of occupational categorization used here. If this latter alternative were true, it would imply that young people who plan on similar occupations share few common values.

The relationships with background factors that were examined in Table 5-4.3 do not reveal any major effects aside from the linearly increasing ability and college plans reported by seniors who aspire to occupations of increasing prestige.

Sex Role Attitudes and Occupational Plans

In this section we will examine a wider range of predictors and plans and explore their joint effects on occupational plans. For that purpose we switch to the Long Form data. Our analytical approach is similar to the one used previously. That is, in a first regression analysis we will examine the impact of the background characteristics that showed a substantial effect in the Monitoring the Future analyses reported above. In a next regression analysis we will in addition include sex role attitudes to test their independent effect on occupational plans. In the next set of regressions we include background characteristics, sex role attitudes, and either preferences for the division of labor, educational plans, occupational values, or job centrality and perceptions of opportunities. Our major criterion is the prestige of the aspired occupation, since many of the relationships we examined in the previous section appear more or less linear.[3]

The bivariate relationships shown in Table 5-3.6 demonstrate a close replication of the findings from the Monitoring the Future analyses. Strong effects are exerted by academic abilities. Somewhat weaker but still substantial are the effects of parental education, a good part of which is mediated through abilities. And self-reported abilities have a slightly stronger impact on young men's than on young women's expected occupational prestige.

The bivariate relationships of occupational values on occupational prestige from the Long Form data can also be checked against the Monitoring the Future data, which were presented in the previous section. As we noted there, only the desired level of responsibility on the job showed a substantial linear relationship with occupational prestige. Therefore, we have little confidence in the several substantial bivariate correlations that we observe in the Long Form data. We are further reminded that the occupational value ratings show a particularly high response effect due to the length of the questionnaire (Chapter 2 and Appendix A). The relationships of the other occupational variables in the analysis cannot be compared with Monitoring the Future findings since these variables were not included in the same Monitoring the Future questionnaire form as the question on expected job at 30. Among them, job centrality and personal competence as worker show positive relationships to occupational prestige.

Among the sex role-related attitudes and preferences, traditional sex role attitudes (as

---

[3]In order not to entirely exclude the attention to specific occupational categories and the possibilities that they could show different patterns than general prestige effects, we also investigated a set of dummy variables for the specific occupational categories of clerical (for females only), craftsman (for males only), professionals with a doctorate, and all professionals. These categories represent the largest categories and the more typical ones for the two sexes. Unfortunately, we were not able to perform similar analyses for the sex-atypical categories because of small number of respondents in those categories. Our findings for these dummy variable regressions showed nothing more than a diluted version of the findings for occupational prestige. Accordingly, we have not included the data here.

reflected in the index) are related negatively, and preference for egalitarian division of home duties are related positively, to the prestige of the expected occupation (using the Long Form data). The strength of these relationships is rather similar for the two sexes. This similarity suggests that the effects are caused by a more general ideological orientation or an even more generalized difference in orientation between the more able and the less able seniors (hence, the omnipresent relationship to abilities), rather than by the conscious attempts on the part of young women to reconcile potentially conflicting roles.

This interpretation receives further support from the finding that the effects of the traditional sex role attitudes and the preferences for the division of labor are substantially reduced when they are included in a multiple regression analysis along with the background factors (Table 5-3.6). In other words, traditional sex role attitudes and preferences for the division of labor in the family do not explain much beyond what is already explained by abilities. When college plans are included in the regression along with background characteristics and sex role attitudes, it becomes clear that effects of abilities largely overlap with effect of educational plans.

Job centrality retains a substantial independent effect on occupational prestige among young men after all the other variables have been included into the analysis, although its effect is considerably reduced. As interesting as this effect among young men may be, the lack of such a relationship among young women is even more interesting, since it suggests that among young women the centrality of the job has little to do with the prestige of the job they aspire to beyond simple effects of ability and educational plans.

SUMMARY

Educational plans of male and female high school seniors are not very different; college is the most popular choice for both. While females are slightly less likely to plan on graduate school or vocational/technical training, they are slightly more likely to plan on entering a 2-year college program.

Educational plans are affected by a number of well-known factors, such as abilities and parental education. While the effect of abilities is stronger

161

on the plans of males, sex role attitudes and preferences for the division of labor in the family provide as little additional explanation for females' as for males' educational plans. In other words, sex role attitudes have little bearing on how women plan their education, and therefore they do not provide the explanatory power that we had expected.

When we turn to occupational plans, it appears that women take work as seriously as men. It is only in comparison to family roles that the difference between the sexes becomes apparent: Young women attribute more importance to family and children than do young men, and they are more likely to expect to modify the work role for the sake of their family roles.

The difference between the sexes is further highlighted by an examination of the kinds of work that women and men aspire to. For example, women attribute more importance to altruistic and people-oriented aspects of a job and to its stimulating and intrinsically rewarding potential, but less to its economic aspects and other external rewards such as the amount of free time off the job. Little change since 1976 and little systematic decline of sex differences is noticeable.

Moreover, young women judge various work settings very differently than young men do. Compared with the males, the females find work in a social service organization and in a school or university much more desirable, self-employment much less desirable. While these preferences for work settings have undergone several cohort changes since 1976, only self-employment shows a decline of sex differences.

In terms of achieving their occupational goals, young women expect their sex to present only a minor hindrance and they judge themselves only very slightly less competent as future workers than young men. Yet they perceive considerable sex discrimination existing in the labor market. Why this apparent contradiction? We believe some of it may be attributable to women's previous adjustments of their occupational plans which led to the overwhelming sex differences observed in our data. The many young women who expect to occupy traditional female occupations are unlikely to view their sex as hindrance in pursuing their chosen occupation, but may well agree that women who pursue less traditional careers may face discrimination.

Finally, when specific occupational categories are examined, young women also show very different plans from young men. As indicated by the index of segrega-

tion, about 50 percent of the males (or females) in
1976 would have had to change plans in order for the
two distributions to become identical. The level of
sex segregation in occupational plans, as measured by
the index, has declined during the last five years, so
that for the class of 1980 only about 36 percent of
males (or females) would need to change plans in order
for the distributions to be identical. The clearest
convergence seems to have occurred in the categories of
clerical and protective service (see also Herzog,
1982). At the same time, no sex differences appear for
mean prestige of the planned occupations. This apparent contradiction is, of course, consistent with
figures on the labor force, reviewed earlier, which indicate a high sex-segregation but similar average prestige for both sexes.

One other trend of considerable importance is the
steadily decreasing proportion of young women who expect to be full-time homemakers at age 30. Among those
expecting to complete college, the proportion has
remained consistently low (five percent in 1976, and
four percent in 1980); but among the non-college bound,
the drop has been substantial (from 22 percent in 1976
to 13 percent in 1979, and down to 9 percent for the
class of 1981). Since virtually no males expect to be
full-time homemakers at age 30, the declining numbers
of females expecting to do so represents another kind
of convergence--another way in which occupational
aspirations are less sex segregated.

In light of the marked sex-segregation of actual
occupational categories plus the sex differences in occupational values, we examined not only predictors of
overall prestige but expended quite some effort to explore potential predictors of single occupational
categories (by analyses of variance for all categories
and by multiple regression analyses predicting to a
single category). Little was learned from those ex-
plorations. The few relationships which emerged seemed
to capture nothing more than prestige. The major
predictors of occupational prestige--already well-known
from the literature--are parental education, abilities,
and college plans. The sex role attitude variables,
which are at the core of this project, show rather
little independent effect on prestige of the aspired
occupation. Neither do preferences for the division of
labor nor occupational values and perceptions show any
significant effects. Thus, sex role attitudes have
little bearing on the status and prestige that a woman
aspires to in her work. Sex role attitudes are only
critical in the decision to work at all and in how
central that work should be.

Table 5-1.1

Educational Plans: Distributions and Trends

| | | 1980 Percentage Distributions | | | | 1976-1980 Trends and Sex Differences | | | | | | | |
| | | | | | | Means | | | | | Zero-order correlation coefficients[1] | |
How likely is it that you will do each of the following things after high school?		Definitely won't (1)	Probably won't (2)	Probably will (3)	Definitely will (4)	1976	1977	1978	1979	1980	Trend	Sex
Attend a technical or vocational school	M:	41.6	29.7	19.3	9.4	2.04	2.03	2.06	2.03	1.97	-.02	-.08
	F:	46.4	28.8	15.5	9.3	1.87	1.87	1.88	1.82	1.88	.00	
Graduate from a two-year college program	M:	39.0	32.6	18.1	10.3	1.92	1.94	1.95	1.97	2.00	.01	.05
	F:	37.7	25.6	21.8	14.8	2.09	2.04	2.03	2.06	2.14	.02	
Graduate from college (four-year program)	M:	23.4	18.6	22.5	35.5	2.48	2.54	2.52	2.52	2.70	.05	-.02
	F:	27.3	18.0	22.5	32.2	2.37	2.42	2.51	2.60	2.60	.07	
Attend graduate or professional school after college	M:	30.7	32.9	25.4	11.0	1.99	2.08	2.01	2.02	2.17	.04	-.04
	F:	35.8	33.0	21.4	9.8	1.90	1.95	1.96	2.03	2.05	.05	

[1]For an explanation of these coefficients, see Chapter 2.

Table 5-1.2

The Role of Paid Work: Distributions and Trends

In the following list you will find some statements about leisure time and work. Please show whether you agree or disagree with each statement

| | | 1980 Percentage Distributions | | | | | Means 1976-1980 Trends and Sex Differences | | | | | Zero-order Correlation Coefficients[2] | |
		Dis-agree (1)	Mostly Dis-agree (2)	Neither (3)	Mostly agree (4)	Agree (5)	1976	1977	1978	1979	1980	Trend	Sex
I like the kind of work you can forget about after the work day is over	M:	16.3	14.1	12.4	22.3	35.0	3.29	3.47	3.47	3.50	3.46	.03	.02
	F:	13.6	13.0	13.3	29.7	30.4	3.45	3.49	3.43	3.56	3.50	.02	
To me, work is nothing more than making a living	M:	37.7	27.5	9.2	12.7	12.9	2.34	2.41	2.33	2.36	2.36	.00	-.10
	F:	47.1	27.5	7.6	10.0	7.9	2.00	2.15	2.08	2.09	2.04	.00	
I expect my work to be a very central part of my life	M:	6.0	6.9	11.6	35.0	40.5	4.00	4.03	3.98	4.00	3.97	-.01	-.04
	F:	4.7	8.5	13.0	37.7	36.1	3.91	3.88	3.92	3.86	3.92	.00	
I want to do my best in my job even if this sometimes means working overtime	M:	2.2	2.2	5.7	30.3	59.6	4.40	4.44	4.46	4.44	4.43	.01	.03
	F:	1.0	1.3	3.4	32.9	61.6	4.45	4.47	4.51	4.47	4.53	.03	
Centrality of Work[1] Index (above 4 items)	M:						3.70	3.65	3.66	3.65	3.65	-.02	.03
	F:						3.73	3.68	3.73	3.67	3.73	.00	

Table 5-1.2 (cont.)

The Role of Paid Work: Distributions and Trends

	1980 Percentage Distributions		1976-1980 Trends and Sex Differences							
	Would want to work (1)	Would not want to work (2)	Means					Zero-order Correlation Coefficients	
			1976	1977	1978	1979	1980	Trend	Sex
If you were to get enough money to live as comfortably as you'd like for the rest of your life, would you want to work?									
M:	79.7	20.3	1.20	1.20	1.18	1.20	1.20	.00	-.02
F:	82.7	17.3	1.19	1.18	1.19	1.16	1.17	-.02	-.02

	1980 Percentage Distributions			1976-1980 Trends and Sex Differences						
	I've thought about it a lot (3)	I've thought about it a little (2)	I haven't thought about it at all (1)	Means					Zero-order Correlation Coefficients	
				1976	1977	1978	1979	1980	Trend	Sex
Have you thought at all about whether you'd like to have children or how many you'd like to have										
M:	26.7	56.3	17.0	2.14	2.08	2.14	2.10	2.10	-.01	-.02
F:	50.9	45.0	4.1	2.50	2.53	2.52	2.50	2.47	-.02	.31

Table 5-1.2 (cont.)

The Role of Paid Work: Distributions and Trends

		1980 Percentage Distributions				1976-1980 Trends and Sex Differences						
		Not impor- tant (1)	Somewhat impor- tant (2)	Quite impor- tant (3)	Extremely important (4)	Means					Zero-order Correlation Coefficients[2]	
						1976	1977	1978	1979	1980	Trend	Sex
How important is each of the following to you in your life?												
Having a good marriage and family life	M:	4.3	9.2	16.9	69.7	3.44	3.48	3.50	3.57	3.52	.03	
	F:	2.7	3.9	11.6	81.7	3.67	3.65	3.70	3.71	3.72	.03	.12
Being successful in my line of work	M:	2.2	9.8	32.8	55.1	3.37	3.39	3.46	3.48	3.41	.04	
	F:	0.5	10.6	33.4	55.4	3.39	3.39	3.42	3.45	3.44	.03	.00
Being able to find steady work	M:	1.8	4.5	25.8	67.8	3.57	3.57	3.58	3.61	3.60	.02	
	F:	0.6	6.7	30.9	61.8	3.51	3.48	3.53	3.53	3.54	.03	-.05

[1]Two items were reversed for inclusion in the index.

[2]For an explanation of these coefficients, see Chapter 2.

167

Table 5-1.3

Occupational Values: Distributions and Trends

Different people may look for different things in their work. Below is a list of some of these things. Please read each one, then indicate how important this thing is for you.

		1980 Percentage Distributions				Means					Zero-order Correlation Coefficients[1]	
		Not important (1)	A little important (2)	Pretty important (3)	Very important (4)	1976	1977	1978	1979	1980	Trend	Sex
A job that has high status and prestige	M:	8.5	25.8	40.0	25.7	2.69	2.77	2.77	2.81	2.83	.05	
	F:	10.0	29.4	36.7	23.9	2.55	2.65	2.67	2.71	2.75	.06	-.06
A job that provides you with a good chance to earn a good deal of money	M:	1.4	7.0	33.8	57.9	3.40	3.43	3.45	3.49	3.48	.04	
	F:	1.6	9.8	38.8	49.8	3.21	3.25	3.28	3.33	3.37	.07	-.11
A job where the chances for advancement and promotion are good	M:	1.1	6.0	27.8	65.1	3.47	3.56	3.57	3.55	3.57	.04	
	F:	0.8	7.8	30.0	61.3	3.40	3.45	3.47	3.55	3.52	.06	-.05
A job that most people look up to and respect	M:	6.0	20.7	37.5	35.8	2.93	2.99	3.00	2.98	3.03	.03	
	F:	4.7	18.5	38.2	38.6	3.05	3.02	3.10	3.07	3.11	.03	.04
Status & Money Index (above 4 items)	M:					3.12	3.19	3.19	3.21	3.23	.06	
	F:					3.05	3.10	3.13	3.16	3.19	.08	-.05
A job that offers a reasonably predictable, secure future	M:	1.9	5.6	29.0	63.5	3.53	3.56	3.58	3.56	3.54	.00	
	F:	0.7	5.1	28.7	65.4	3.53	3.54	3.54	3.56	3.59	.03	.00
A job which allows you to establish roots in a community and not to have to move from place to place	M:	10.0	16.5	33.6	40.0	3.02	3.01	3.07	3.06	3.04	.01	
	F:	11.0	19.4	31.0	38.5	3.03	3.03	2.97	2.93	2.97	-.03	-.03
Stability & Security Index (above 2 items)	M:					3.27	3.29	3.32	3.31	3.29	.01	
	F:					3.28	3.29	3.25	3.24	3.28	-.01	-.02

Table 5-1.3 (cont.)

Occupational Values: Distributions and Trends

| | | 1980 Percentage Distributions | | | | 1976-1980 Trends and Sex Differences | | | | | | |
		Not impor- tant (1)	A little important (2)	Pretty impor- tant (3)	Very impor- tant (4)	Means 1976	1977	1978	1979	1980	Zero-order Correlation Coefficients[1] Trend	Sex
A job where you get a chance to participate in decision making	M:	5.1	20.7	43.8	30.4	2.92	2.92	2.99	3.01	3.00	.04	.04
	F:	5.0	24.0	42.9	28.1	2.86	2.86	2.88	2.95	2.94	.04	-.04
A job where most problems are quite difficult and challenging	M:	15.0	34.0	42.9	14.2	2.45	2.44	2.51	2.49	2.50	.02	.04
	F:	16.9	36.3	35.3	11.5	2.31	2.34	2.37	2.40	2.42	.04	-.06
Responsibility Index (above 2 items)	M:					2.68	2.68	2.75	2.75	2.75	.04	.05
	F:					2.58	2.60	2.63	2.67	2.68	.05	-.06
A job where you have more than two weeks vacation	M:	17.4	31.2	27.2	24.2	2.51	2.60	2.49	2.56	2.58	.01	.02
	F:	23.8	40.0	24.8	11.3	2.18	2.23	2.19	2.24	2.24	.02	-.17
A job which leaves a lot of time for other things in your life	M:	1.5	12.1	42.3	44.1	3.22	3.29	3.29	3.29	3.29	.03	.01
	F:	3.2	19.6	42.0	35.1	3.05	3.09	3.09	3.08	3.09	.01	-.12
A job with an easy pace that lets you work slowly	M:	28.3	40.2	20.1	11.3	2.13	2.18	2.18	2.18	2.15	.00	-.01
	F:	27.3	38.0	27.6	7.0	2.12	2.17	2.14	2.08	2.14	-.01	-.02
A job which leaves you mostly free of supervision by others	M:	7.7	22.1	40.6	29.6	2.82	2.95	2.94	2.92	2.92	.02	.04
	F:	9.8	28.3	39.0	22.9	2.63	2.70	2.75	2.73	2.75	.04	-.11
Easy Pace Index (above 4 items)	M:					2.67	2.76	2.72	2.74	2.73	.02	.02
	F:					2.49	2.55	2.54	2.53	2.55	.02	-.15

Table 5-1.3 (cont.)

Occupational Values: Distributions and Trends

| | | 1980 Percentage Distributions | | | | 1976-1980 Trends and Sex Differences | | | | | | | |
| | | Not impor- tant (1) | A little important (2) | Pretty impor- tant (3) | Very impor- tant (4) | Means | | | | | Zero-order Correlation Coefficients¹ | |
						1976	1977	1978	1979	1980	Trend	Sex
A job where you have the chance to be creative	M:	6.2	25.3	35.2	33.3	2.93	2.95	2.99	3.00	2.96	.01	
	F:	5.3	21.5	35.2	38.0	3.04	3.08	3.11	3.06	3.06	.00	.06
A job which is interesting to do	M:	0.7	1.3	13.0	84.9	3.80	3.86	3.85	3.86	3.82	.01	
	F:	0.2	1.2	8.0	90.6	3.91	3.90	3.90	3.89	3.89	-.02	.08
A job where you do not have to pretend to be a type of person that you are not	M:	5.7	6.3	23.4	64.7	3.46	3.43	3.45	3.45	3.47	.01	
	F:	3.5	2.6	12.5	81.4	3.73	3.74	3.75	3.71	3.72	-.01	.17
A job where you can learn new things. Learn new skills	M:	1.4	12.6	42.0	44.0	3.24	3.25	3.27	3.30	3.29	.03	
	F:	0.9	10.1	36.5	52.6	3.40	3.41	3.39	3.41	3.41	.00	.09
A job where you can see the results of what you do	M:	0.9	9.2	35.9	53.9	3.44	3.43	3.50	3.47	3.43	.01	
	F:	0.6	5.5	30.4	63.5	3.52	3.56	3.56	3.55	3.57	.02	.08
A job which uses your skills and abilities & lets you do the things you do best	M:	0.7	3.5	27.5	68.3	3.59	3.64	3.63	3.66	3.63	.02	
	F:	0.2	2.8	20.6	76.4	3.73	3.76	3.71	3.70	3.73	-.02	.08
A job where the skills you learn will not go out of date	M:	4.3	11.6	32.6	51.5	3.39	3.39	3.35	3.34	3.31	-.03	
	F:	4.1	11.7	30.3	54.0	3.32	3.36	3.27	3.32	3.34	.00	-.02
Stimulation and Mastery Index (above 7 items)	M:					3.41	3.42	3.43	3.44	3.42	.01	
	F:					3.52	3.54	3.53	3.52	3.53	.00	.13

Table 5-1.3 (cont.)

Occupational Values: Distributions and Trends

		1980 Percentage Distributions				1976-1980 Trends and Sex Differences						Zero-order Correlation Coefficients[1]	
		Not impor- tant (1)	A little important (2)	Pretty impor- tant (3)	Very impor- tant (4)	Means						Trend	Sex
						1976	1977	1978	1979	1980			
A job that gives you an opportunity to be directly helpful to others	M:	4.4	19.0	43.2	33.4	3.13	3.09	3.10	3.11	3.06		-.02	.25
	F:	0.7	8.5	30.4	60.4	3.52	3.52	3.51	3.48	3.51		-.01	
A job that is worthwhile to society	M:	5.0	18.5	40.3	36.2	3.10	3.15	3.10	3.12	3.08		-.01	.15
	F:	1.5	12.4	35.6	50.5	3.35	3.37	3.34	3.35	3.35		.00	
Altruism Index (above 2 items)	M:					3.12	3.12	3.10	3.11	3.07		-.02	.24
	F:					3.44	3.44	3.43	3.41	3.43		-.01	
A job that gives you a chance to make friends	M:	2.7	10.9	39.7	46.6	3.26	3.33	3.30	3.34	3.30		.02	.13
	F:	1.6	8.6	30.7	59.1	3.50	3.51	3.50	3.51	3.47		-.01	
A job that permits contact with a lot of people	M:	11.1	27.3	36.0	25.7	2.76	2.76	2.79	2.79	2.76		-.01	.19
	F:	5.7	18.0	35.8	40.4	3.15	3.13	3.12	3.14	3.11		-.01	
Contact with Others Index (above 2 items)	M:					3.01	3.05	3.04	3.07	3.03		.01	.19
	F:					3.33	3.32	3.31	3.32	3.29		-.01	

[1]For an explanation of these coefficients, see Chapter 2.

Table 5-1.4

Perceptions About Success Potentials: Distributions and Trends

		1980 Percentage Distributions						1976-1980 Trends and Sex Differences						
		Poor (1)	Not so Good (2)	Fairly Good (3)	Good (4)	Very Good (5)	Don't know	Means					Zero-order correlation coefficients[1]	
								1976	1977	1978	1979	1980	Trend	Sex
These next questions ask you to guess how well you might do in different situations. How good do you think you would be . . .														
as a husband or a wife?	M:	1.1	1.7	9.7	40.4	42.6	4.5	4.14	4.16	4.26	4.18	4.28	.04	
	F:	1.0	1.7	7.3	33.6	52.9	3.5	4.29	4.35	4.33	4.37	4.41	.05	.09
As a parent?	M:	0.9	1.8	9.6	38.1	43.4	6.1	4.13	4.14	4.22	4.16	4.29	.06	
	F:	1.4	2.1	8.4	34.4	49.5	4.3	4.15	4.21	4.21	4.24	4.34	.06	.02
As a worker on a job?	M:	0.3	0.2	3.9	27.5	66.5	1.5	4.53	4.49	4.58	4.56	4.62	.06	
	F:	0.3	0.3	5.5	33.2	59.2	1.7	4.43	4.44	4.46	4.51	4.53	.05	-.06

Table 5-1.4 (cont.)

Perceptions About Success Potentials: Distributions and Trends

| | | 1980 Percentage Distributions | | | | | 1976-1980 Trends and Sex Differences | | | | | | |
		Poorly (1)	Not so well (2)	Fairly well (3)	Well (4)	Very well (5)	Means 1976	1977	1978	1979	1980	Zero-order correlation coefficients Trend	Sex
How well do you think your experiences and training (at home, school, work, etc.) have prepared you to be a good. . .													
Husband or wife?	M:	2.5	6.4	26.7	42.1	22.4	3.68	3.65	3.68	3.74	3.76	.03	
	F:	1.6	4.9	18.3	40.6	34.5	4.03	4.00	3.97	4.02	4.02	.00	.16
Parent?	M:	3.2	7.9	26.3	38.5	24.2	3.65	3.67	3.67	3.73	3.73	.03	
	F:	1.5	5.5	20.5	35.9	36.5	3.98	3.96	3.96	3.95	4.00	.01	.14
Worker on a job?	M:	0.9	2.9	13.0	40.0	43.2	4.09	4.15	4.19	4.22	4.22	.05	
	F:	0.6	3.0	14.8	39.5	42.2	4.13	4.13	4.13	4.19	4.20	.03	-.01

Table 5-1.4 (cont.)

Perceptions About Success Potentials: Distributions and Trends

		1980 Percentage Distributions										1976-1980 Trends and Sex Differences						
		A (9)	A- (8)	B+ (7)	B (6)	B- (5)	C+ (4)	C (3)	C- (2)	D (1)		Means					Zero-order correlation coefficients[1]	
												1976	1977	1978	1979	1980	Trend	Sex
Which of the following best describes your average grade so far in high school?	M:	7.0	7.6	14.9	21.8	16.1	14.7	10.4	5.2	2.3		5.46	5.42	5.37	5.53	5.48	.01	
	F:	10.4	11.9	19.6	23.6	12.6	11.0	6.9	3.0	0.8		6.21	6.09	6.02	6.02	6.13	-.02	.17

Table 5-1.4 (cont.)

Perceptions About Success Potentials: Distributions and Trends

| | 1980 Percentage Distributions | | | | | | | 1976-1980 Trends and Sex Differences | | | | | | |
| | Far below average (1) | Below average (2) | Slightly below average (3) | Average (4) | Slightly above average (5) | Above average (6) | Far above average (7) | Means | | | | | Zero-order correlation coefficients | |
								1976	1977	1978	1979	1980	Trend	Sex
Compared with others your age throughout the country, how do you rate yourself on school ability? M:	0.8	2.3	4.9	35.6	23.3	26.3	6.8	4.84	4.84	4.84	4.88	4.87	.01	
F:	0.3	1.5	4.3	37.8	24.3	26.7	5.0	4.85	4.83	4.83	4.81	4.89	.01	.00
How intelligent do you think you are compared with others your age? M:	0.5	1.1	4.5	31.5	24.5	28.6	9.3	4.95	4.96	4.97	5.01	5.01	.02	
F:	0.2	0.9	4.1	37.9	24.6	27.0	5.5	4.83	4.83	4.82	4.77	4.84	.00	-.08

Table 5-1.4 (cont.)

Perceptions About Success Potentials: Distributions and Trends

| | | 1980 Percentage Distributions | | | | | | 1976-1980 Trends and Sex Differences | | | | | | |
| | | Not at all (1) | Very little (2) | Some (3) | A good deal (4) | A great deal (5) | Don't know | Means | | | | | Zero-order correlation coefficients[1] | |
								1976	1977	1978	1979	1980	Trend	Sex
These questions are about whether you think women are discriminated against in each of the following areas. To what extent are women discriminated against...														
In getting a college education?	M:	54.4	27.3	7.3	2.1	1.3	7.6	1.74	1.65	1.66	1.66	1.58	-.05	.11
	F:	39.4	36.8	13.9	2.5	1.7	5.7	1.90	1.84	1.84	1.89	1.84	-.01	
In gaining positions of leadership over men and women?	M:	9.5	17.2	37.3	23.3	7.6	5.1	3.17	3.12	3.06	3.01	3.03	-.05	.21
	F:	3.9	9.7	34.6	29.1	16.7	5.9	3.60	3.52	3.49	2.56	3.48	-.03	
In obtaining executive positions in business?	M:	10.4	17.4	31.7	24.8	7.8	7.7	3.25	3.16	3.13	3.04	3.02	-.07	.13
	F:	5.8	14.6	31.8	26.0	14.9	6.9	3.53	3.49	3.37	3.44	3.32	-.06	
In obtaining top jobs in the professions?	M:	12.6	22.8	29.0	20.8	7.2	7.5	3.04	2.93	2.93	2.95	2.86	-.04	.14
	F:	7.8	19.4	29.1	24.0	14.3	5.3	3.35	3.28	3.24	3.32	3.19	-.03	
In getting skilled labor jobs?	M:	11.8	22.3	32.0	18.2	7.2	8.6	3.02	2.97	3.00	2.89	2.85	-.05	.09
	F:	8.9	17.6	31.9	21.0	9.9	10.6	3.23	3.15	3.17	3.14	3.06	-.04	
In getting elected to political office?	M:	7.8	15.5	26.0	24.1	20.6	6.0	3.45	3.28	3.30	3.25	3.36	-.02	.24
	F:	2.6	8.4	18.6	26.6	37.6	6.1	3.98	3.85	3.87	3.87	3.94	-.01	
In getting equal pay for equal work?	M:	24.2	24.6	23.4	13.3	9.2	5.3	2.74	2.75	2.75	2.68	2.56	-.05	.23
	F:	11.2	19.1	25.5	19.5	19.5	5.3	3.33	3.40	3.26	3.37	3.18	-.04	

Table 5-1.4 (cont.)

Perceptions About Success Potentials: Distributions and Trends

	1980 Percentage Distributions				1976-1980 Trends and Sex Differences							
	Not at all (1)	Somewhat (2)	A lot (3)	Don't know	Means					Zero-order correlation coefficients[1]	
					1976	1977	1978	1979	1980	Trend	Sex
To what extent do you think the things listed below will prevent you from getting the kind of work you would like to have?											
Your sex M:	87.9	7.6	2.8	1.7	1.17	1.13	1.15	1.13	1.14	-.02	
F:	66.4	26.5	4.5	2.7	1.34	1.40	1.33	1.33	1.36	-.01	.20

[1]For an explanation of these coefficients, see Chapter 2.

Table 5-1.5

Preferred Work Settings: Distributions and Trends

Apart from the particular kind of work you want to do, how would you rate each of the following settings as a place to work?

| | | 1980 Percentage Distributions | | | | 1976-1980 Trends and Sex Differences | | | | | | |
| | | Not at all acceptable (1) | Somewhat acceptable (2) | Acceptable (3) | Desirable (4) | Means | | | | | Zero-order correlation coefficients[1] | |
						1976	1977	1978	1979	1980	Trend	Sex
Working in a large corporation	M:	5.0	26.1	47.8	21.1	2.66	2.70	2.78	2.81	2.85	.08	
	F:	6.5	26.7	47.7	19.0	2.61	2.68	2.69	2.80	2.79	.08	-.03
Working in a small business	M:	4.6	23.2	51.9	20.3	2.82	2.84	2.88	2.86	2.88	.03	
	F:	3.9	21.7	51.5	22.8	2.93	2.91	2.89	2.93	2.93	.00	.04
Working in a government agency	M:	22.0	32.4	32.0	13.6	2.47	2.43	2.32	2.37	2.37	-.03	
	F:	19.0	33.4	31.6	16.0	2.49	2.55	2.44	2.48	2.45	-.02	.05
Working in the military service	M:	44.8	30.5	16.1	8.5	2.10	1.96	1.94	1.87	1.88	-.07	
	F:	54.0	26.7	14.4	4.8	1.97	1.87	1.84	1.76	1.70	-.10	-.06
Working in a school or university	M:	28.8	35.2	28.4	7.6	2.22	2.12	2.04	2.13	2.15	-.02	
	F:	17.8	31.0	35.6	15.6	2.64	2.55	2.46	2.53	2.49	-.04	.20
Working in a police department or police agency	M:	33.3	34.1	22.6	9.8	2.25	2.15	2.14	2.11	2.09	-.05	
	F:	29.7	34.3	26.1	9.9	2.38	2.26	2.30	2.25	2.16	-.06	.06
Working in a social service organization	M:	31.0	41.8	21.6	5.6	2.17	2.04	2.01	1.98	2.02	-.06	
	F:	8.4	30.0	37.9	23.6	2.93	2.87	2.81	2.80	2.77	-.06	.40
Working with a small group of partners	M:	8.7	26.6	44.6	20.2	2.74	2.69	2.74	2.74	2.76	.01	
	F:	9.2	29.7	39.9	21.3	2.62	2.63	2.65	2.65	2.73	.04	-.04
Working on your own (self-employed)	M:	5.0	13.3	30.2	51.5	3.24	3.25	3.26	3.27	3.28	.02	
	F:	11.5	19.7	28.5	40.2	2.77	2.77	2.83	2.95	2.97	.08	-.20

[1]For an explanation of these coefficients, see Chapter 2.

178

Occupational Aspirations: Distributions and Trends

		1976-1980 Trends and Sex Differences				
		Percentage				
		1976	1977	1978	1979	1980
What kind of work do you think you will be doing when you are 30 years old? Mark the one that comes closest to what you expect to be doing.						
(1) Laborer (car washer, sanitary worker, farm laborer)	M:	0.7	0.6	0.6	0.8	0.7
	F:	0.0	0.0	0.3	0.1	0.1
(2) Service worker (cook, waiter, barber, janitor, gas station attendant, practical nurse, beautician)	M:	0.6	1.0	0.8	0.6	0.6
	F:	4.5	4.8	4.6	5.0	4.8
(3) Operative or semi-skilled worker (garage worker, taxi-cab, bus or truck driver, assembly line worker, welder)	M:	7.6	7.7	5.4	6.4	4.9
	F:	0.3	0.6	0.2	0.8	0.3
(4) Sales clerk in a retail store (shoe salesperson, department store clerk, drug store clerk)	M:	0.5	0.8	0.6	0.8	0.6
	F:	3.2	2.6	2.0	2.9	2.4
(5) Clerical or office worker (bank teller, bookkeeper, secretary, typist, postal clerk or carrier, ticket agent)	M:	1.8	1.4	1.9	1.5	2.2
	F:	23.3	22.3	21.3	19.3	19.8
(6) Protective service (police officer, fireman, detective)	M:	7.3	4.4	4.1	4.4	2.8
	F:	1.1	1.5	1.3	0.9	0.9
(7) Military service	M:	4.8	5.0	4.2	3.6	3.3
	F:	1.0	1.0	0.7	1.0	0.6
(8) Craftsman or skilled worker (carpenter, electrician, brick layer, mechanic, machinist, tool & die maker, telephone installer)	M:	22.0	21.7	23.9	23.8	21.5
	F:	0.5	0.6	0.6	1.0	1.2

		1976-1980 Trends and Sex Differences				
		Percentage				
		1976	1977	1978	1979	1980
(9) Farm owner, farm manager	M:	3.7	4.0	4.0	4.1	3.4
	F:	1.6	0.8	0.8	0.9	0.8
(10) Owner of small business (restaurant owner, shop owner)	M:	6.3	5.4	8.1	7.1	5.7
	F:	1.5	2.5	3.9	2.5	3.2
(11) Sales representative (insurance agent, real estate broker, bond salesman)	M:	1.6	1.6	2.6	2.1	2.3
	F:	0.2	0.6	1.1	1.3	1.4
(12) Manager or administrator (office manager, sales manager, school administrator, government official)	M:	5.3	6.1	7.0	6.4	8.7
	F:	3.8	3.6	5.6	5.1	7.3
(13) Professional without doctoral degree (registered nurse, librarian, engineer, architect, social worker, technician, accountant, actor, artist, musician)	M:	23.4	26.6	24.2	25.7	29.2
	F:	35.1	37.0	36.5	37.9	36.4
(14) Professional with doctoral degree or equivalent (lawyer, physician, dentist, scientist, college professor)	M:	14.3	13.6	12.5	12.5	13.9
	F:	10.8	10.5	10.5	13.0	12.7
(15) Full-time homemaker or Housewife	M:	0.1	0.0	0.0	0.1	0.1
	F:	13.2	11.7	10.7	8.4	7.9
Index of Segregation (Not including housewife)		49.8	45.8	44.7	44.0	36.3

Table 5-1.7

Prestige of Aspired Occupation: Trends

		1976-1980 Trends and Sex Differences						Zero-order Correlation Coefficients	
		Means						Trend	Sex
		1976	1977	1978	1979	1980			
Occupational Prestige	M:	9.72	9.89	9.96	9.93	10.36		.05	
	F:	9.69	9.77	9.95	10.09	10.12		.04	-.01

Table 5-2.1

Educational Plans: Effects of Background Characteristics

			Zero-Order Correlation Coefficients											Multiple Correlation Coefficients
		Race	Live with Mother	Live with Father	Mother Worked	Father Educ.	Mother Educ.	Urbani-city	Acad. Ability	Grades	Coll. Plans	Polit. Orient.	Relig. Commit.	Dating Freq.	
Vocational/ technical	M:	.05	-.05	-.04	.04	-.17	-.14	-.12	-.23	-.20	-.38	.01	-.04	.06	.40
	F:	.09	-.05	-.04	.05	-.17	-.13	-.10	-.17	-.14	-.35	-.02	.00	.04	.37
2-year college	M:	.04	-.02	-.02	.01	-.02	-.03	.01	-.08	-.07	.00	.02	-.03	.02	.09
	F:	.03	-.01	-.03	.06	-.05	-.05	.01	-.08	-.05	-.12	.03	-.01	.03	.14
4-year college	M:	.03	.07	.05	-.04	.35	.29	.25	.45	.41	.91	-.01	.13	-.05	.91'
	F:	.10	.09	.04	-.01	.35	.32	.15	.39	.34	.92	.03	.11	-.16	.92'
Graduate school	M:	.05	.03	.03	-.02	.32	.26	.23	.42	.37	.60	.02	.09	-.04	.65
	F:	.13	.06	.00	.00	.26	.24	.13	.35	.28	.59	.05	.07	-.14	.62

'Extremely high values are due to the inclusion of college plans as predictor of educational plans.

Table 5-2.2

The Role of Paid Work: Effects of Background Characteristics

		Race	Live with Mother	Live with Father	Mother Worked	Father Educ.	Mother Educ.	Urbani-city	Acad. Ability	Grades	Coll. Plans	Polit. Orient	Relig. Commit.	Dating Freq.	Multiple Correlation Coefficients
								Zero-Order Correlation Coefficients							
Housewife at 30	M:	--	--	--	--	--	--	--	--	--	--	--	--	--	--
	F:	-.09	-.07	-.01	-.09	-.05	-.08	-.06	-.11	-.09	-.21	-.09	.05	.07	.26
Like work you can forget	M:	.02	.00	-.03	-.02	.08	.06	.01	.13	.13	.12	-.02	.04	-.02	.17
	F:	.09	-.01	-.02	-.02	.07	.08	.02	.15	.10	.17	.02	.03	-.08	.22
Work nothing than making a living	M:	-.16	.06	.07	-.04	.12	.10	.00	.19	.20	.16	-.03	.08	.03	.27
	F:	-.16	.02	.06	-.05	.13	.12	.02	.20	.20	.20	.01	.07	-.04	.30
Work central part of life	M:	.07	.00	.00	.04	-.02	-.02	-.04	.01	.02	.03	-.06	.05	-.01	.11
	F:	.14	-.02	-.05	.03	-.04	-.02	-.06	.03	.02	.06	-.01	.04	-.04	.16
Best job, even if overtime	M:	.04	.00	.00	.02	-.02	-.02	-.06	.03	.03	-.01	-.06	.06	.05	.12
	F:	.04	.00	-.02	.04	-.01	.00	-.05	.07	.06	.03	-.03	.06	.00	.10
Work Centrality Index (above 4 items)	M:	-.02	.02	.02	-.01	.08	.06	-.03	.15	.16	.13	-.06	.09	.01	.21
	F:	.03	.00	-.01	-.01	.07	.08	-.02	.19	.15	.19	.01	.08	-.07	.25
Would stop work if enough money	M:	.00	-.01	-.03	.01	-.02	-.02	.06	-.02	-.06	-.01	.06	-.10	.00	.12
	F:	-.03	-.01	.01	-.01	-.04	-.04	.01	-.07	-.06	-.12	-.01	-.04	.07	.13
Thought about having children	M:	.07	-.01	-.03	.02	.00	-.01	.01	.08	.05	.07	-.02	.11	.18	.24
	F:	-.03	-.02	.02	.01	-.01	-.01	.02	.06	.03	-.02	-.01	.04	.14	.16
Good marriage/family important	M:	-.02	.02	.03	-.03	.00	-.01	.00	.08	.08	.08	-.14	.20	.11	.26
	F:	-.06	.01	.04	-.04	-.02	-.05	-.02	-.01	.01	-.01	-.17	.15	.16	.27
Success in work important	M:	.03	.04	.03	-.02	.05	.04	.01	.13	.10	.12	-.06	.09	.06	.19
	F:	.10	.01	-.01	.04	.04	.03	.01	.13	.11	.13	-.01	.05	-.01	.19
Steady work important	M:	.05	.03	.00	.01	-.04	-.04	.00	-.02	-.03	-.02	-.08	.06	.08	.13
	F:	.10	.02	-.02	.08	-.05	-.06	.00	-.01	-.01	-.02	-.01	.01	.04	.13

Table 5-2.3

Occupational Values: Effects of Background Characteristics

		Zero-Order Correlation Coefficients													Multiple Correlation Coefficients
		Race	Live with Mother	Live with Father	Mother Worked	Father Educ.	Mother Educ.	Urbani- city	Acad. Ability	Grades	Coll. Plans	Polit. Orient	Relig. Commit	Dating Freq.	
Status	M:	.13	-.02	-.03	.05	-.02	-.01	.02	.00	-.02	.04	-.04	.05	.05	.16
	F:	.21	-.04	-.07	.09	-.09	-.09	.02	-.06	-.11	-.04	.00	.01	.05	.24
Income	M:	.11	-.03	-.02	.06	-.08	-.06	-.01	-.10	-.14	-.12	-.03	-.06	.10	.22
	F:	.20	-.05	-.06	.09	-.13	-.13	.02	-.15	-.17	-.15	-.02	-.08	.11	.31
Advancement	M:	.05	.01	.00	.05	-.01	-.01	.01	-.03	-.03	.00	-.04	.03	.10	.13
	F:	.12	-.02	-.04	.05	-.06	-.07	.06	-.04	-.06	-.07	-.03	-.04	.09	.19
Respect by Others	M:	.10	.00	-.04	.03	.00	.01	-.01	.01	.00	.05	-.05	.10	.04	.14
	F:	.15	-.04	-.05	.04	-.04	-.05	-.02	-.02	-.06	-.01	-.07	.08	.04	.19
Status & Money Index	M:	.14	-.01	-.03	.06	-.04	-.02	.00	-.03	-.06	.00	-.05	.04	.09	.19
	F:	.23	-.05	-.08	.09	-.11	-.11	.02	-.09	-.13	-.09	-.04	.00	.09	.29
Job Security	M:	.03	.02	.00	.03	-.03	-.03	.00	-.03	.00	-.04	-.07	.07	.07	.13
	F:	.09	.00	-.02	.05	-.10	-.09	-.02	-.07	-.02	-.06	-.10	.05	.06	.18
No Transfer	M:	.00	.00	-.01	.03	-.09	-.04	-.11	-.12	-.07	-.11	-.08	.11	.09	.22
	F:	.07	-.02	-.01	.02	-.12	-.11	-.09	-.10	-.07	-.15	-.11	.10	.08	.25
Stability & Security Index	M:	.02	-.02	-.01	.04	-.08	-.05	-.08	-.09	-.05	-.10	-.09	.12	.10	.22
	F:	.10	-.01	-.01	.04	-.14	-.12	-.08	-.11	-.07	-.14	-.13	.10	.09	.27
Participate in Decisions	M:	.07	.00	-.01	.01	.09	.08	.03	.13	.08	.12	-.02	.07	.04	.19
	F:	.11	.00	-.02	.03	.08	.07	.04	.10	.04	.14	.05	.02	.02	.19
Difficult Problems	M:	.02	-.01	-.01	-.01	.09	.05	.06	.15	.10	.12	.00	.03	.02	.17
	F:	.06	.00	-.01	.02	.10	.08	.03	.15	.09	.17	.06	.03	-.03	.20
Responsibility Index	M:	.06	-.01	-.01	.00	.11	.08	.06	.17	.11	.15	-.01	.06	.03	.22
	F:	.10	.00	-.01	.03	.11	.09	.05	.15	.09	.19	.07	.03	-.01	.24

Table 5-2.3 (cont.)

Occupational Values: Effects of Background Characteristics

		Zero-Order Correlation Coefficients													Multiple Correlation Coefficients
		Race	Live with Mother	Live with Father	Mother Worked	Father Educ.	Mother Educ.	Urbani-city	Acad. Ability	Grades	Coll. Plans	Polit. Orient	Relig. Commit	Dating Freq.	
Much Vacation	M:	.04	-.04	.00	-.01	.02	.03	.04	-.01	-.06	.00	.02	.00	.00	.09
	F:	.11	-.01	-.03	.01	.02	-.01	.03	-.02	-.06	.01	.02	.01	-.01	.12
Much Free Time	M:	-.01	.00	.01	.00	-.01	-.01	.00	.00	-.06	.01	.02	.01	.04	.08
	F:	.05	-.02	-.02	.01	-.01	-.01	-.01	-.03	-.04	-.04	.02	.01	.05	.08
Easy Pace on Job	M:	.09	-.02	-.02	.04	-.06	-.06	-.02	-.10	-.09	-.05	.02	.02	.02	.14
	F:	.06	-.03	-.03	.01	-.08	-.09	-.03	-.15	-.14	-.10	-.04	.00	-.04	.18
No Supervision	M:	-.01	-.03	-.01	.00	.00	.01	.00	.01	-.04	-.02	.04	-.05	.05	.08
	F:	.07	-.01	-.04	.03	.00	.01	.01	.00	-.05	-.01	.07	-.08	.02	.12
Easy Pace Index	M:	.04	-.03	-.01	.01	-.02	-.01	.01	-.04	-.09	-.03	.04	-.01	.01	.09
	F:	.11	-.03	-.05	.02	-.03	-.04	.00	-.08	-.11	-.05	.03	-.02	.02	.14
Be Creative	M:	.03	-.02	-.01	.00	.03	.04	.05	.09	.04	.04	.07	.03	.01	.12
	F:	.03	-.01	-.02	.02	.03	.05	.04	.06	.02	.08	.10	.01	.01	.13
Interesting Work	M:	-.05	.08	.06	-.01	.05	.02	.02	.10	.05	.07	.01	.03	.03	.14
	F:	-.07	.04	.04	-.01	.04	.04	.00	.07	.07	.06	.02	.02	.00	.11
Be Yourself	M:	-.01	.03	.02	.00	.01	.01	.00	.06	.04	.05	.03	.08	.03	.11
	F:	-.03	.02	.05	.00	.03	.04	.00	.07	.08	.03	.00	.04	-.01	.09
Learn New Things	M:	.12	-.03	-.05	.03	-.08	-.07	-.02	-.10	-.09	-.11	-.01	.05	.02	.17
	F:	.14	-.03	-.05	.05	-.06	-.06	.02	-.03	-.07	-.02	.01	.05	.01	.16
See Results	M:	.07	.00	-.02	.02	-.01	.02	-.01	.02	.00	.00	-.01	.07	.04	.10
	F:	.06	-.02	-.01	.04	-.01	-.01	-.01	.05	.03	.06	-.01	.06	.02	.10
Use Skills	M:	.03	.01	.01	-.01	.01	.00	-.01	.05	.04	.03	-.01	.08	.02	.09
	F:	-.01	.01	.01	.02	.03	.02	-.01	.08	.06	.06	.00	.05	-.01	.09
Skills Not Out-of-Date	M:	.06	.00	-.01	.02	-.08	-.05	-.02	-.03	-.04	-.08	.03	.03	.06	.12
	F:	.07	-.04	-.03	.04	-.05	-.07	.00	-.03	-.02	-.04	.00	.01	.04	.10
Stimulation & Mastery Index	M:	.07	.01	-.01	.02	-.02	-.01	.01	.04	.04	-.01	.04	.09	.05	.13
	F:	.07	-.01	-.01	.05	-.01	-.01	.01	.06	.03	.05	.04	.06	.02	.12

Table 5-2.3 (cont.)

Occupational Values: Effects of Background Characteristics

		Zero-Order Correlation Coefficients													Multiple Correlation Coefficients
		Race	Live with Mother	Live with Father	Mother Worked	Father Educ.	Mother Educ.	Urbani-city	Acad. Ability	Grades	Coll. Plans	Polit. Orient	Relig. Commit	Dating Freq.	
Help People	M:	.12	.00	-.04	.04	.00	.00	.00	.00	.01	.03	-.01	.18	.04	.21
	F:	.07	.00	-.02	.02	-.06	-.05	-.03	-.02	-.01	.03	.00	.14	.03	.17
Job Worthwhile to Society	M:	.06	-.01	-.02	.01	.00	.00	-.02	.04	.06	.05	-.04	.16	.02	.17
	F:	.02	.01	.00	-.01	.03	.02	-.02	.06	.08	.10	-.01	.13	.00	.16
Altruism Index	M:	.10	-.01	-.04	.03	.00	.00	-.01	.02	.04	.05	-.03	.20	.03	.22
	F:	.05	.00	-.01	.01	-.02	-.02	-.03	.02	.05	.08	.00	.16	.01	.18
Make Friends	M:	-.04	.05	.03	-.01	.02	.01	.00	.00	.01	.03	-.01	.11	.02	.12
	F:	-.12	.03	.04	-.05	.02	.01	-.03	.00	.04	-.01	-.01	.09	.01	.15
Meet Others	M:	.05	-.01	-.01	.02	.06	.05	.05	.02	.01	.10	.02	.13	.03	.17
	F:	-.04	.04	.02	.00	.04	.03	.02	.03	.02	.08	.02	.11	.02	.14
Contact with Others Index	M:	.02	.02	.01	.01	.05	.04	.03	.01	.02	.08	.01	.14	.03	.16
	F:	-.09	.04	.03	-.03	.03	.02	.00	.02	.03	.04	.00	.11	.02	.16

Table 5-2.4

Perceptions About Success Potential: Effects of Background Characteristics

		Zero-Order Correlation Coefficients													Multiple Correlation Coefficients
	Race	Live with Mother	Live with Father	Mother Worked	Father Educ.	Mother Educ.	Urbani-city	Acad. Ability	Grades	Coll. Plans	Polit. Orient.	Relig. Commit.	Dating Freq.	
How good do you think you would be...														
as a husband or a wife? — M:	-.02	.04	.04	-.01	.05	.04	.06	.18	.12	.12	-.07	.17	.13	.28
F:	.00	-.01	.04	-.03	.04	-.01	.04	.11	.07	-.02	-.08	.12	.12	.23
as a parent? — M:	.06	.01	.00	.02	.03	.02	.07	.13	.07	.10	-.05	.14	.10	.23
F:	.11	-.01	-.03	.00	.01	-.01	.07	.05	.01	.01	-.07	.12	.06	.20
as a worker on a job? — M:	-.01	.04	.03	.01	.04	.02	.04	.12	.08	.04	-.05	.07	.10	.17
F:	.09	.02	.02	.03	.05	.04	.06	.23	.19	.11	-.02	.06	-.02	.27
How well have your experiences prepared you to be a good . . .														
Husband or Wife? — M:	.09	-.01	.00	.04	.02	.02	.01	.14	.11	.09	-.07	.16	.12	.26
F:	.03	.00	.04	.04	-.01	.00	-.01	.10	.07	.00	-.08	.14	.09	.21
Parent? — M:	.14	.00	-.03	.04	.00	.01	.03	.12	.08	.10	-.07	.15	.07	.25
F:	.11	-.01	.01	.03	-.02	.00	.02	.08	.03	.03	-.07	.16	.05	.21
Worker on a job? — M:	.09	.00	.00	.04	-.03	.00	-.05	.08	.09	.02	-.07	.09	.08	.19
F:	.06	.02	.01	.05	.01	.01	.04	.16	.12	.05	-.06	.08	.02	.21

187

Table 5-2.4 (cont.)

Perceptions About Success Potential: Effects of Background Characteristics

		Zero-Order Correlation Coefficients													Multiple Correlation Coefficients
		Race	Live with Mother	Live with Father	Mother Worked	Father Educ.	Mother Educ.	Urbanicity	Acad. Ability	Grades	Coll. Plans	Polit. Orient	Relig. Commit	Dating Freq.	
Women discriminated against. . .															
In getting college education	M:	.09	-.08	-.09	.04	-.04	-.03	-.03	-.06	-.03	-.07	.01	-.06	-.01	.15
	F:	.07	-.04	-.05	.01	.03	.05	.02	.06	.01	.07	.08	-.04	-.06	.14
In gaining leadership positions	M:	.06	.00	-.02	.04	.02	.00	.03	.01	.02	.03	.07	-.03	-.05	.12
	F:	.06	.00	-.04	.01	.02	.02	.05	.04	.00	.05	.12	-.06	-.02	.15
In obtaining exec. positions in bus.	M:	.01	.03	.01	.00	.05	.04	.05	.08	.07	.07	.06	-.02	-.05	.12
	F:	.02	-.01	-.02	-.01	.05	.07	.03	.10	.06	.11	.10	-.05	-.06	.17
In obtain. top jobs in the professions	M:	.03	-.02	-.02	.02	.02	.00	.02	.01	.02	.01	.07	-.04	-.04	.09
	F:	.06	-.02	-.03	-.00	.04	.04	.02	.05	.01	.07	.09	-.04	-.05	.13
In getting skilled labor jobs	M:	.04	-.02	-.01	.02	-.02	-.01	.02	-.01	.00	.01	.07	-.02	-.01	.08
	F:	.05	-.02	-.02	.00	.02	.03	.04	.02	.01	.05	.07	-.06	-.02	.11
In getting elected to political off.	M:	.04	.00	-.02	.02	-.05	-.04	.01	-.01	.01	.00	.05	-.03	-.02	.08
	F:	.01	.01	-.01	.01	.02	.01	.04	.03	.02	.02	.07	-.05	.01	.08
In getting equal pay for equal work	M:	.09	-.02	-.05	.03	-.03	-.02	.00	-.06	-.03	-.01	.05	-.04	-.03	.11
	F:	.06	-.01	-.05	.01	.00	.01	.02	-.02	-.04	.02	.06	-.05	-.04	.10
Index Perceived Sex Discrimination (above 7 items)	M:	.06	-.02	-.03	.03	-.01	-.02	.03	-.01	.01	.01	.09	-.05	-.04	.12
	F:	.06	-.02	-.04	.00	.04	.05	.05	.05	.01	.07	.12	-.07	-.05	.17
To what extent will your sex prevent you from getting the kind of job you would like to have?	M:	.03	-.04	-.05	.01	-.02	-.04	-.04	-.08	-.06	-.06	-.03	-.02	-.01	.10
	F:	.01	-.01	.01	-.02	.07	.05	.05	.05	.02	.10	.05	-.07	-.05	.14

Table 5-2.5

Preferred Work Settings: Effects of Background Characteristics

			Zero-Order Correlation Coefficients												Multiple Correlation Coefficients
		Race	Live with Mother	Live with Father	Mother Worked	Father Educ.	Mother Educ.	Urbani-city	Acad. Ability	Grades	Coll. Plans	Polit. Orient.	Relig. Commit.	Dating Freq.	
Large Corporation	M:	.12	.03	.00	.05	-.01	-.01	.05	.07	.07	.09	-.06	.04	.04	.18
	F:	.10	.01	-.01	.04	-.02	-.03	.05	.07	.05	.02	-.06	.03	.03	.16
Small Business	M:	-.11	.04	.06	-.05	.06	.04	-.03	.05	.06	.02	-.02	.02	-.01	.13
	F:	-.16	.02	.07	-.05	.04	.06	-.08	.05	.07	-.04	-.07	.04	.05	.21
Government Agency	M:	.15	.00	-.04	.07	.00	.00	.05	.10	.11	.14	-.02	.07	-.02	.23
	F:	.11	.04	-.01	.04	.01	.01	.06	.14	.11	.11	.00	.08	-.01	.21
Military Service	M:	.12	-.02	-.05	.07	-.09	-.09	-.06	-.06	-.04	-.10	-.07	.02	-.03	.18
	F:	.15	-.02	-.04	.05	-.10	-.09	-.05	-.04	-.05	-.05	-.06	.06	-.07	.20
School or University	M:	.12	.00	-.03	.03	.10	.07	.06	.20	.19	.30	.04	.10	-.05	.34
	F:	.05	.01	.01	.00	.05	.06	.01	.16	.16	.28	.00	.12	-.08	.30
Police Department	M:	-.06	.00	.01	.01	-.05	-.05	.03	-.04	-.02	-.03	-.05	.06	.03	.14
	F:	-.01	.00	.01	.00	-.04	-.04	.02	.01	.02	.02	-.02	.07	-.02	.09
Social Service Organization	M:	.16	-.02	-.05	.03	-.01	-.01	.04	.03	.05	.11	.06	.11	-.01	.22
	F:	.03	.00	-.02	.00	.01	.02	.01	.04	.05	.09	.07	.09	.02	.15
Small Group of Partners	M:	-.07	.05	.04	-.01	.12	.10	.01	.14	.10	.10	.07	.04	-.01	.19
	F:	-.11	.01	.04	-.06	.10	.11	.00	.11	.10	.10	.01	.02	.00	.18
Self-employed	M:	-.06	.01	.01	-.02	.02	.03	-.05	.06	.02	-.03	.03	-.05	.06	.14
	F:	.00	-.02	-.02	-.01	.06	.05	-.02	.10	.06	.07	.06	-.04	.04	.14

Table 5-2.6

Prestige of Aspired Occupation: Effects of Background Characteristics

			Live with Mother	Live with Father	Mother Worked	Father Educ.	Mother Educ.	Urbani- city	Acad. Ability	Grades	Coll. Plans	Polit. Orient.	Relig. Commit.	Dating Freq.	Multiple Correlation Coefficients
		Race													
								Zero-Order Correlation Coefficients							
Occupational	M:	.00	.05	.05	-.04	.28	.23	.20	.43	.36	.56	.04	.09	-.03	.61
prestige	F:	-.03	.05	.02	-.03	.28	.25	.12	.31	.25	.54	.05	.04	-.10	.57

190

Table 5-3.1

Plans for 4-year College: Effects of Predictors

		Bivariate Coefficients[1]	Multivariate Coefficients[2]		
Race	M: F:	-.06 .06	.01 .12*	.01 .14*	.02 .12*
Father's Education	M: F:	.29* .30*	.13 .17*	.13 .17*	.13 .17*
Mother's Education	M: F:	.28* .31*	.09 .18*	.09 .17*	.09 .17*
Urbanicity	M: F:	.05 -.04	.07 -.06	.07 -.06	.07 -.05
Acad. Ability Comp.	M: F:	.47* .37*	.39* .28*	.37* .24*	.37* .24*
Relig. Commitment	M: F:	.25* .18*	.17* .10	.19* .13*	.19* .13*
Dating Frequency	M: F:	-.07 -.11	-.03 -.10	-.02 -.10	-.02 -.10
Trad. Sex Role Att.	M: F:	-.18* -.22*		-.10 -.09	-.13 -.06
Equal Opp. Attitudes	M: F:	.12 .10		-.01 .01	-.01 .02
Parenting Attitudes	M: F:	.01 -.07		-.03 -.08	-.03 -.07
Div. Paid Work	M: F:	-.04 .12			-.07 .05
Div. Home Duties	M: F:	.12 .16*			-.06 .03
R (adj.)	M: F:		.52 .48	.52 .49	.52 .48
R² (adj.)	M: F:		.27 .23	.27 .24	.27 .24

Note: *p < .05

[1]Entries are zero-order correlation coefficients.

[2]Entries are standardized regression coefficeints.

191

Table 5-3.2

Plans for Graduate/Professional School: Effects of Predictors

		Bivariate Coefficients[1]		Multivariate Coefficients[2]					
Race	M: F:	.04 .24*	.13* 	.11 .11	.19* .08	.11 .11	.21* .08	.12 .11	.20* .08
Father's Education	M: F:	.24* 	.21* 						
Mother's Education	M: F:	.26* 	.30* 	.11 	.25* 	.11 	.24* 	.12 	.24*
Urbanicity	M: F:	.02 	.02 	.02 	-.01 	.01 	-.02 	.01 	-.01
Acad. Ability Comp.	M: F:	.43* 	.25* 	.39* 	.18* 	.37* 	.15* 	.37* 	.14*
Dating Frequency	M: F:	-.06 	-.08 	-.02 	-.06 	-.02 	-.05 	-.02 	-.06
Trad. Sex Role Att.	M: F:	-.18* 	-.22* 			-.09 	-.12 	-.09 	-.05
Equal Opp. Attitudes	M: F:	.12 	.08 			-.01 	.00 	-.01 	-.01
Parenting Attitudes	M: F:	.00 	-.11 			-.02 	-.11 	-.02 	-.10
Pref. Div. Paid Work	M: F:	.02 	.17* 					-.04 	.07
Pref. Div. Home Duties	M: F:	.14 	.19* 					.02 	.10
R (adj.)	M: F:	.45 	.39 	.45 	.39 	.45 	.41 	.44 	.42
R² (adj.)	M: F:	.21 	.15 	.21 	.15 	.20 	.17 	.20 	.17

Note: *p < .05

[1] Entries are zero-order correlation coefficients.

[2] Entries are standardized regression coefficients.

192

Table 5-3.3

Plans for Being a Housewife at 30:   Effects of Predictors

		Bivariate Coefficients[1]	Multivariate Coefficients[2]	
Acad. Ability Comp.	M:	-.06	.04	.04
	F:		.09	.08
Trad. Sex Role Att.	M:	.34*	.35*	.29*
	F:		.34*	.28*
Equal Opp. Attitudes	M:	-.11	.04	.03
	F:		.04	.03
Parenting Attitudes	M:	.16*	.09	.07
	F:		.09	.07
Pref. Div. Paid Work	M:	-.24*		-.12
	F:			-.11
Pref. Div. Home Duties	M:	-.18*		-.04
	F:			-.04
College Plans	M:	-.17*		
	F:		-.14	-.13
R (adj.)	M:	.00	.33	.34
	F:		.35	.35
R² (adj.)	M:	.00	.11	.11
	F:		.12	.12

Note: *p < .05

[1]Entries are zero-order correlation coefficients.

[2]Entries are standardized regression coefficients.

Table 5-3.4

Job Centrality Index: Effects of Predictors

		Bivariate Coefficients[1]		Multivariate Coefficients[2]									
Acad. Ability Comp.	M: F:	.31* .27*		.31* .27*		.29* .22*		.29* .21*		.23* .17*		.23* .16*	
Trad. Sex Role Att.	M: F:	-.06 -.24*				.02 -.18*		.03 -.11		.04 -.16*		.05 -.09	
Equal Opp. Attitudes	M: F:	.14* .10				.08 -.01		.07 -.01		.09 .00		.08 .00	
Parenting Attitudes	M: F:	.07 .00				.04 .05		.03 .05		.04 .05		.03 .05	
Pref. Div. Paid Work	M: F:	-.03 -.14*						-.03 .09				-.02 .07	
Pref. Div. Home Duties	M: F:	.11 .21*						.04 .10				.04 .10	
College Plans	M: F:	.23* .26*								.13 .16*		.13 .16*	
R (adj.)	M: F:			.30 .27		.29 .30		.28 .31		.30 .33		.29 .33	
R² (adj.)	M: F:			.09 .07		.08 .09		.08 .09		.09 .11		.09 .11	

Note: *p < .05

[1]Entries are zero-order correlation coefficients.

[2]Entries are standardized regression coefficients.

Table 5-3.5

Perceived Sex Discrimination Index: Effects of Predictors
*

		Bivariate Coefficients[1]		Multivariate Coefficients[2]								
		M	F	M	F	M	F	M	F	M	F	
Political Orientation	M:/F:	.03	.00	.04	-.01	.03	-.02	.03	.00	.03	-.01	
Trad. Sex Role Att.	M:/F:	-.09	-.04	-.13	.00	-.16	.09	-.14	.03	-.17	.10	
Equal Opp. Attitudes	M:/F:	-.04	.11	-.10	.12	-.10	.11	-.10	.12	-.10	.11	
Parenting Attitudes	M:/F:	.07	-.01	.10	.00	.10	.00	.10	.00	.10	.00	
Pref. Div. Paid Work	M:/F:	-.02	.05			-.04	.06			-.05	.05	
Pref. Div. Home Duties	M:/F:	-.01	.13			-.06	.13	-.06		-.05	.12	
College Plans	M:/F:	-.04	.10					-.06	.10	-.06	.09	
R (adj.)	M:/F:	.00	.00	.00	.00	.00	.04	.00	.00	.00	.07	
R² (adj.)	M:/F:	.00	.00	.00	.00	.00	.00	.00	.00	.00	.00	

Note: *p < .05. The index is described in the text.

[1] Entries are zero-order correlation coefficients.

[2] Entries are standardized regression coefficients.

Table 5-3.6

Occupational Prestige: Effects of Predictors

		Bivariate Coefficients[1]	Multivariate Coefficients[2]						
Father's Education	M:	.22*	.04	.03	.03	-.03	.02	.03	-.03
	F:	.25*	.16*	.17*	.17*	.12	.17*	.17*	.11
Mother's Education	M:	.28*	.14	.14	.15	.12	.13	.14	.13
	F:	.20*	.04	.03	.03	-.03	.01	.03	-.04
Urbanicity	M:	.10	.10	.10	.09	.07	.09	.09	.06
	F:	-.03	-.03	-.02	-.02	.00	-.02	-.02	.01
Acad. Ability Comp.	M:	.49*	.44*	.40*	.40*	.27*	.38*	.34*	.23*
	F:	.38*	.33*	.30*	.30*	.19*	.25*	.28*	.16*
Dating Frequency	M:	-.12	-.08	-.08	-.07	-.06	-.10	-.07	-.07
	F:	-.03	-.03	-.03	-.03	.01	-.02	-.03	.02
Trad. Sex Role Att.	M:	-.26*		-.13	-.17*	-.09	-.11	-.13	-.09
	F:	-.22*		-.12	-.14	-.09	-.09	-.11	-.10
Equal Opp. Attitudes	M:	.21*		.06	.06	.09	.03	.05	.05
	F:	.09		-.04	-.04	-.02	-.04	-.03	-.03
Parenting Attitudes	M:	-.02		-.03	-.03	-.03	-.11	-.05	-.11
	F:	-.02		.01	.01	.02	-.02	.01	-.02
Pref. Div. Paid Work	M:	-.05			-.09				-.04
	F:	.00			-.05				-.10
Pref. Div. Home Duties	M:	.15*			-.04				-.05
	F:	.17*			.02				.03
College Plans	M:	.53*				.35*			.31*
	F:	.50*				.40*			.39*
Occ.Val: Status	M:	.17*					-.05		-.09
	F:	.09					.00		.04
Occ.Val: Stabil.	M:	.13					-.01		.02
	F:	.03					-.03		-.02
Occ.Val: Respon.	M:	.25*					.07		.02
	F:	.24*					.11		.04
Occ.Val: Easy Pace	M:	.12					.05		.10
	F:	-.02					-.07		-.07
Occ.Val: Stimul.	M:	.30*					.16		.17
	F:	.21*					.01		.01
Occ.Val: Altruism	M:	.22*					.03		-.01
	F:	.26*					.20*		.17
Occ.Val: Contact	M:	.24*					.05		.03
	F:	.11					-.03		-.03
Job Centrality	M:	.35*						.21*	.17*
	F:	.20*						.09	-.02
Perc. Sex Discrim.	M:	.01						.06	.06
	F:	-.02						-.03	-.07
Personal Compet.	M:	.15						.04	.02
	F:	.11						-.01	-.02
R (adj.)	M:		.50	.52	.51	.60	.54	.54	.62
	F:		.39	.39	.38	.53	.41	.38	.52
R² (adj.)	M:		.25	.27	.26	.35	.29	.30	.38
	F:		.15	.15	.14	.28	.16	.14	.27

Note: *p < .05

[1]Entries are zero-order correlation coefficients.

[2]Entries are standardized regression coefficients.

Table 5-4.1

Occupational Values: Interrelationships
Between Indices and Single Variables

	Easy Pace Index		Status & Money Index		Altruism Index		Stimulation & Mastery Index		Contact with Others Index		Stability & Security Index		Responsibility Index	
	M	F	M	F	M	F	M	F	M	F	M	F	M	F
Mean	2.72	2.53	3.19	3.13	3.10	3.43	3.42	3.53	3.04	3.31	3.30	3.27	2.73	2.63
Standard Deviation	.63	.63	.59	.61	.73	.61	.42	.37	.74	.69	.67	.67	.72	.72
Product-Moment Correlations:														
Much Vacation	.74	.75	.34	.34	.09	.06	.13	.13	.18	.13	.15	.14	.18	.16
Much Free Time	.65	.70	.24	.24	.07	.03	.19	.17	.14	.14	.22	.22	.11	.08
Easy Pace	.70	.67	.22	.20	.08	.06	.12	.13	.20	.14	.18	.20	.10	.06
No Supervision	.64	.67	.22	.24	.07	.06	.21	.20	.15	.10	.19	.17	.23	.23
Easy Pace Index			.37	.37	.11	.07	.23	.22	.25	.18	.26	.26	.23	.19
Status	.24	.25	.78	.80	.19	.11	.18	.17	.21	.10	.19	.19	.24	.19
Income	.33	.34	.68	.73	.02	-.02	.13	.13	.09	.02	.26	.26	.09	.07
Advancement	.20	.20	.65	.69	.16	.09	.26	.24	.17	.09	.26	.24	.18	.17
Respect by Others	.29	.30	.74	.71	.28	.22	.26	.24	.35	.26	.24	.23	.31	.25
Status & Money Index	.37	.37			.24	.14	.29	.26	.30	.17	.32	.31	.30	.24
Help People	.08	.03	.21	.10	.85	.82	.40	.33	.44	.41	.18	.14	.31	.21
Job Worthwhile	.11	.09	.20	.14	.86	.85	.42	.37	.37	.31	.22	.18	.31	.29
Altruism Index	.11	.07	.24	.14			.48	.42	.48	.43	.24	.19	.36	.30
Be Creative	.19	.16	.14	.10	.33	.25	.65	.64	.26	.23	.04	.02	.33	.32
Interesting Work	.07	.08	.12	.00	.19	.17	.45	.39	.16	.19	.14	.08	.13	.09
Be Yourself	.09	.07	.07	.00	.22	.16	.55	.48	.18	.17	.15	.13	.15	.08
Learn Things	.15	.10	.23	.22	.35	.29	.61	.59	.29	.25	.20	.17	.29	.31
See Results	.05	.07	.18	.20	.29	.29	.56	.54	.18	.21	.14	.13	.25	.24
Use Skills	.12	.12	.17	.15	.33	.28	.58	.57	.26	.23	.20	.16	.24	.25
Skills Not Out-of-Date	.18	.20	.24	.21	.19	.16	.55	.56	.16	.14	.22	.23	.14	.13
Stimulation & Mastery Index	.23	.22	.29	.26	.48	.42			.38	.37	.27	.24	.39	.38
Make Friends	.21	.18	.22	.12	.39	.32	.36	.35	.81	.81	.21	.15	.23	.16
Meet Others	.21	.14	.28	.16	.41	.40	.27	.28	.87	.88	.14	.08	.36	.31
Contact Index	.25	.18	.30	.17	.48	.43	.38	.37			.21	.13	.36	.29
Security	.20	.19	.35	.37	.22	.17	.31	.27	.18	.10	.70	.69	.15	.10
No Transfer	.22	.23	.20	.17	.18	.15	.16	.15	.16	.10	.88	.89	.05	.02
Stability & Security Index	.26	.26	.32	.31	.24	.19	.27	.24	.21	.13			.11	.06
Make Decisions	.28	.26	.33	.28	.34	.28	.36	.40	.34	.28	.14	.11	.79	.80
Difficult Problems	.10	.06	.16	.11	.25	.21	.28	.24	.25	.20	.04	.00	.83	.83
Responsibility Index	.23	.19	.30	.24	.36	.30	.39	.38	.36	.29	.11	.06		

Table 5-4.2

Perceptions of Discrimination: Interrelationships Between Items

	College Education		Leader-ship		Executive Positions		Top Professions		Skilled Labor		Political Office	
	M	F	M	F	M	F	M	F	M	F	M	F
Leadership	.26	.32										
Executive Position	.28	.35	.66	.64								
Top Professions	.30	.36	.58	.57	.68	.72						
Skilled Labor	.24	.27	.43	.39	.46	.45	.52	.49				
Political Office	.14	.13	.49	.49	.48	.46	.46	.45	.41	.39		
Equal Pay	.36	.30	.41	.42	.46	.44	.47	.47	.41	.39	.33	.35

Note: Entries are product-moment correlations.

Table 5-4.3

Occupational Aspirations: Relationships with Occupational Values,
Preferences for the Division of Labor, and Background Characteristics

| | Percentage of Total | | Occupational Values | | | | | | | | | | | | | |
| | | | Status/ Money | | Stabil-ity | | Respon-sibility | | Easy Pace | | Stimul./ Master | | Altru-ism | | Contact With Others | |
	M	F	M	F	M	F	M	F	M	F	M	F	M	F	M	F
Laborer	0.7	0.1	2.98	2.96	3.20	3.35	2.63	2.13	3.05	2.79	3.24	3.53	2.76	3.14	3.06	2.70
Service Worker	0.7	5.3	3.28	3.17	3.33	3.41	2.69	2.45*	2.88	2.56	3.39	3.54	3.17	3.48	3.33	3.41
Operative or Semi-skilled Worker	6.3	0.5	3.14	3.12	3.28	3.22	2.49	2.34	2.73	2.35	3.35	3.38	2.99	3.04	2.98	2.82
Sales Clerk in Retail Store	0.7	2.9	3.12	3.14	3.46	3.42	2.57	2.39	2.68	2.56	3.44	3.47	3.10	3.29*	3.33	3.26
Clerical or Office Worker	1.8	23.6	3.38*	3.28	3.48*	3.45*	2.63	2.51	2.65	2.56	3.38	3.53	3.15	3.35	3.12	3.30
Protective Service	4.5	1.3	3.25	2.98	3.41	3.26	2.79	2.81	2.63	2.42	3.42	3.58	3.38*	3.67*	3.25*	3.50
Military Service	4.2	0.9	3.25	3.29	3.08*	3.16	2.84	2.69	2.66	2.58	3.47	3.59	3.16	3.45	3.03	3.36
Craftsman or Skilled Worker	22.7	0.9	3.17	3.00	3.43	3.16	2.59	2.70	2.74	2.58	3.46	3.66	3.01	3.18	2.91	3.09
Farm Owner, Farm-Manager	3.9	1.1	3.02*	2.85*	3.42	3.20	2.64	2.61	2.62	2.67	3.37	3.54	3.03	3.33	2.83*	2.99*
Owner of Small Business	6.6	3.1	3.19	3.23	3.32	3.16	2.74	2.77	2.81	2.58	3.41	3.58	3.02	3.36	3.09	3.40
Sales Representative	2.1	1.1	3.41*	3.37	3.46	3.25	2.81	2.71	2.76	2.76	3.40	3.58	3.09	3.37	3.26*	3.44
Manager or Administrator	6.8	5.7	3.36*	3.25	3.36	3.18	2.90	2.81	2.75	2.47	3.42	3.52	3.16	3.60	3.20	3.31
Professional without Doctoral Degree	25.8	40.8	3.15	3.02	3.21	3.19	2.77	2.70	2.67	2.48	3.46	3.54	3.10	3.50	3.02	3.36
Professional with Doctoral Degree	13.3	12.8	3.20	3.12	3.20	3.14	3.02*	3.01	2.69	2.45	3.44	3.56	3.29	3.56	3.16	3.34
Overall Mean			3.19	3.13	3.30	3.26	2.75	2.68	2.71	2.54	3.43	3.54	3.11	3.44	3.04	3.33
Standard Deviation			.58	.61	.66	.67	.71	.71	.63	.63	.41	.35	.73	.60	.73	.68
Eta (adj.)			.13	.19	.16	.18	.21	.23	.08	.08	.08	.06	.15	.15	.16	.10
r			.01	-.12	-.08	-.17	.16	.19	-.03	-.06	.05	.03	.06	.10	.04	.03

Table 5-4.3 (cont.)

Occupational Aspirations: Relationships with Occupational Values, Preferences for the Division of Labor, and Background Characteristics

	Index Div. Childcare, couple work		Index Div. Housework, couple work		Perceptions of Obstacles Sex	
	M	F	M	F	M	F
Laborer	2.30	2.60	2.13	2.46	1.45	1.55
Service Worker	2.39	2.51	2.29	2.38*	1.31	1.14*
Operative or Semi-Skilled Worker	2.35*	2.54	2.19	2.58	1.15	1.73
Sales Clerk in Retail Store	2.56	2.48*	2.33	2.29*	1.19	1.28
Clerical or Office Worker	2.58	2.55	2.37	2.34*	1.10	1.23
Protective Service	2.48	2.67	2.26	2.55	1.16	1.87*
Military Service	2.51	2.36*	2.37	2.31	1.15	1.35
Craftsman or Skilled Worker	2.44	2.67	2.24	2.56	1.17	1.70*
Farm Owner, Farm Manager	2.37	2.64	2.17	2.47	1.16	1.54
Owner of Small Business	2.43	2.63	2.28	2.54	1.12	1.29
Sales Representative	2.42	2.62	2.21	2.45	1.10	1.41
Manager or Administrator	2.46	2.67	2.25	2.54	1.08	1.53*
Professional without Doctoral degree	2.52	2.66	2.35	2.53	1.08	1.30
Professional with Doctoral degree	2.54	2.70	2.34	2.62*	1.11	1.54*
Overall Mean	2.48	2.63	2.29	2.48	1.12	1.33
Standard Deviation	.44	.36	.46	.42	.40	.55
Eta (adj.)	.12	.17	.12	.24	.12	.25
r	.09	.16	.08	.21	-.09	.11

Table 5-4.3 (cont.)

Occupational Aspirations: Relationships with Occupational Values,
Preferences for the Division of Labor, and Background Characteristics

| | Background Characteristics | | | | | | | | | | | | | |
| | Race | | Live with Mother | | Live with Father | | Mother Worked | | Father's Educ. | | Mother's Educ. | | Urbani- city | |
	M	F	M	F	M	F	M	F	M	F	M	F	M	F
Laborer	.04	.41	.75	1.00	.77	.60	1.95	1.77	2.82*	2.56	2.93	2.84	2.83*	3.36
Service Worker	.10	.15	.78	.92	.71	.82	2.18	2.28	2.97	2.76*	3.14	2.96*	3.95	3.29*
Operative or Semi- skilled Worker	.08	.00*	.92	.95	.81	.79	2.18	2.69	2.86*	2.48*	2.93*	2.68	3.30*	2.64*
Sales Clerk in Retail Store	.13	.20	.89	.92	.83	.79	2.21	2.27	2.94	2.69*	3.20	2.77*	3.86	3.59
Clerical or Office Worker	.21	.16	.95	.93	.80	.81	2.10	2.25	3.40	2.92*	3.22	2.89*	3.80	3.68
Protective Service	.06	.12	.95	.95	.80	.84	2.30	2.14	3.13*	3.45	3.19	3.13	3.85	4.05
Military Service	.25*	.35*	.91	.89	.79	.65	2.30	2.62	3.27	2.69*	3.18	2.68*	3.62	3.43
Craftsman or Skilled Worker	.09	.14	.91	.85	.82	.71	2.16	2.44	3.05*	3.24	3.05*	3.16	3.53	3.72
Farm Owner, Farm-Manager	.03	.06	.90	.79	.88	.72	1.81*	2.22	3.07*	3.66	3.27	3.40	2.26*	3.43
Owner of Small Business	.09	.07	.91	.94	.83	.83	2.14	2.27	3.42	3.48	3.34	3.24	3.81	3.90
Sales Representative	.03	.12	.90	.94	.84	.75	2.13	2.44	3.96*	3.57	3.68	3.75	3.97	3.88
Manager or Administrator	.14	.16	.93	.95	.85	.80	2.06	2.27	3.78	3.57	3.44	3.49	3.98	3.97
Professional without Doctoral Degree	.10	.12	.94	.95	.84	.82	2.08	2.19	3.77	3.64	3.55	3.49	3.94	3.78
Professional with Doctoral Degree	.08	.17	.94	.95	.86	.81	2.05	2.23	4.33*	4.06	3.93*	3.79*	4.10*	4.02
Overall Mean	.10	.14	.92	.94	.83	.81	2.11	2.23	3.52	3.43	3.38	3.32	3.73	3.76
Standard Deviation	.30	.35	.26	.24	.38	.39	1.08	1.12	1.45	1.45	1.18	1.22	1.12	1.07
Eta (adj.)	.13	.09	.08	.08	.05	.05	.07	.12	.31	.29	.25	.26	.34	.17
r	.00	-.03	.05	.05	.05	.02	-.04	-.03	.28	.28	.23	.25	.20	.12

201

Table 5-4.3 (cont.)

Occupational Aspirations: Relationships with Occupational Values,
Preferences for the Division of Labor, and Background Characteristics

	Background Characteristics											
	Academic Ability		Grades		College Plans		Polit. Orient.		Relig. Commit.		Dating Freq.	
	M	F	M	F	M	F	M	F	M	F	M	F
Laborer	4.18*	3.88	4.40	3.31	.07*	.24	3.26	3.23	25.02	26.75	3.05	3.11
Service Worker	4.12*	4.30*	4.35*	5.21*	.27*	.14*	2.87	3.18	25.23	28.66	2.66*	3.81
Operative or Semi-skilled Worker	4.09*	4.48	4.21*	4.78*	.05*	.00*	3.19	2.98	12.95*	27.89	3.50	4.40
Sales Clerk in in Retail Store	4.29*	4.37*	4.26*	5.08*	.23*	.12*	3.35	3.15	28.25	28.57	3.42	3.80
Clerical or Office Worker	5.08	4.65	5.91	5.91	.59	.22*	2.81*	3.11	29.75*	29.71	3.11	3.82
Protective Service	4.53*	4.73	4.81*	5.48*	.46	.51	3.11	3.25	27.18	27.64	3.56	3.48
Military Service	4.78	4.37*	5.20	5.07*	.36*	.34*	3.21	3.29	26.98	29.81	3.00	3.35
Craftsman or Skilled Worker	4.49*	4.63	4.86*	5.60	.16*	.38	3.22	3.29	26.00	24.47*	3.57	3.18
Farm Owner, Farm-Manager	4.68	4.58	5.33	5.56	.31*	.41*	2.89*	3.26	28.87	26.23*	3.17	3.75
Owner of Small Business	4.74	4.71	5.02*	5.74*	.48	.41	3.23	3.16	27.76	28.17	3.47	3.84
Sales Representative	4.96	4.73	5.21	5.40*	.74*	.56	3.28	3.39	27.76	27.32	3.77*	4.08
Manager or Administrator	5.09	5.13	4.74	6.51	.77*	.74*	3.04	3.24	28.27	29.74	3.51	3.57
Professional without Doctoral Degree	5.33*	5.06	6.09*	6.47	.81*	.74*	3.25	3.22	27.56	30.24	3.31	3.49
Professional with Doctoral Degree	5.81*	5.47*	6.91*	6.99*	.95*	.91*	3.27	3.30	27.86	29.60	3.20	3.30
Overall Mean	4.96	4.92	5.53	6.21	.54	.56	3.20	3.21	27.04	29.63	3.38	3.59
Standard Deviation	1.08	.95	1.95	1.80	.50	.50	1.11	.95	9.74	8.73	1.52	1.65
Eta (adj.)	.47	.34	.41	.29	.08	.55	.08	.05	.12	.09	.11	.09
r	.43	.31	.36	.25	.56	.54	.04	.05	.09	.04	-.03	-.10

Note: Entries in main body of table are means. For explanation of asterisk, refer to text.

202

CHAPTER 6

MARITAL AND FAMILY PLANS

Dramatic changes have occurred in recent decades
in the nature of major family roles. For example, over
the last twenty-five years age at first marriage has
increased by one and one-half years; and since this increase has been more substantial for women, the
traditional sex gap in age at first marriage has been
partially closed (Glick and Norton, 1977). The birth
rate has declined to reach the widely prevalent number
of two children per couple, while the divorce rate has
been climbing (Glick, 1979). A combination of the increasing number of divorces and the higher age at marriage is presumably responsible for the recent explo-
sion of one-adult households, both with and without
children.

Although these changes are expected to slow down
over the next decades (Glick, 1979), the traditional
form of the family has undergone significant changes,
some of which are part of the changes that have occurred in women's roles; i.e., as women's participation
in the work force increases, the extent of their family
roles seem to decrease. Specifically, lower fertility
has repeatedly been found to be related to employment
(Smith-Lovin and Tickamyer, 1978; Waite and Stolzenberg, 1976), and marital timing to educational attainment (Marini, 1978b), indicating certain modifications
of roles presumably to increase compatibility between
them.

Changes in family characteristics are most often
examined from a population perspective and explained by
objective contingencies, i.e., fertility as a function
of socioeconomic level, employment, income, or family
size; marital timing as a function of level of education, socioeconomic status; and the like. But we know
much less about the marital and family plans that
precede actual engagement in those roles; about how
they are formed and how they have been changing. Plans
never correspond perfectly to eventual behaviors, and
data on plans have often been discounted for that very
reason; nevertheless, as mentioned in the introduction,
in the related research area of status attainment,

plans and aspirations have been assigned a prominent
position and have generally been found to exert a
moderately important effect on early attainments
(Featherman and Carter, 1976; Otto and Haller, 1979;
Sewell and Hauser, 1975). Indeed, it has been argued
that it is probably at the end of high school more than
at any other point in the life span that plans have a
significant bearing on later outcomes (Otto, 1979;
Spenner and Featherman, 1978). At this critical stage
in their lives young people make decisions--based to
some degree on plans--which set the stage for much of
their future lives; later they are increasingly locked
in by contingencies resulting from earlier decisions.
We therefore believe that the concepts of marital and
family plans deserve more attention than presently
given.

Of course, given the complex interdependence of
family and occupational roles, it is necessary to investigate family and marital plans in conjunction with
work and educational plans. It seems likely that most
young women are aware of the potential conflict between
these roles and thus make some effort to coordinate
their future role involvements and the sequencing of
those roles. We do not mean to imply that these
processes are entirely rational or carefully thought
out, but we do expect them to result in a certain level
of interrelatedness.

Contingencies set by educational and occupational
roles may be less obvious for young men. But even for
them, some level of financial independence associated
with holding a job and having completed schooling is
important in planning marriage and in starting a family.

Although not entirely consistent, existing
research supports the interdependence of roles. For
example, some studies suggest that plans for timing of
marriage are related to educational aspirations, for
young women more so than for young men (Bayer, 1969a,b;
Gaskell, 1977-1978; Shea et al., 1971). Other studies
indicate that fertility plans of young women are related to their planned labor force participation (Gustavus and Nam, 1970; Waite and Stolzenberg, 1976; Westoff and Potvin, 1967; Whelpton et al., 1966) and their
career commitment (Falbo et al., 1978; Farley, 1970).
These relationships are, of course, consistent with
relationships observed between actual behaviors within
the adult population, as noted above. What is interesting about the consistency is the implication that
the relationships are to some degree based on plans
rather than just on the situations that exist when
women actually take jobs and have babies.

Several alternative interpretations remain open after demonstrating such interrelationships. First, the direction of causation remains undetermined. Recent attempts at disentangling the predominant direction of causation underlying the well-established relationship between women's fertility and labor force participation, utilizing non-recursive path models, have led to inconsistent findings (Smith-Lovin and Tickamyer, 1978; Waite and Stolzenberg, 1976). These inconsistencies may be due to methodological problems such as multicollinearity or misspecification, as Cramer (1980) has pointed out. In addition, empirical relationships between plans do not necessarily imply direct causation, since the relationship may be attributable to one or more prior causal factors that are shared.

What then are some of the correlates of marital and family plans? Although not entirely consistent, sex role attitudes appear to be related to some of the marital and fertility plans as well as the educational and occupational plans (Eagly and Anderson, 1974; Gaskell, 1977-1978; Scanzoni, 1976). This is consistent with the view that plans are part of a more general ideological orientation, and thus their interrelationships are effects of a general ideology rather than the result of the recognition that the specific roles are incongruent. Smith-Lovin and Tickamyer (1978) have followed up that hypothesis by controlling sex role attitudes when examining the relationship between labor force participation and fertility; they found the strength of the relationship to be only slightly affected by such controls.

Political orientation and religious commitment are two other ideological dimensions which we might expect to relate to family and marital plans. Religion, in fact, emerges as one of the more pervasive predictors; Catholic adolescents desire earlier marriages, earlier family formation, and larger families (Brackbill and Howell, 1974; Paterson, 1972; Westoff and Potvin, 1967).

Ability differences are another source of differential plans. Characteristics such as high academic ability, high self-esteem, a sense of control over one's life, high achievement motivation, independence, and self-concepts which are not sex-stereotyped, are all thought to be associated with less traditional choices of occupational roles--e.g., a female's choice of full-time employment over part-time employment or home-making, or her choice of a typically male over a typically female occupation. One could argue by implication that these same abilities and personality factors are likely to be associated also with less traditional marital and family plans. In fact, among female college students a non-sex stereotypical self-concept does appear to be related to the desire for fewer children (Allgeier, 1975; Vogel, Rosenkrantz, Broverman, Broverman, and Clarkson, 1975). The underlying argument is that the choice of non-traditional roles requires higher abilities, more self-confidence, and lesser concern about the approval of others.

Several correlates tap the impact of socialization on marital and fertility plans; among them, number of siblings and parental socioeconomic status emerge repeatedly as predictors of fertility (Gustavus, 1973; Gustavus and Nam, 1970; Paterson, 1972; Simmons and Turner, 1976). Presumably, young people form many of their attitudes, expectations, and ideals after their parents; the family size that their parents chose would therefore become a direct model for their own fertility plans. Socioeconomic status probably does not affect plans directly, but exerts its influence indirectly through its effects on education, life style, and economic well-being, all of which tend to delay marriage and decrease fertility.

Finally, indicators of demographic variation--race and sex--show many and substantial relationships with fertility, age at marriage, wife's labor force participation, and division of labor in the family (Chapter 4; Kuvlesky and Obordo, 1972). Of course, as mentioned above, their effects are possibly mediated by personality, ability, and attitudinal variables.

MARITAL PLANS

According to the Monitoring the Future data, about 82 percent of female seniors and 74 percent of male seniors expect to get married "in the long run." This sex difference does not occur primarily because more young men are opposed to getting married; instead, it reflects the fact that higher proportions of males than females indicate that they "have no idea" about whether they will choose to marry (Table 6-1.1). Most of the seniors expect to stay married to the same person throughout their adult life; about 60 percent judge this as very likely, another 20 percent as fairly likely (Table 6-1.2). Again, female seniors are more likely to believe that they would stay married than male seniors, and the sex difference is due to young men being somewhat more uncertain than women, but not more negative. Sex differences are even stronger with respect to the expected timing of marriage; females plan on getting married sooner after leaving high school than males do (Table 6-1.3).'

These sex differences should not, however, over-shadow the fact that a large majority of seniors of both sexes are expecting to get married and stay married. In fact, these marital plans and expectations are impressive in their uniformity, and vary substantially only in the expected timing of marriage.

Trends

The marital plans measured in the Monitoring the Future study have changed little over the last five high school cohorts, except for a faint trend towards plans for later marriage, which is consistent with an increase in actual age at first marriage observed in the last few years (Glick, 1979).

Background Characteristics

The possibility of getting married and the stability of marriage is judged more skeptically by young blacks--in particular young black women--than by whites (Table 6-2.1). Heightened skepticism is also apparent among less religious and among more politically liberal seniors. These three variables plus academic abilities explain about 12 and 10 percent of variance in females' and males' expected marital stability, respectively, and about 8 percent of variance in their plans to wed.

The variation in plans for the actual timing of marriage is explained to a considerably greater extent by the standard set of predictors included in these analyses. About 30 percent of the variance in females' plans, and 16 percent of the variance in males' plans, can be explained. The critical predictors are a set of ability and aspiration factors. Young people who judge themselves as more able, who have higher educational aspirations, and whose parents are more highly educated plan, on the average, on later marriages. Since educational aspirations are related to abilities and both of them to socio-economic background, all these variables capture to some degree the same variance if included simultaneously in a regression analysis. More

---

'Early analyses of follow-up data indicate that these expectations are correct.

specifically, parental education and abilities exert
their influence in large measure through college plans,
as demonstrated by regression results that are not
reported here in detail. On the other hand,
urbanicity--youngsters from urban settings planning on
later marriages--seems to function only partly through
college plans. Finally, dating frequency operates almost completely independently of college plans. As
suggested by the multiple correlation coefficients,
these predictors have a somewhat stronger effect on the
planned marital timing of young women than young men.
This is particularly true for the two major
predictors--college plans and dating frequency. These
sex differences are not due to variance differences
since females' responses regarding timing of marriage
have somewhat higher variance than males'.

FAMILY PLANS

About 80 percent of the seniors want to have
children (Table 6-1.4). The actual number of children
that are desired is reported as two by almost half of
the seniors, and as three by another fifth, while very
few seniors desire only one child, or four children (5
and 12 percent, respectively). While the sexes do not
differ in their hope to become parents, young women on
the average desire slightly higher numbers of children
than men (Table 6-1.5).

With respect to the timing of the first birth, a
majority of the seniors would wait one or two years
after marriage (Table 6-1.6). Interestingly, young
women--who are inclined to get married sooner after
high school than men, as shown above--are more likely
to prefer longer delays of the first child after marriage. In the Monitoring the Future questionnaire the
timing of the first birth is asked in terms of desired
delay after marriage. Therefore, the desired age at
first birth must be estimated by combining the desired
age at marriage with the desired delay of first birth
after marriage. If this were done, the sex differences
no doubt would be weaker, since to a certain extent
they cancel each other out. (These remarks point to a
potential weakness of the Monitoring the Future measure
of expected timing of birth. The delay of the first
birth after marriage may not capture the most significant aspect of birth timing; more critical in terms
of its social significance would probably be the expected age at first birth.)

208

In sum, family plans--much like marital plans--
show impressively little variation. Most of today's
young people want children, want two of them, and want
them one or two years after getting married.

Trends

No overall changes in the above parental plans
have occurred over the last five high school cohorts.

Background Characteristics

The plans for having children at all, as well as
the actual number preferred, are affected by the
religiosity of the respondents: young men and women who
are more religious are more likely to plan on a family
and want larger families than the less religious
seniors. None of the other standard background variables shows any sizeable effect (Table 6-2). In
evaluating this lack of predictors, we need to remember
the uniformity of these plans; such a lack of variation
limits the strengths of relationships that may be observed.

INTERRELATIONSHIPS BETWEEN MARITAL AND FAMILY PLANS

Table 6-3 reveals an overall level of positive
interrelationships which suggest the existence of a
general family orientation. For example, female and
male seniors who want to get married are also more
likely to expect to stay married and to have children
and desire somewhat larger numbers of children. In
other words, commitment to a stable marriage and to
children go hand in hand.

Moreover, the desired timing of these plans is
related to the commitment to them, although the
relationships are somewhat weaker than the ones between
marital and family plans reported in the previous
paragraph. Earlier marriages are anticipated by those
seniors who definitely want to get married and expect a
stable marriage than those who are less sure about
their marital intentions and the stability of a
prospective marriage. This negative relationship between marital timing plans and marital stability expectations is in direct contradiction to the positive
relationship observed for age at marriage and marital
stability (Otto, 1979): however, it should be noted

that such a negative relationship is usually obtained for the entire age range, while our findings are based on high school seniors only. Our data thus exclude many of the married seventeen year-olds, because many of them presumably dropped out before graduation, and these "very" early marriages may be the ones which are most endangered.

Likewise, the seniors who are most certain that they want to have children and who want larger numbers of them also want to start child bearing sooner after getting married than less child-oriented seniors. Interestingly, there is no relationship between plans for timing of marriage and plans for timing of child bearing after marriage. In other words, seniors who hope on getting married early are no more--and no less--likely to plan on immediate child bearing than seniors who plan on later marriages.

SEX ROLE ATTITUDES AND MARITAL AND FAMILY PLANS

Marital Plans

We will first examine young women's expectations about whether they will be getting married "in the long run" (Table 6-4.1). It should be recalled that responses to this question vary mostly between plans to get married and uncertainty about such plans. Young women who are white, religiously committed, and date frequently are more likely to expect to get married than those who are black, less religious, and date less frequently. These effects were observed in the Monitoring the Future analyses, are replicated here, and hold up in multivariate analyses. On the other hand, the bivariate relationships with political beliefs and living with the father, observed in the Monitoring the Future analyses and replicated here, are considerably reduced when other background factors are controlled. These reductions are most likely due to the relationships between political beliefs and religious commitment, and between living with father and race.

Now let us turn to sex role, educational, and occupational variables, and examine how they affect young women's marital expectations. The importance that young women attribute to parenting, as captured by our index, relates clearly to their expectations of getting married: Young women who place a high value on parenting are more likely to expect to get married than are young women who value parenting less highly. The importance of parenting contributes to marital plans, independently of background factors, as shown by the increase in the explained variance when sex role variables are included in the regression equations, and by the significant regression coefficient of the importance of parenting in those regressions. Preferences for egalitarian division of labor show a slight tendency for negative relationships with marital plans; the more sex-segregated the preferences, the higher the certainty of getting married. However, this effect does not contribute independently to the explanation of marital plans among young women, which is most likely due to the conceptual similarity and empirical inter-relationship between the two division of labor indices that was noted in Chapter 4.

Among young men, the patterns of relationship between importance of parenting, background characteristics and marriage expectations are mostly similar to those of females. The few exceptions are academic ability and--more central to this report--the value of occupational stability, both of which are somewhat stronger predictors among males and contribute independently to the explanation of marital plans. With regard to the latter predictor, it appears that young men who are looking for a stable and secure job are also more likely to look for stability in the relationship between the sexes by planning to get married.

Expectations to stay married to the same person are related to similar predictors as are expectations to get married in the first place, and the background factors impact at least as strongly on young men's as on young women's expectations (Table 6-4.2). Race, political orientation, religious commitment, and--among young men--academic abilities contribute clearly to the expectation of marital stability. These effects tend to replicate the findings for the Monitoring the Future data, reported above, and retain their strength when included in a multiple regression.[2]

Among the variables of central interest in this report, several show a modest relationship with expected marital stability: importance of parenting, preferences for the division of labor, college plans, occupational value of job stability, and expected competence as worker. But in the multivariate analyses

---

[2]The stronger relationships involving males' academic abilities (and also their college plans) are not, however, a replication; they may, in fact, be idiosyncratic in the Long Form sample.

all of these variables tend to be of marginal importance, as reflected by their marginal statistical significance and by the small or non-existent increase in explained variance after they have been added to the background factors in the regression equation. In other words, they add little to what can be explained by the background factors alone.

As noted in the Monitoring the Future analyses, most variation in marital plans occurs in the expected timing of this event; and the expected timing of marriage can be explained to a considerable extent by background factors. The most important findings from the analysis of the Monitoring the Future data are replicated in the analyses of the Long Form data; academic abilities and frequency of dating emerge again as the major independent predictors among the background characteristics (Table 6-4.3). Parental education--particularly mother's education--also exerts a positive influence on marital timing, although part of that effect is indirect through academic achievements.

Some sex role attitudes are also related to timing of marriage and contribute to its explanation in addition to background factors. Interestingly, the specific attitudes are not the same for young women and men. While more traditional women are more likely to expect early marriages than their less traditional female classmates, traditional sex role attitudes show no such effects for young men. Among young men it is more clearly the importance attributed to parenting that prompts some of them to desire early marriages. This difference in predictors implies that young women plan marriage in accordance with the priorities they assign to various adult roles. If they view women's roles in a traditional way--and thereby marriage and child rearing as first-order priorities--they also plan on entering the marital role sooner than if they view women's lives as consisting of a multitude of roles including the work role. Young men, on the other hand, plan the timing of marriage in accordance with their affinity to the parental role. At a second look, the two mechanisms may not be as divergent as they first appear. In both cases, plans for early marriage appear related to the importance attributed to family roles, parenting in particular among males, more general marital and family roles among females.

College plans represent another major factor in determining plans for the timing of marriage among young men and women. The effect is somewhat stronger among young women--presumably because educational activities are more likely to interfere with women's family roles than with men's. Among both sexes college plans mediate a good part of the effect of academic abilities, as shown by the decrease in strength of the ability coefficients when college plans are entered into the regression equation. At the same time, very little of the effect of sex role attitudes is mediated by college plans. In other words, able young women and men desire on the average later marriages partly because they expect to attend college, while less traditional young women and less child-oriented young men are not planning to postpone marriage to accommodate a college education but presumably because of a certain lack of interest in these roles.

Some occupational plans and attitudes are also related to the expected timing of marriage, but more strongly among young women than among young men. Particularly the centrality of the work role and the prestige of the planned occupation show clear positive relationships with marital timing, which are independent of the effects of background factors and sex role variables. The interpretation of these occupational effects are, of course, entirely consistent with the previously reported effects of sex role attitudes: the more central and demanding a work role they expect, the more likely young women are to plan on delaying marriage. However, occupational prestige does not retain an independent significant effect when all other variables are controlled. This indicates that the prestige of the aspired occupation is related to marital timing only by virtue of its association with other variables in the final regression equation (e.g., college plans).

Family Plans

As we noted in a previous section, family plans display little variance, since most of the seniors want to have children and plan on two of them, and such a limitation in variance places restrictions on the possible size of correlations. This should be born in mind when interpreting the results of the multivariate analyses to be reported below.

Still, there is some variation by background factors (Table 6-4.4). Religious commitment is positively related to the desire to have children, a relationship which replicates the findings from the Monitoring the Future analyses. More important, some sex role attitudes and preferences also display a significant impact on the desire for children. The importance of parenting is the more obvious one: young people of both sexes who attribute high importance to parenting are more likely to want children of their

own. It is somewhat less obvious that sex role
traditionality and preference for sex-segregated division of home duties contribute to the desire for
children. The effect of traditional sex role attitudes
is reduced to a non-significant level when preferences
for the division of labor are included in the regression equation, indicating that preferences mediate a
good part of the effect of sex role attitudes on desire
for children. In turn, sex role attitudes and importance of parenting appear to mediate a small part of
the effect of religious commitment as shown by the
decrease in its coefficients when sex role variables
are included along with the background factors in the
regression equation.

Among occupational variables, the value of job
stability and security exerts a weak influence on
desire for children, an effect which is partly independent of sex role and background variables.

When we turn to the actual number of children
that seniors would like to have (Table 6-4.5), we find
that the most prominent background predictor for young
women is their religious commitment, and the one for
young men is race. The effect of religious commitment
replicates the finding from the Monitoring the Future
analyses, except that in those analyses it was important for both sexes. This inconsistency cautions us
against overemphasizing the sex difference in the effect of religious commitment observed in the analysis
of the Long Form data. The differential effect of
race, on the other hand, was also noticeable in the
Monitoring the Future analyses, although at a much
weaker level, and inspires somewhat more confidence.
Therefore, we conclude that black young men desire
somewhat more children than white young men, while no
such race difference exists for young women.

Aside from these effects, the importance of
parenting emerges as a predictor in the planning of the
number of children. Young men and women who assign
higher importance to parenting are more likely to want
children, as shown before, and also to want slightly
larger numbers of them. Among females, sex role
traditionality is also positively associated with
desired number of children.

Also, the job value of stability affects males'
(and, to a slight extent, females') desired number of
children. This job value, in combination with the
values of contact with others, being able to help
others, and easy pace, explains an additional amount of
variance in males' desired number of children, above
the variance that is explained by sex role attitudes

214

and background factors. Again, then, it appears that young men who desire a stable and secure occupational situation are more family-oriented.[3]

The measure of preferred timing of first child showed no significant relationships with occupational variables. Only one of the other predictors showed a significant relationship: young men who prefer a working wife also prefer a greater-than-average delay in birth of first child. This modest relationship ($r = .15$) remains significant after controlling on other variables. (The usual table of multivariate relationships is not presented because of the lack of other significant findings, and also because some of the multivariate coefficients are unstable and potentially misleading due to a high degree of multicollinearity among some of the job attitude dimensions.)

SUMMARY

The rather dramatic changes in major family roles that have occurred in recent decades have prompted many to question the survival of the American family. The responses of young women and men who are about to assume major adult roles provide little indication for such a conclusion. Most of these young people expect to marry and hope for a stable marriage. Moreover, most of them want two or more children. Thus, the overall commitment to the institutions of marriage and family appears to be alive and well, and has shown no deterioration during the last five years. The enduring commitment to marriage does not imply, however, that the roles of the spouses have remained unchanged. As we have shown before, major changes toward more egalitarian or less-sex-segregated roles are taking place: Young women and men increasingly believe that women should participate in some form in the breadwinner role and that men should be involved in child care and housework.

The major purpose of the multivariate analyses reported here is to investigate the ways in which high school seniors' specific plans for marriage and parenthood are related to their more general sex role attitudes, their personal preferences for division of labor in the family, and their occupational aspira-

---

[3]Clearly, there is no single causal direction implied.

tions. The marital and family plans that are measured in the Monitoring the Future study--plans to get and stay married, plans to have children, the number of children expected, and the expected timing of marriage and first birth--are not critically affected by the occupational variables investigated here. Two exceptions to this generalization must be mentioned. First, young men who highly value a stable and secure job are somewhat more likely to plan on getting married and starting a family than men who are less concerned about stability and security. Second, young women who plan on attending college and who expect work to play a major role in their life prefer to delay marriage a bit longer than other young women do. This finding suggests that young women attempt to sequence roles according to their priorities: if education and work are to be important, and thus presumably require more time and effort devoted to them, marriage is expected to be postponed.

A similar interpretation can account for several of the sex role-related findings. Women who express less traditional sex role attitudes, which for them translate into higher relative importance of work, are planning on postponing marriage; young men who value parenting highly expect to get married early; young men and women who value parenting highly are more likely to want to get married, to have children and to have larger numbers of them.

These effects of family and work priorities on the choice and sequencing of roles are not mere spurious relationships due to common antecedents such as religiosity or college plans, since any potential antecedents among the background factors were controlled in the multivariate analyses. (Because the background measures served primarily as controls in the multivariate analyses, and because the Monitoring the Future findings discussed above provide much more reliable estimates, we do not dwell on the effects of the background characteristics except to say that in most respects they replicate the Monitoring the Future findings reasonably well and thus inspire confidence in the multivariate findings reported here.)

Table 6-1.1

Likelihood of Getting Married: Distributions and Trends

| | 1980 Percentage Distributions | | | | 1976-1980 Trends and Sex Differences | | | | | | |
| | | | Not | | Means | | | | | Zero-order Correlation Coefficients[1] | |
	Getting married (3)	I have no idea	getting married (2)	Already married (1)	1976	1977	1978	1979	1980	Trend	Sex
Which do you think you are most likely to choose in the long run? M: F:	73.6 81.8	20.4 12.5	5.7 3.8	0.3 2.0	2.63 2.77	2.67 2.74	2.68 2.75	2.68 2.78	2.68 2.80	.02 .03	.09

[1]For an explanation of these coefficients, see Chapter 2.

Table 6-1.2

Likelihood of Staying Married: Distributions and Trends

| | 1980 Percentage Distributions | | | | | 1976-1980 Trends and Sex Differences | | | | | | |
| | | | | | | Means | | | | | Zero-order Correlation Coefficients[1] | |
	Very likely (5)	Fairly likely (4)	Uncertain (3)	Fairly unlikely (2)	Very unlikely (1)	1976	1977	1978	1979	1980	Trend	Sex
How likely do you think it is that you would stay married to the same person for life? M:	56.7	24.6	15.5	1.7	1.6	4.35	4.34	4.33	4.41	4.33	.01	
F:	69.4	18.2	9.9	1.4	1.0	4.49	4.45	4.56	4.55	4.53	.03	.10

[1]For an explanation of these coefficients, see Chapter 2.

218

Table 6-1.3

Preferred Timing of Marriage: Distributions and Trends

		1980 Percentage Distributions					1976-1980 Trends and Sex Differences						
		Within the next year or so (1)	Two or three years from now (2)	Four or five years from now (4)	Over five years from now (6)	I don't want to marry	Means					Zero-order Correlation Coefficients[1]	
							1976	1977	1978	1979	1980	Trend	Sex
If it were just up to you, what would be the ideal time for you to get married?	M:	3.5	17.4	35.3	37.6	6.2	4.09	4.37	4.37	4.31	4.32	.03	
	F:	10.2	26.9	35.7	24.1	3.1	3.36	3.48	3.50	3.55	3.63	.03	-.23

[1]For an explanation of these coefficients, see Chapter 2.

Table 6-1.4

Preference for Having Children: Distributions and Trends

| | 1980 Percentage Distributions | | | | | | 1976-1980 Trends and Sex Differences | | | | | | |
| | | | | | | | Means | | | | | Zero-order correlation coefficients[1] | |
	Very Likely (5)	Fairly Likely (4)	Uncertain (3)	Fairly Unlikely (2)	Very Unlikely (1)	Already have children	1976	1977	1978	1979	1980	Trend	Sex
How likely is it that you would want to have children? M:	58.7	24.4	11.8	2.3	2.5	0.3	4.32	4.27	4.32	4.32	4.35	.02	-.02
F:	60.6	17.0	12.7	3.2	3.7	2.9	4.27	4.20	4.27	4.29	4.32	.02	

[1]For an explanation of these coefficients, see Chapter 2.

Table 6-1.5

Preferred Number of Children: Distributions and Trends

	1980 Percentage Distributions								1976-1980 Trends and Sex Differences						
	None (0)	One (1)	Two (2)	Three (3)	Four (4)	Five (5)	Six or more (6)	Don't know	Means					Zero-order correlation coefficients[1]	
									1976	1977	1978	1979	1980	Trend	Sex
All things considered, if you could have exactly the number of children you want, what number would you choose to have? M:	4.6	5.0	42.7	21.2	10.4	2.9	2.6	10.6	2.58	2.48	2.58	2.54	2.53	-.01	
F:	4.1	4.3	45.5	20.5	13.3	2.4	3.5	6.5	2.68	2.73	2.76	2.63	2.60	-.03	.06

[1]For an explanation of these coefficients, see Chapter 2.

Table 6-1.6

Preferred Timing of First Child: Distributions and Trends

	1980 Percentage Distributions								1976-1980 Trends and Sex Differences					Zero-order correlation coefficients[1]	
									Means						
	Don't want child	Would not wait at all (0)	Would wait 1 year (1)	Would wait 2 years (2)	Would wait 3 years (3)	Would wait 4 or 5 years (4)	Would wait 5+ years (6)	DK or already have a child	1976	1977	1978	1979	1980	Trend	Sex
If it were just up to you how soon after getting married would you want to have your first child? M:	5.3	5.7	28.7	28.0	12.0	6.5	1.9	11.9	1.93	1.90	1.90	1.90	1.91	.00	.14
F:	4.4	1.6	22.4	36.7	16.4	10.4	1.8	6.1	2.26	2.26	2.19	2.24	2.21	-.01	

[1]For an explanation of these coefficients, see Chapter 2.

222

Table 6-2

Marital and Family Plans: Effects of Background Characteristics

			Live with Mother	Live with Father	Mother Worked	Father Educ.	Mother Educ.	Urbani-city	Acad. Ability	Grades	Coll. Plans	Polit. Orient.	Relig. Commit.	Dating Freq.	Multiple Correlation Coefficients
		Race													
Marital Plans															
Think will get married	M:	-.13	.06	.07	-.03	.02	.03	.02	.10	.11	.09	-.09	.16	.14	.28
	F:	-.17	.03	.10	-.07	.05	.03	.00	.08	.09	-.01	-.14	.11	.15	.29
Likely to stay married	M:	-.09	.07	.09	-.05	.02	.04	-.03	.07	.12	.06	-.11	.25	.08	.31
	F:	-.17	.04	.14	-.09	.01	-.01	-.06	.09	.13	-.01	-.15	.22	.09	.34
When want to get married	M:	.05	.01	-.02	.01	.19	.17	.21	.17	.12	.27	.09	-.07	-.21	.40
	F:	.06	.04	-.01	-.03	.23	.22	.21	.22	.14	.44	.07	-.02	-.31	.54
Family Plans															
Likely to have children	M:	.03	.04	.00	.01	-.02	-.01	.02	.03	.05	.07	-.09	.16	.09	.21
	F:	-.04	.03	.06	-.06	.01	.01	.03	-.02	.00	.00	-.10	.15	.08	.21
Number of children want	M:	.10	.00	-.02	-.02	.00	.00	.04	.03	.03	.08	-.03	.18	.01	.21
	F:	-.04	.04	.04	-.06	.03	.02	.07	-.01	-.01	.05	-.05	.17	.01	.21
When want first child	M:	-.11	.01	.01	-.02	.08	.07	-.02	.06	.08	.03	.02	-.04	.05	.16
	F:	-.09	.00	-.01	.00	.06	.06	-.01	.08	.08	.04	.04	-.07	.11	.18

Zero-Order Correlation Coefficients

Table 6-3

Interrelationships Between Marital and Family Plans

		Think will marry	Likely stay married	When married	Likely have children	Number of children	When 1st child
Think will marry	M:		.35		.36		
	F:		.36		.40		
Likely stay married	M:	.43			.33		
	F:	.45			.30		
When married	M:	-.23	-.15			.00	.08
	F:	-.34	-.26			-.04	.06
Likely have children	M:	.29	.28	-.09			
	F:	.41	.38	-.22			
Number of children	M:	.21	.13	.00	.46		-.20
	F:	.21	.19	-.03	.41		-.23
When 1st child	M:	-.02	.05	.00	-.27	-.16	
	F:	-.01	-.03	.03	-.23	-.16	

Note: Above the diagonal are product-moment correlations for MtF data; below diagonal for Long Form data.

224

Table 6-4.1

Likelihood of Getting Married: Effects of Predictors

Predictor		Bivariate Coefficients[1]	Multivariate Coefficients[2]							
Race	M:	-.14*	-.09	-.09	-.09	-.09	-.12	-.10	-.10	-.13
	F:	-.19*	-.16*	-.18*	-.19*	-.17*	-.17*	-.18*	-.18*	-.19*
Live with Father	M:	.18*	.10	.12	.12	.12	.10	.12	.12	.10
	F:	.16*	.10	.09	.09	.09	.09	.09	.09	.08
Acad. Ability Comp.	M:	.17*	.13	.10	.11	.14	.13	.14	.12	.15
	F:	.08	.04	.06	.07	.06	.08	.07	.06	.08
Political Orient.	M:	-.10	-.09	-.07	-.07	-.08	-.05	-.08	-.07	-.06
	F:	-.12	-.08	-.07	-.06	-.07	-.06	-.07	-.07	-.06
Religious Commit.	M:	.15*	.11	.10	.10	.11	.08	.12	.10	.10
	F:	.18*	.16*	.13*	.12	.13*	.14*	.14*	.13*	.14*
Dating Frequency	M:	.06	.07	.06	.06	.06	.08	.05	.06	.07
	F:	.15*	.15*	.14*	.13*	.14*	.13*	.13*	.14*	.12*
Trad. Sex Role Att.	M:	-.09		-.08	-.09	-.10	-.10	-.07	-.09	-.09
	F:	.05		.04	-.01	.04	.03	.02	.04	-.02
Equal Opp. Attitudes	M:	.08		.01	.01	.00	.01	.02	.01	.02
	F:	.02		.02	.03	.02	.03	.02	.02	.03
Parenting Attitudes	M:	.13		.10	.10	.09	.12	.09	.09	.10
	F:	.16*		.14*	.15*	.14*	.15*	.14*	.14*	.16*
Pref. Div. Paid Work	M:	-.05			-.01					-.02
	F:	-.10			.00					.00
Pref. Div. Home Duties	M:	.09			-.02					.01
	F:	-.08			-.12					-.11
College Plans	M:	.04				-.09				-.06
	F:	.00				-.02				-.00
Occ.Val: Status	M:	-.03					.04			.07
	F:	.02					.06			.04
Occ.Val: Stabil.	M:	.14*					.20*			.19*
	F:	.07					-.01			-.02
Occ.Val: Respon.	M:	-.11					-.14			-.14
	F:	-.07					-.07			-.06
Occ.Val: Easy Pace	M:	-.04					-.05			-.08
	F:	-.01					.00			.00
Occ.Val: Stimul.	M:	.00					-.10			-.11
	F:	.01					-.03			.00
Occ.Val: Altruism	M:	.04					.10			.12
	F:	-.01					-.06			-.05
Occ.Val: Contact	M:	-.07					-.13			-.14
	F:	.03					.03			.02
Job Centrality	M:	-.01						-.10		-.08
	F:	-.07						-.11		-.07
Perc. Sex Discrim.	M:	.05						.07		.08
	F:	.00						.01		.03
Personal Compet.	M:	.03						.00		.03
	F:	.06						.06		.06
Occ. Prestige	M:	.08							-.04	.05
	F:	.01							.00	.03
R (adj.)	M:		.24	.24	.22	.24	.30	.24	.23	.27
	F:		.30	.32	.32	.31	.29	.32	.31	.27
R² (adj.)	M:		.06	.06	.05	.06	.09	.06	.05	.07
	F:		.09	.10	.10	.10	.08	.10	.10	.08

Note: *p < .05

[1] Entries are zero-order correlation coefficients.

[2] Entries are standardized regression coefficients.

Table 6-4.2

Likelihood of Staying Married: Effects of Predictors

		Bivariate Coefficients[1]	Multivariate Coefficients[2]							
Race	M:	-.17*	-.14	-.14*	-.14*	-.14*	-.15*	-.16*	-.15*	-.18*
	F:	-.18*	-.16*	-.19*	-.20*	-.19*	-.17*	-.19*	-.19*	-.19*
Live with Father	M:	.17*	.03	.04	.04	.03	.03	.03	.04	.01
	F:	.17*	.08	.08	.08	.08	.09	.08	.08	.08
Acad. Ability Comp.	M:	.24*	.19*	.17*	.17*	.15*	.18*	.17*	.21*	.18*
	F:	.09	.04	.08	.10	.08	.09	.08	.08	.08
Political Orient.	M:	-.21*	-.20*	-.19*	-.19*	-.18*	-.18*	-.19*	-.19*	-.18*
	F:	-.22*	-.17*	-.15*	-.14*	-.15*	-.13*	-.15*	-.15*	-.13*
Religious Commit.	M:	.29*	.24*	.23*	.23*	.22*	.21*	.24*	.24*	.22*
	F:	.23*	.18*	.15*	.14*	.15*	.14*	.15*	.15*	.14*
Trad. Sex Role Att.	M:	-.04		-.04	-.03	-.02	-.04	-.02	-.05	-.03
	F:	.11		.10	.04	.10	.08	.08	.10	.03
Equal Opp. Attitudes	M:	.08		.00	.00	.01	.00	.01	.01	.02
	F:	-.04		-.01	.00	-.01	-.02	-.01	-.01	-.02
Parenting Attitudes	M:	.13		.05	.05	.06	.05	.03	.05	.01
	F:	.15*		.11	.12	.11	.11	.10	.11	.11
Pref. Div. Paid Work	M:	-.07		-.01						-.02
	F:	-.13*		.00						-.01
Pref. Div. Home Duties	M:	.12		.00						.00
	F:	-.13*		-.13						-.10
College Plans	M:	.20*				.06				.11
	F:	.03				.00				.01
Occ. Val: Status	M:	.01					.02			.01
	F:	-.01					.00			-.03
Occ.Val: Stabil.	M:	.12					.14			.14
	F:	.15*					.15*			.13
Occ.Val: Respon.	M:	-.01					-.05			-.05
	F:	-.02					.03			.05
Occ.Val: Easy Pace	M:	-.03					-.06			-.06
	F:	-.07					-.10			-.10
Occ.Val: Stimul.	M:	.05					-.15			-.13
	F:	.02					-.03			-.01
Occ.Val: Altruism	M:	.14*					.15			.16
	F:	-.01					-.11			-.10
Occ.Val: Contact	M:	.04					.00			-.04
	F:	.05					.07			.06
Job Centrality	M:	.09						-.05		-.05
	F:	-.06						-.10		-.10
Perc. Sex Discrim.	M:	-.02						.05		.06
	F:	-.04						-.04		-.03
Personal Compet.	M:	.17*						.13		.15*
	F:	.11						.11		.11
Occ. Prestige	M:	.11							-.08	-.12
	F:	.01							.00	.01
R (adj.)	M:		.40	.39	.38	.39	.39	.40	.39	.40
	F:		.33	.35	.35	.34	.35	.36	.34	.35
R² (adj.)	M:		.16	.15	.14	.15	.15	.16	.15	.16
	F:		.11	.12	.13	.12	.12	.13	.12	.12

Note: *p < .05

[1] Entries are zero-order correlation coefficients.

[2] Entries are standardized regression coefficients.

Table 6-4.3

Preferred Timing of Marriage: Effects of Predictors

		Bivariate Coefficients[1]	Multivariate Coefficients[2]							
Father's Education	M:	.04	-.04	-.06	-.05	-.09	-.08	-.06	-.06	-.09
	F:	.11	.03	.03	.03	-.01	.02	.03	.00	-.01
Mother's Education	M:	.12	.10	.11	.11	.10	.12	.11	.11	.11
	F:	.19*	.15*	.12	.12	.07	.11	.11	.11	.08
Urbanicity	M:	-.03	-.04	-.05	-.04	-.06	-.05	-.05	-.05	-.05
	F:	.01	.01	.02	.02	.04	.03	.02	.02	.04
Acad. Abilit. Comp.	M:	.20*	.16*	.18*	.19*	.11	.18*	.15	.16	.12
	F:	.19*	.14*	.08	.08	.00	.04	.03	.03	-.05
Dating Frequency	M:	-.32*	-.31*	-.29*	-.29*	-.28*	-.31*	-.29*	-.29*	-.29*
	F:	-.31*	-.31*	-.30*	-.31*	-.28*	-.29*	-.30*	-.30*	-.27*
Trad. Sex Role Att.	M:	-.04		.01	-.02	.04	.03	.01	.02	.01
	F:	-.29*		-.21*	-.19*	-.19*	-.17*	-.18*	-.19*	-.15
Equal Opp. Attitudes	M:	.03		-.01	.01	.00	-.02	-.02	-.01	.00
	F:	.13*		.01	.01	.02	.01	.01	.02	.03
Parenting Attitudes	M:	-.20*		-.19*	-.17*	-.19*	-.20*	-.20*	-.19*	-.18*
	F:	-.13*		-.07	-.07	-.07	-.08	-.08	-.07	-.08
Pref. Div. Paid Work	M:	.04			.01					.04
	F:	.10			.03					-.02
Pref. Div. Home Duties	M:	-.08			-.10					-.13
	F:	.18*			.03					.00
College Plans	M:	.25*				.20*				.21*
	F:	.37*				.29*				.24*
Occ.Val: Status	M:	-.02					-.08			-.15
	F:	.02					-.03			-.01
Occ.Val: Stabil.	M:	-.10					-.11			-.09
	F:	-.08					-.14*			-.13
Occ.Val: Respon.	M:	.04					.10			.08
	F:	.20*					.08			.00
Occ.Val: Easy Pace	M:	-.02					.08			.12
	F:	.00					.00			.05
Occ.Val: Stimul.	M:	.00					.08			.12
	F:	.18*					.12			.11
Occ.Val: Altruism	M:	-.05					-.05			-.08
	F:	.17*					.10			.04
Occ.Val: Contact	M:	-.01					.02			.01
	F:	.10					-.03			-.03
Job Centrality	M:	.16*						.09		.11
	F:	.28*						.20*		.14*
Perc. Sex Discrim.	M:	-.08						-.01		-.02
	F:	.04						.00		-.03
Personal Compet.	M:	.03						.03		.03
	F:	.10						.05		.04
Occ. Prestige	M:	.17*							.06	-.07
	F:	.25*							.16*	.03
R (adj.)	M:		.35	.38	.38	.41	.36	.37	.38	.39
	F:		.37	.43	.42	.50	.45	.46	.45	.50
R² (adj.)	M:		.12	.14	.14	.17	.13	.14	.14	.15
	F:		.14	.18	.18	.25	.20	.21	.20	.25

Note: *p < .05

[1] Entries are zero-order correlation coefficients.

[2] Entries are standardized regression coefficients.

Table 6-4.4

Preference for Having Children: Effects of Predictors

		Bivariate Coefficients[1]	Multivariate Coefficients[2]							
Political Orient.	M:	-.02	-.01	.03	.01	.03	.03	.02	.03	.01
	F:	-.12	-.08	-.05	-.05	-.06	-.04	-.05	-.05	-.04
Religious Commit.	M:	.16*	.16*	.12	.13	.12	.11	.14*	.12	.12
	F:	.19*	.17*	.13*	.12*	.14*	.11	.13*	.13*	.11
Trad. Sex Role Att.	M:	.14*		.12	.04	.12	.11	.12	.13	.06
	F:	.14*		.09	.02	.08	.10	.09	.09	.04
Equal Opp. Attitudes	M:	-.03		-.02	.01	-.02	.00	.00	-.02	.02
	F:	-.02		.06	.07	.06	.04	.07	.06	.06
Parenting Attitudes	M:	.20*		.18*	.19*	.18*	.16*	.17*	.18*	.18*
	F:	.30*		.25*	.25*	.25*	.24*	.25*	.25*	.24*
Pref. Div. Paid Work	M:	-.08		-.04						-.04
	F:	-.13*		-.04						-.03
Pref. Div. Home Duties	M:	-.15*		-.17*						-.15
	F:	-.15*		-.12						-.10
College Plans	M:	.03			.03					.03
	F:	-.04			-.05					-.06
Occ.Val: Status	M:	.10					.06			.04
	F:	.02					-.04			-.04
Occ.Val: Stabil.	M:	.18*					.17			.16
	F:	.15*					.11			.09
Occ.Val: Respon.	M:	.00					-.10			-.10
	F:	.00					.00			.02
Occ.Val: Easy Pace	M:	.08					.03			.00
	F:	.00					-.06			-.05
Occ.Val: Stimul.	M:	.05					-.21			-.19
	F:	.06					-.05			-.03
Occ.Val: Altruism	M:	.13					.10			.12
	F:	.09					.02			.01
Occ.Val: Contact	M:	.09					.08			.08
	F:	.09					.09			.08
Job Centrality	M:	-.07						-.10		-.10
	F:	.01						.00		.00
Perc. Sex Discrim.	M:	.01						.02		.02
	F:	-.08						-.08		-.06
Personal Compet.	M:	.05						.02		.01
	F:	.06						.04		.04
Occ. Prestige	M:	.02							.04	.06
	F:	-.01							.00	.02
R (adj.)	M:		.13	.22	.25	.21	.24	.21	.21	.24
	F:		.18	.31	.32	.31	.30	.31	.31	.28
R² (adj.)	M:		.02	.05	.06	.05	.06	.04	.05	.06
	F:		.03	.10	.10	.10	.09	.10	.09	.08

Note: *p < .05

[1] Entries are zero-order correlation coefficients.

[2] Entries are standardized regression coefficients.

Table 6-4.5

Preferred Number of Children: Effects of Predictors

Predictor		Bivariate Coefficients[1]	Multivariate Coefficients[2] (1)	(2)	(3)	(4)	(5)	(6)	(7)	(8)
Race	M:	.20*	.20*	.19*	.18*	.19*	.20*	.19*	.20*	.20*
	F:	-.03	-.04	-.06	-.03	-.08	-.06	-.07	-.07	-.04
Religious Commit.	M:	.07	.07	.04	.05	.02	.04	.04	.02	.00
	F:	.21*	.21*	.17*	.18*	.14*	.15*	.17*	.16*	.13*
Trad. Sex Role Att.	M:	.05		.03	.05	.04	.02	.05	.05	.05
	F:	.13*		.10	.10	.13	.13	.10	.12	.14
Equal Opp. Attitudes	M:	-.02		-.01	.00	-.01	-.02	-.01	-.02	-.02
	F:	-.02		.05	.03	.04	.03	.04	.04	.02
Parenting Attitudes	F:	.14*		.12	.13	.13	.05	.12	.13	.09
	F:	.22*		.18*	.16*	.19*	.16*	.18*	.18*	.14*
Pref. Div. Paid Work	M:	.03		.01						.03
	F:	-.17*		-.10						-.08
Pref. Div. Home Duties	M:	-.07		-.06						-.06
	F:	.01		.09						.08
College Plans	M:	.08				.10				.08
	F:	.15*				.16*				.16*
Occ.Val: Status	M:	.12					-.07			-.10
	F:	-.02					-.17*			-.15
Occ.Val: Stabil.	M:	.21*					.16			.16
	F:	.12					.07			.08
Occ.Val: Respon.	M:	.03					-.14			-.15
	F:	.07					.07			.04
Occ.Val: Easy Pace	M:	.17*					.13			.14
	F:	.05					.03			.02
Occ.Val: Stimul.	M:	.13					-.06			-.07
	F:	.11					.11			.09
Occ.Val: Altruism	M:	.18*					.13			.13
	F:	.11					.05			.05
Occ.Val: Contact	M:	.14*					.12			.11
	F:	.05					-.06			-.04
Job Centrality	M:	-.01						-.01		-.01
	F:	-.01						-.02		-.08
Perc. Sex Discrim.	M:	-.05							-.06	-.06
	F:	-.01							-.01	-.03
Personal Compet.	M:	.07							.02	.00
	F:	.05							.04	.04
Occ. Prestige	M:	.07							.11	.07
	F:	.07							.08	-.02
R (adj.)	M:		.18	.18	.16	.19	.27	.15	.20	.23
	F:		.19	.27	.28	.30	.27	.25	.27	.28
R² (adj.)	M:		.03	.03	.03	.04	.07	.02	.04	.06
	F:		.04	.07	.08	.09	.07	.06	.08	.08

Note: *p < .05

[1] Entries are zero-order correlation coefficients.

[2] Entries are standardized regression coefficients.

REFERENCES

Alexander, K. L., & Eckland, B. K. Sex differences in
    the educational attainment process. American
    Sociological Review, 1974, 39, 668-682.

Allgeier, E. R. Beyond sowing and growing: The
    relationship of sex-typing to socialization,
    family plans, and future orientation. Journal
    of Applied Social Psychology, 1975, 5, 217-226.

Aneshensel, C. S., & Rosen, B. C. Domestic roles and
    sex differences in occupational expectations.
    Journal of Marriage and the Family, 1980, 42,
    121-131.

Angrist, S. S., Mickelsen, R., & Penna, A. N. Sex dif-
    ferences in sex-role conceptions and family
    orientation of high school students. Journal
    of Youth and Adolescence, 1977, 6, 179-186.

Bachman, J. G., & Johnston, L. D. The Monitoring the
    Future project: Design and procedures
    (Monitoring the Future Occasional Paper 1).
    Ann Arbor, MI: The Institute for Social
    Research, 1978.

Bachman, J. G., Johnston, L. D. & O'Malley, P. M.
    Monitoring the Future: Questionnaire responses
    from the nation's high school seniors, 1980.
    Ann Arbor, MI: The Institute for Social
    Research, 1981.

Bachman, J. G., & Johnston, L. D. Fewer rebels, fewer
    causes. (Monitoring the Future Occasional
    Paper 4). Ann Arbor, MI: The Institute for
    Social Research, 1979.

Bayer, A. E. Marriage plans and educational aspira-
    tions. American Journal of Sociology, 1969,
    75, 239-244. (a)

Bayer, A. E. Life plans and marriage age: An applica-
    tion of path analysis. Journal of Marriage and
    the Family, 1969, 31, 551-558. (b)

Bayer, A. E. Sexist students in American colleges: A descriptive note. Journal of Marriage and the Family, 1975, 37, 391-397.

Bednarzik, R. W., & Klein, D. P. Labor force trends: A synthesis and analysis. Monthly Labor Review, 1977, 100, 3-11.

Bernard, J. Women and the public interest: An essay on policy and protest. Chicago: Aldine-Atherton, 1971.

Bernard, J. Women, wives, mothers. Chicago: Aldine, 1975.

Blau, F. D., & Hendricks, W. E. Occupational segregation by sex: Trends and prospects. The Journal of Human Resources, 1979, 14, 197-210.

Blau, F., & C. L. Jusenius. Economists' approaches to sex segregation in the labor market: An appraisal. Sigus, 1976, 1(suppl.), 181-199.

Blood, R. O., & Hamblin, R. L. The effect of the wife's employment on the family power structure. Social Forces, 1958, 36, 347-352.

Blood, R. O., & Wolfe, D. M. Husbands and wives. New York: Free Press, 1960.

Bowen, W. G., & Finegan, T. A. The economics of labor force participation. Princeton, NJ: Princeton University Press, 1969.

Brackbill, Y., and Howell, E. M. Religious differences in family size among American teenagers. Sociological Analysis, 1974, 35, 35-44.

Brim, O. G. Adult socialization. In J. A. Clausen (Ed.), Socialization and society. Boston: Little, Brown, & Co., 1968.

Bush, D. E., Simmons, R. G., Hutchinson, B., & Blyth, D. A. Adolescent perception of sex roles in 1968 and 1975. Public Opinion Quarterly, 1977-1978, 41, 459-474.

Cramer, J. C. Fertility and female employment: Problems of causal direction. American Sociological Review, 1980, 45, 167-190.

Christensen, H. T. Lifetime family and occupational role projections of high school students. Marriage and Family Living, 1961, 23, 181-183.

Davis, H. Employment gains of women by industry, 1968-78. Monthly Labor Review, 1980, 103, 3-9.

Duncan, O. D., & Duncan, B. Residential distribution and occupational stratification. American Journal of Sociology, 1955, 60, 493-503.

Dunn, M. S. Marriage role expectations of adolescents. Marriage and Family Living, 1960, 22, 99-111.

Eagly, A. H., & Anderson, P. Sex role and attitudinal correlates of desired family size. Journal of Applied Social Psychology, 1974, 4, 151-164.

Ericksen, J. A., Yancey, W. L., & Ericksen, E. P. The division of family roles. Journal of Marriage and the Family, 1979, 41, 301-313.

Falbo, T., Graham, J. S., & Gryskiewicz, S. S. Sex roles and fertility in college women. Sex Roles, 1978, 4, 845-851.

Farkas, G. Cohort, Age and period effects upon the employment of white females: Evidence for 1957-1968. Demography, 1977, 14, 33-42.

Farley, J. Graduate women: Career aspirations and desired family size. American Psychologist, 1970, 25, 1099-1100.

Featherman, D. L., & Carter, T. M. Discontinuties in schooling and the socioeconomic life cycle. In W. Sewell, R. M. Hauser, and D. L. Featherman (Eds.), Schooling and achievement in American society. New York: Academic Press, 1976.

Featherman, D. L., & Hauser, R. M. Sexual inequalities and socioeconomic achievement in the U. S., 1962-1973. American Sociological Review, 1976, 41, 462-483.

Ferree, M. M. A woman for president. Public Opinion Quarterly, 1974, 38, 390-391.

Fuchs, V. R. Differences in hourly earnings between men and women. Monthly Labor Review, 1971, 94, 10-14.

Garrison, H. H. Gender differences in the career aspirations of recent cohorts of high school seniors. Social Problems, 1979, 27, 170-184.

Gaskell, J. Sex-role ideology and the aspirations of high-school girls. <u>Interchange</u>, 1977-1978, <u>8</u>, 43-53.

Glick, P. C. Updating the life cycle of the family. <u>Journal of Marriage and the Family</u>, 1977, <u>39</u>, 3-15.

Glick, P. C. <u>The future of the American family</u>. Current Population Reports, Series P-23, No. 78. Washington, D.C.: U.S. Government Printing Office, 1979.

Glick, P. C. & Norton, A. J. Marrying, divorcing, and living together in the U.S. today. <u>Population Bulletin</u>, 1977, <u>32</u>.

Golladay, M. <u>The condition of education</u>. National Center for Education Statistics, Washington, D.C.: U.S. Government Printing Office, 1976.

Golladay, M. <u>The condition of education</u>. National Center for Education Statistics, Volume 3, Part 1. Washington, D.C.: U.S. Government Printing Office, 1977.

Gottfredson, L. S. <u>Race and sex differences in occupational aspirations: Their development and consequences for occupational segregation</u>. Report No. 254, Center for Social Organization of Schools, Baltimore, MD: The John Hopkins University, 1978.

Gottlieb, D. <u>Youth and the meaning of work</u>. Report prepared for Manpower Administration, U.S. Department of Labor. Springfield, VA: National Technical Information Service, 1973.

Gustavus, S. The family size preference of young people: A replication and longitudinal follow-up study. <u>Studies in Family Planning</u>, 1973, <u>4</u>, 335-342.

Gustavus, S. O., & Nam, C. B. The formation and stability of ideal family size among young people. <u>Demography</u>, 1970, <u>7</u>, 43-51.

Hartley, R. E. Children's concepts of male and female roles. <u>Merrill-Palmer Quarterly</u>, 1959-1960, <u>6</u>, 83-92.

Hartley, R. E. A developmental view of female sex-role definition and identification. <u>Merrill-Palmer Quarterly</u>, 1964, <u>10</u>, 3-16.

Hershey, M. R., & Sullivan, J. L. Sex role attitudes, identities, and political ideology. Sex Roles, 1977, 3, 37-57.

Herzog, A. R. High school seniors' plans and values: Trends in sex differences 1976 through 1980. Sociology of Education, 1982, 55, 1-13.

Herzog, A. R., & Bachman, J. G. Description of a special survey using a single combined form of the Monitoring the Future questionnaire (Monitoring the Future Occasional Paper Series No. 6). Ann Arbor, MI: The Institute for Social Research, 1979.

Herzog, A. R., Bachman, J. G. & Johnston, L. D. High school seniors' preferences for sharing work and family responsibilities between husband and wife (Monitoring the Future Occasional Paper Series No. 3). Ann Arbor, MI: The Institute for Social Research, 1979.

Herzog, A. R., & Bachman, J. G. Effects of questionnaire length on response quality. Public Opinion Quarterly, 1981, 45, 549-559.

Hoffman, L. W., & Nye, F. I. Working mothers. San Francisco, CA: Jossey-Bass, 1974.

Holmstrom, L. L. The two-career family. Cambridge, MA: Schenkman, 1972.

Hout, M., & Morgan, W. R. Race and sex variations in the causes of the expected attainments of high school seniors. American Journal of Sociology, 1975, 81, 364-394.

Kagan, J., & Moss, H. A. Birth to Maturity. New York: Wiley, 1962.

Kanter, R. M. Work and family in the United States: A critical review and agenda for research and policy. New York: Russell Sage Foundation, 1977.

Kellerman, J., & Katz, E. R. Attitudes toward the devision of child rearing responsibility. Sex Roles, 1978, 4, 505-512.

Kohlberg, L. A. A cognitive developmental analysis of children's sex-role concepts and attitudes. In E. Maccoby (Ed.), The development of sex differences. Stanford, CA: Stanford University Press, 1966.

Kreps, J. _Sex in the marketplace: American women at work_. Baltimore: John Hopkins University Press, 1971.

Kuvlesky, W. P., & Obordo, A. S. A racial comparison of teen-age girls' projections for marriage and procreation. _Journal of Marriage and the Family_, 1972, _34_, 75-84.

Laws, J. L. Work aspirations of women: False leads and new starts. In M. Blaxall and B. Regan (Eds.), _Women and the workplace_. Chicago, IL: University of Chicago Press, 1976.

Lipman-Blumen, J. How ideology shapes women's lives. _Scientific American_, 1972, _266_, 34-42.

Lipman-Blumen, J., & Tickamyer, A. R. Sex roles in transition: A ten-year perspective. In A. Inkeles, J. Coleman, & N. Smelser (Eds.), _Annual review of sociology_. Palo Alto, CA: Annual Reviews, Inc., Vol. 1, 1975.

Lueptow, L. B. Social change and sex-role change in adolescent orientations toward life, work, and achievement: 1964-1975. _Social Psychology Quarterly_, 1980, _43_, 48-59.

Maccoby, E. E., & Jacklin, C. N. _The psychology of sex differences_. Stanford, CA: Stanford University Press, 1974.

Macke, A. S., & Morgan, W. R. Maternal employment, race, and work orientation of high school girls. _Social Forces_, 1978, _57_, 187-204.

Marini, M. M. The transition to adulthood: Sex differences in educational attainment and age at marriage. _American Sociological Review_, 1978, _43_, 483-507. (b)

Marini, M. M. Sex differences in the determination of adolescent aspirations: A review of research. _Sex Roles_, 1978, _4_, 723-753. (a)

Marini, M. M. Sex differences in the process of occupational attainment: A closer look. _Social Science Research_, 1980, _9_, 307-361.

Marini, M. M., & Greenberger, E. Sex differences in educational aspirations and expectations. _American Educational Research Journal_, 1978, _15_, 67-79. (a)

Marini, M. M., & Greenberger, E. Sex differences in occupational aspirations and expectations. Sociology of Work and Occupations, 1978, 5, 147-178. (b)

Mason, K. O. & Bumpass, L. L. U.S. women's sex-role ideology, 1970. American Journal of Sociology, 1975, 80, 1212-1219.

Mason, K. O., Czajka, J. L., & Arber, S. Change in U.S. women's sex role attitudes, 1964-1974. American Sociological Review, 1976, 41, 573-596.

McClendon, J. J. The occupational status attainment process of males and females. American Sociological Review, 1976, 41, 52-64.

McLaughlin, S. Expected family size and perceived status deprivation among high school senior women. Demography, 1974, 11, 57-73.

Meissner, M., Humphreys, E. W., Meis, S. M., & Scheu, W. J. No exit for wives: Sexual division of labour and the cumulation of household demands. Canadian Review of Sociology and Anthropology, 1975, 12, 424-439.

Nelson, H. Y., & Goldman, P. R. Attitudes of high school students and young adults toward the gainful employment of married women. The Family Coordinator, 1969, 18, 251-255.

Oaxaca, R. Sex discrimination in wages. In Ashenfelter, O., and A. Rees (Eds.), Discrimination in labor markets. Princeton, NJ: Princeton University, 1973.

Oppenheimer, V. K. The sex-labeling of jobs. Industrial Relations, 1968, 7, 219-234.

Orcutt, J. D., & Bayer, A. E. Student protest and sex role attitude change, 1967-1971: a log-linear analysis of longitudinal data. Sex Roles, 1978, 4, 267-280.

Osmond, M. W., & Martin, P. Y. Sex and sexism: a comparison of male and female sex-role attitudes. Journal of Marriage and the Family, 1975, 37, 744-758.

Otto, L. B., & Haller, A. O. Evidence for a social psychological view of the status attainment process: Four studies compared. <u>Social Forces</u>, 1979, <u>57</u>, 887-914.

Otto, L. B. Antecedents and consequences of marital timing. In W. R. Burr, R. Hill, F. I. Nye, and I. L. Reiss (Eds.), <u>Contemporary theories about the family</u>. New York: Free Press, 1979.

Parelius, A. P. Emerging sex-role attitudes, expectations, and strains among college women. <u>Journal of Marriage and the Family</u>, 1975, <u>37</u>, 146-153.

Parsons, T., & Bales, R. F. (Eds.). <u>Family socialization and interaction process</u>. Glencoe, IL: The Free Press, 1955.

Paterson, N. Adolescent family size preferences. <u>International Journal of Sociology of the Family</u>, 1972, <u>2</u>, 231-245.

Payne, R. Adolescents' attitudes toward the working wife. <u>Marriage and Family Living</u>, 1956, <u>18</u>, 345-348.

Pleck, J. H. <u>Men's two roles in the family: Housework and child care</u>. Unpublished manuscript, 1976.

Pleck, J. H. The work-family role system. <u>Social Problems</u>, 1977, <u>24</u>, 417-427.

Psathas, G. Toward a theory of occupational choice for women. <u>Sociology and Social Research</u>, 1968, <u>52</u>, 253-268.

Quinn, R. P., & Staines, G. L. <u>The 1977 Quality of Employment survey</u>. Ann Arbor, MI: Survey Research Center, 1979.

Rainwater, L. <u>Family design</u>. Chicago: Aldine, 1965.

Rebecca, M., Hefner, R., & Oleshansky, B. A model of sex-role transcendence. <u>Journal of Social Issues</u>, 1976, <u>32</u>, 197-206.

Robinson, J. P. <u>How Americans use time</u>. New York: Praeger, 1977.

Rosen, B. C., & Aneshensel, C. S. Sex differences in the educational-occupational expectation process. <u>Social Forces</u>, 1978, <u>57</u>, 164-186.

Rosenfeld, R. A. Women's employment patterns and occupational achievements. Social Science
Research, 1978, 7, 61-80.

Rosenfeld, R. A., & Sorensen, A. B. Sex differences in
patterns of career mobility. Demography, 1979,
16, 89-101.

Safilios-Rothschild, C. Sex role socialization and sex
discrimination: A synthesis and critique of the
literature. Final report to the National Institute of Education, U.S. Department of
Health, Education and Welfare. Washington,
D.C.: U.S. Government Printing Office, 1979.

Scanzoni, J. H. The black family in modern society.
Boston, Mass.: Allyn and Bacon, 1971.

Scanzoni, J. Sex role change and influences on birth
intentions. Journal of Marriage and the Family, 1976, 38, 43-58.

Scanzoni, J., & Fox, G. L. Sex roles, family, and
society: The seventies and beyond. Journal of
Marriage and the Family, 1980, 42, 743-756.

Sewell, W. H. Inequality of opportunity for higher
education. American Sociological Review, 1971,
36, 793-809.

Sewell, W. H., & Hauser, R. M. Education, occupation
and earnings: Achievement in the early career.
New York: Academic Press, 1975.

Sewell, W. H., Hauser, R. M., & Wolf, W. C. Sex,
schooling, and occupational status. American
Journal of Sociology, 1980, 86, 551-583.

Sewell, W. H., & Shah, V. P. Socioeconomic status, intelligence, and the attainment of higher education. Sociology of Education, 1967, 40, 1-23.

Sewell, W. H., & Shah, V. P. Parents' education and
children's educational aspirations and achievements. American Sociological Review, 1968, 33,
191-209.

Shapiro, D., & Carr, T. J. Investments in human capi-
tal and the earnings of young women. In
F. Mott (Ed.), Years for decision, Vol. 4. U.S.
Department of Labor, R & D Monograph 24.
Washington, D.C.: U.S. Government Printing Of-
fice, 1978.

Shea, J. R., Roderick, R. D., Zeller, F. A., & Kohen, A. I. Years for decision. Vol. I. Columbus, Ohio: The Ohio State University, 1971.

Simmons, A. B., & Turner, J. E. The socialization of sex-roles and fertility ideals: A study of two generations in Toronto. Journal of Comparative Family Studies, 1976, 7, 255-271.

Smith, R. E. The movement of women into the labor force. In R. E. Smith (Ed.), The Subtle Revolution. Washington, D.C.: The Urban Institute, 1979.

Smith-Lovin, L., & Tickamyer, A. R. Nonrecursive models of labor force participation, fertility behavior and sex role attitudes. American Sociological Review, 1978, 43, 541-557.

Spenner, K. I., & Featherman, D. L. Achievement ambitions. In R. H. Turner, J. Coleman, & R. C. Fox (Eds.), Annual Rview of Sociology. Palo Alto, CA: Annual Reviews, 1978.

Spitze, G., & Huber, J. Changing attitudes toward women's nonfamily roles: 1938 to 1978. Sociology of Work and Occupations, 1980, 7, 317-336.

Sweet, J. A. Women in the labor force. New York: Seminar Press, 1973.

Tangri, S. S. Determinants of occupational role innovation among college women., Journal of Social Issues, 1972, 28, 177-199.

Theodore, A. The professional woman: Trends and prospects. In A. Theodore (Ed.), The professional woman. Cambridge, MI: Schenkman, 1971.

Thornton, A., & Freedman, D. Changes in the sex role attitudes of women, 1962-1977: Evidence from a panel study. American Sociological Review, 1979, 44, 831-842.

Treiman, D. J., & Terrell, K. Women, work, and wages: Trends in the female occupational structure. In K. Land & S. Spilerman (Eds.), Social indicator models. New York: Russell Sage Foundation, 1975. (a)

Treiman, D. J., & Terrell, K. Sex and the process of status attainment: A comparison of working women and men. American Sociological Review, 1975, 40, 174-200. (b)

Turner, R. H. Some aspects of women's ambition. _American Journal of Sociology_. 1964, _70_, 271-285.

U.S. Bureau of the Census. _Population alphabetical index of industries and occupations_. Washington, D.C.: U.S. Government Printing Office, 1971.

U.S. Bureau of the Census. _Statistical abstracts of the United States: 1976 (97th ed.)_. Washington, D.C.: U.S. Government Printing Office, 1976.

U.S. Department of Education, National Center for Education Statistics. _The Condition of Education_. Washington, D.C.: U.S. Government Printing Office, 1980.

U.S. Department of Labor, Bureau of Labor Statistics. _U.S. Working Women_. Bulletin 1880. Washington, D.C.: U.S. Government Printing Office, 1975. (a)

U.S. Department of Labor, Women's Bureau. _1975 Handbook of Women Workers_. Bulletin 297. Washington, D.C.: U.S. Government Printing Office, 1975. (b)

U.S. Department of Labor, Employment and Training Administration. _Women and work_. Research and Development Monograph 46. Washington, D.C.: U.S. Government Printing Office, 1977.

Vanfossen, B. E. Sexual stratification and sex-role socialization. _Journal of Marriage and the Family_, 1977, _39_, 563-574.

Vogel, S. R., Rosenkrantz, P. S., Broverman, I. K., Broverman, D. M., & Clarkson, F. E. Sex-role self-concepts and life style plans of young women. _Journal of Consulting and Clinical Psychology_, 1975, _43_, 427.

Waite, L. J., & Stolzenberg, R. M. Intended childbearing and labor force participation of young women: Insights from nonrecursive models. _American Sociological Review_, 1976, _41_, 235-252.

Weil, M. W. An analysis of the factors influencing married women's actual and planned work participation. _American Sociological Review_, 1961, _26_, 91-96.

Westoff, C. F., & Potvin, R. H. <u>College women and fer-</u><u>tility values</u>. Princeton, NJ: Princeton University Press, 1967.

Westoff, C. F., & Ryder, N. B. <u>The contraceptive</u> <u>revolution</u>. Princeton, NJ: Princeton University Press, 1977.

Whelpton, P. K., Campbell, A. A., & Patterson, J. E. <u>Fertility and family planning in the United</u> <u>States</u>. Princeton, NJ: Princeton University Press, 1966.

Willie, C. V., & Greenblatt, S. L. Four "classic" studies of power relationships in black families: A review and look to the future. <u>Journal of Marriage and the Family</u>, 1978, <u>40</u>, 691-694.

Wolf, W. C., & Fligstein, N. D. Sex and authority in the working place: The causes of sexual ine-quality. <u>American Sociological Review</u>, 1979, <u>44</u>, 235-252.

Yankelovich, D. <u>The new morality</u>. New York: McGraw-Hill, 1974.

Young, M. D., & Willmott, P. <u>The symmetrical family</u>. New York: Pantheon Books, 1973.

APPENDIX A

STRAIGHT-LINE RESPONDING

This appendix describes in more detail than was possible in Chapter 2 one specific difference that we observed between data from the Long Form data collection and data from the Monitoring the Future survey. The difference manifests itself as an increased tendency, towards later parts of the Long Form questionnaire, to use an identical response category for most or all items in the same set. In other words, respondents are increasingly more likely to show some form of position bias in later parts of the questionnaire.

In Table A sets of 10 or more items which appeared in sequence and used a common response scale (e.g., agree-disagree) are listed in the order of their occurrence in the long questionnaire. In columns A through C the exact numbers of items per set are indicated, as well as the location in the long questionnaire and the location in the short questionnaire. Column D shows the percentages of Long Form respondents who answered each item in the set using a single response category (e.g., response of "mostly disagree" to all items in a set).' The table shows quite clearly that while few respondents adopted such a "straight-line" stereotypical response strategy at the outset of the questionnaire, increasing numbers showed the straight-line pattern in the second half of the questionnaire.

Although the content of the question set seems to influence its "susceptibility" to the straight-line response pattern, the data in Table A clearly indicate that question content is not the sole cause of the pattern. The same question sets appear in the long form and in the five different short forms, but show quite

---

'Thirteen sets of items for which some form of entirely identical responding appeared reasonable were omitted from Table A; most of those item sets dealt with use of various types of drugs, and many respondents indicated "no use" of any drug.

different proportions of straight-line responders. The
factor which determines these differences, in large
measure, is questionnaire length. Even within the
short questionnaires the degree of straight-line
responding varies somewhat. Of particular interest to
the present argument--and in agreement with it--is the
tendency towards an increase in straight-line responding that shows up within three of the five forms.[2]
All in all, data from the long form in combination with
data from the short forms suggest quite strongly that
straight-line responding increases gradually as the
time spent in responding grows longer.

A more detailed examination of the responses to
the item sets listed in Table A revealed that the particular response categories chosen by the straight-line
responders reflect neither random choice nor a simple
and consistent position bias (data not shown). Rather,
it appears that straight-line responses tend toward
whatever is the modal response category for the general
sample of respondents, provided that the same one or
two response categories turn out to be modal for all
items in a particular set. For example, in the set of
12 items dealing with competence of various institutions, just under half of the straight-line responders
gave all institutions "fair" ratings and most of the
rest gave them all "good" ratings; and these same
ratings were the modal categories employed by the full
sample in their (non-straight-line) ratings of each of
the institutions. A different pattern emerged,
however, when we examined item sets which used agree-
disagree response scales (and also showed considerable
variation in modal patterns across the various items in
the set). For such agree-disagree item sets, the large
majority of all straight-line responders (about 80 percent) employed the middle category consisting of a non-
committal "neither," even though that category was infrequently chosen by the other respondents. In sum,
the particular response category chosen for the great
majority of stereotypical responding appears to be that
which is most "middle-of-the-road"--either in terms of
sticking with the most common (i.e., modal) category or
in terms of the non-committal category. These patterns
suggest that respondents did not stop reading al-

---

[2]The most striking instance is the set of questions about honesty of institutions, which produced 2.6
percent straight-line responders in the short form
(when it appeared in the tenth of 12 pages and followed
a lot of demographic items), compared with 1.4 percent
straight-line responders in the long form version
(where it appeared on page nine of a 36-page questionnaire).

together; rather, when they found a long set of relatively less interesting items they tended to slip into
a comfortable "groove" that allowed them, in effect, to
skip on to the next questions.

Given the above observations, it should come as no
surprise that the tendency toward stereotypical
responding is not limited to a totally straight-line
pattern; it also reveals itself in a more subtle way as
a general tendency toward nearly uniform patterns of
responding, which we can refer to as an "almost-
straight line" pattern. Table B presents a clear illustration of this phenomenon: 4.0 percent of Long Form
respondents, versus only 0.7 percent of short form
respondents, produced a straight-line pattern of
response to all 23 items in the question set; more importantly, the all-but-one identical responses pattern
appeared more often among Long Form respondents, as
well as the all-but-two, all-but-three, and all-but-
four patterns. Other item sets that we have examined
show similar patterns.

Effects of Bias on Substantive Results. Given the
increased tendency towards stereotypical responding for
long sets of items that is suggested by these data, the
critical issue then becomes the potential bias of substantive results based on the data collected by such a
long questionnaire. We will explore that issue for
both means and correlations, in each case comparing
Long Form items with the corresponding items from the
short forms. In order to limit the size of the task,
and also to focus attention where the problems are
likely to be most severe, our comparisons made use of
the last four items in each of the long item sets.

In order to assess the differences in means, each
difference between a mean of the short form and a mean
of the long form was divided by the standard deviation
for the short form to provide a "standardized" measure
of the difference. The absolute values of these differences were then averaged across items within each
set. Averaged standardized differences in means from
large item sets are displayed in Table A Column G.
These results are quite clear; among long item sets the
average absolute differences grow larger in later parts
of the Long Form questionnaire, reflecting most likely
the increasingly substantial impact of the response
bias. While at the beginning of the questionnaire all
average differences remained less than a tenth of a
standard deviation, in later parts many of them ex-

ceeded that level, and a few reached as much as two tenths of a standard deviation.[3]

Since these overall differences could be caused by any form of inaccurate reporting that increasingly occurs towards the end of a lengthy questionnaire rather than specifically by straight-line responding, it is useful to consider some additional evidence. When we examined means of randomly selected items that were not part of large item sets, and thus by definition could not be affected by straight-line responding, we found only small differences between long form and short form data, and no trend towards increasing differences in later parts of the long questionnaire (data not shown).

For assessing the effect of straight-line responding on correlations, we examined long form versus short form differences in three types of averaged correlations: (a) all pair-wise correlations involving the last four items within each large item set, (b) correlations pairing each of the last four items in one large item set with each of the last four items in another large item set, and (c) correlations pairing each of the last four items of large sets with each of several (usually four) single items.

We expect the problems generated by straight-line responding to be most severe in the case of correlations between two items within the same larger set. This is the case because straight-line responding involves positively correlated measurement errors, which have the effect of biasing correlations in a positive direction. Thus, to the extent that straight-line responding occurs in a set of items, we would expect

---

[3]While we recognize the desirability for estimates of statistical significance levels for these differences, any such estimate is afflicted by the difficulty of making reasonable assumptions about design effects in the data collected with the Long Form, short of extensive and costly computations. While we estimate the design effect for these kinds of analyses of the Monitoring the Future data to be approximately 1.5 (see Bachman, Johnston, and O'Malley, 1981, for design effect estimates), for the Long Form data it may range from 2 up to 7, depending on how much a particular item is related to school and regional characteristics, since the Long Form respondents were highly clustered on those dimensions. If we assume a Long Form design effect of 2.5 for these data based on males and females combined, a difference of .11 of a standard deviation would reach statistical significance ($p < .05$, two-tailed).

the long form correlations to be more positive (or less negative) than the corresponding short form correlations. Expectations are less clear for correlations pairing items across sets, or pairing one item from a set with a single item.

Findings concerning correlations between items from the same set match our expectations quite well (Table A, Column J). In the beginning of the long questionnaire, where little if any straight-line responding was taking place, differences between averaged signed correlations per set from the long form and short form are small and inconsistent in their direction (i.e., in the first quarter of the questionnaire no single difference exceeded .05).[4] After the first quarter of the long questionnaire the differences start to become larger and consistent in their direction. The correlations among items in the long questionnaire are consistently more positive than the comparable correlations in the short forms, the differences ranging from .04 to .20.

With regard to correlations across large item sets we were again interested in the size of the differences as well as in their direction. As it turned out, we found generally small and unsystematic differences. In fact, their distribution approximates a random distribution, assuming a design effect of 2.5 for the data collected with the Long Form (data not shown). For those correlations which paired a single item with an item from a long set, the general thrust of the findings is similar; we found no evidence for anything except random differences between correlations (data not shown).

In conclusion, the reported data suggest that due to what we assume is a decline in motivation, people respond in somewhat more stereotypical ways in later parts of the long questionnaire used in the Long Form data collection, as reflected in straight-line or almost-straight-line responding. However, the effect is less pervasive than might be anticipated. First, the straight-line responding occurs by no means with certainty, since even at the very latest part of the two-hour-plus questionnaire some item sets show very little straight-line responding. Second, although

---

[4]Similar considerations concerning design effect estimates as noted in footnote 3 also apply to the estimation of statistical significance of differences in correlations. A difference of .11 would just about reach statistical significance (p < .05, two-tailed) given a Long Form design effect of 2.5.

means appear biased according to the level of straight-
line responding, correlations are much less affected.
Specifically, only correlations between items from the
same set appear to be substantially altered, while correlations between items belonging to different sets appear much less altered.

Of course, expanding the capability for correlational analyses was the main rationale for collect-
ing data with the Long Form in the first place: Because
questions are contained in five different Monitoring
the Future questionnaire forms and therefore cannot be
correlated with questions in other forms, data were
needed from respondents who answered all five questionnaires. On the other hand, estimates of means and
standard deviations are available from the full
Monitoring the Future sample. And given the potential
bias in means of items from the Long Form questionnaire, only Monitoring the Future data should be used
for those estimates.

Table A

Comparison of Long and Monitoring the Future Questionnaires:
Straight-Line Responding, Means, and Within-Set Correlations

	No. of items in set (A)	Location of Set		% Straight-line Responders			Average Diff. in Means[1] (G)	Average Within-set Correlations[2]		
		Long Form (B)	MtF Form (C)	Long Form (D)	MtF Form (E)	Diff. (F)		Long Form (H)	MtF Form (I)	Diff. (J)
Satisfaction with various areas of life	14	9-22	F1: 9-22	0.1	0.1	0.0	.02	.32	.32	.00
Importance of life values	14	23-36	F1: 23-36	0.1	0.2	-0.1	.03	.19	.22	-.03
Mixed set of agree-disagree items	10	40-49	F1: 40-49	0.2	0.4	-0.2	.07	.12	.11	.01
Frequency of various activities	16	50-65	F2: 2-17	0.0	0.0	0.0	.07	.13	.10	.03
Honesty of various institutions	12	205-216	F2: 197-208	1.4	2.6	-1.2	.06	.48	.52	-.04
Competence of various institutions	12	301-312	F3: 48-59	4.3	1.0	3.3	.16	.43	.37	.06
Importance of various possessions	12	496-507	F3: 245-256	2.1	1.0	1.1	.05	.46	.42	.04
Mixed set of agree-disagree items	11	528-538	F4: 6-16	6.2	0.2	6.0	.18	.17	.06	.11
Importance of various job characteristics	23	540-562	F4: 18-40	4.0	0.7	3.3	.23	.30	.19	.11

Table A (cont.)

	No. of items in set (A)	Location of Set		% Straight-line Responders			Average Diff. in Means[1] (G)	Average Within-set Correlations[2]		
		Long Form (B)	MtF Form (C)	Long Form (D)	MtF Form (E)	Diff. (F)		Long Form (H)	MtF Form (I)	Form Diff. (J)
Power of various institutions	10	588-597	F4: 68-77	6.7	1.5	5.2	.14	.51	.42	.09
Agreement with parents on various issues	15	657-671	F4: 214-228	2.4	1.4	1.0	.06	.48	.43	.05
Frequency of worrying about various social issues	11	703-713	F5: 3-13	6.5	0.6	5.9	.13	.42	.22	.20
Mixed set of agree-disagree items	14	744-757	F5: 45-58	5.5	0.2	5.3	.21	.14	.06	.08
Mixed set of personality characteristics	22	807-828	F5: 184-205	1.8	0.3	1.5	.15	.05	-.03	.08

Note: Only sets of ten or more items were included.

[1] For each of the last four items in a given set, the difference between the long form and the short form mean was divided by the short form standard deviation. The absolute values for these standardized differences were then averaged across the four items.

[2] Each entry in columns H and I is the mean of the six product-moment correlations for all pair-wise combinations of the last four items in the item set. The signs of the correlations (plus or minus) were retained in the computations of these averages (see text for rationale).

Table B

Percentages of Respondents Answering with
Identical or Nearly Identical Response Categories to an
Entire Set of Items in the Long Form and the Monitoring the Future Questionnaires

	Long Form	Short Form
All identical response categories	4.0%	0.7%
All-but-one identical response category	2.9%	0.6%
All-but-two identical response categories	2.6%	0.8%
All-but-three identical response categories	3.1%	1.0%
All-but-four identical response categories	4.0%	1.1%

NOTE: The analyses utilized the special weights discussed in the text. The set consists of 23 items on the importance of various job characteristics.